The Narrative Integrity
of Mark 13:24–27

Australian College of Theology Monograph Series

SERIES EDITOR GRAEME R. CHATFIELD

The ACT Monograph Series, generously supported by the Board of Directors of the Australian College of Theology, provides a forum for publishing quality research theses and studies by its graduates and affiliated college staff in the broad fields of Biblical Studies, Christian Thought and History, and Practical Theology with Wipf and Stock Publishers of Eugene, Oregon. The ACT selects the best of its doctoral and research masters theses as well as monographs that offer the academic community, scholars, church leaders and the wider community uniquely Australian and New Zealand perspectives on significant research topics and topics of current debate. The ACT also provides opportunity for contributors beyond its graduates and affiliated college staff to publish monographs which support the mission and values of the ACT.

Rev. Dr. Graeme Chatfield
Series Editor and Associate Dean

The Narrative Integrity
of Mark 13:24–27

PETER G. BOLT

WIPF & STOCK · Eugene, Oregon

THE NARRATIVE INTEGRITY OF MARK 13:24–27

Australian College of Theology Monograph Series

Copyright © 2021 Peter G. Bolt. All rights reserved. Except for brief quotations in critical publications or reviews, no part of this book may be reproduced in any manner without prior written permission from the publisher. Write: Permissions, Wipf and Stock Publishers, 199 W. 8th Ave., Suite 3, Eugene, OR 97401.

Wipf & Stock
An Imprint of Wipf and Stock Publishers
199 W. 8th Ave., Suite 3
Eugene, OR 97401

www.wipfandstock.com

PAPERBACK ISBN: 978-1-6667-3079-1
HARDCOVER ISBN: 978-1-6667-2272-7
EBOOK ISBN: 978-1-6667-2273-4

10/15/21

To Kathryn

exalted
the Son of Man
gives gifts to man
the news abounds
true love is found
late in life but
in eternity
early

Contents

List of Tables | ix
Preface | xi
Abbreviations | xv
Introduction | xix

1   The Referential Problem of Mark 13:24–27 | 1
       1. The Problem   1
       2. Three Readings of Mark 13:24–27   2
       3. Interpreting Mark 13:24–27 as a Problem of Method   14
       4. Reading Mark 13:24–27   15

2   The Literary Method | 16
       1. The New Paradigm   16
       2. Reader-Response Method   18
       3. The Method in Action   27

3   Mark 13 in Anticipation (Mark 1–12) | 28
       1. The Narrative of Mark 1–12   28
       2. The Anticipation of Mark 13   49

4   Mark 13: A First Reading | 51
       1. A Narrative Pause   51
       2. The Linking Scene (vv.1–2)   53

CONTENTS

    3. The Apocalyptic *Discourse* 56
    4. The *Apocalyptic* Discourse 64
    5. The Three Readings: A Preliminary Assessment 68

5   Mark 13: A Close Reading | 69
    1. A Misguided Attitude (vv.1–4) 69
    2. A Warning for the Time of Distress (vv.5–23) 78
    3. What to Look for (vv.24–27) 106
    4. Watch for It (vv.28–37) 113
    5. Reading with Apocalyptic Expectation 126

6   Mark 13 in Retrospect (Mark 14–16) | 127
    1. Mark 13 as Part of the Rising Action 127
    2. Mark 13 and the Passion Narrative 128
    3. Mark 13: The Apocalyptic Precursor to the Passion Narrative 146

7   Conclusion | 147
    1. Mark 13:24–27: In Search of a Referent 147
    2. Mark 13:24–27: Narrative Integrity 148
    3. Mark 13:24–27: A Referent Discovered 149

Appendix 1: The Parallels | 151
    1. Support from the Parallels 151
    2. The Synoptic Parallels and Acts 151
    3. Other New Testament Material 156
Appendix 2: A Brief Note on Timothy J. Geddert, Watchwords | 158
Bibliography | 163
Modern Author Index | 175
Ancient Document Index | 180

Tables

Table 1: Interrelation of the Parties in a Narrative Transaction   24

Figure 1: Intratextual Relationships & Narrative Levels in Mark 13   25

Table 2: The Forms of Mark 13   58

Table 3: Rhetorical Structure of Mark 13   59

Table 4: The Syntactical Structure of Mark 13:11   88

Table 5: The Quotation of Daniel 12:1 in Mark 13:19   100

Preface

THIS BOOK BEGAN LIFE as a thesis submitted to the Australian College of Theology in December 1991 as a partial requirement for the MTh awarded me in the following year. I am therefore pleased that, thirty years after it was first submitted, it can be published as part of the Australian College of Theology Monograph Series.

Apart from the addition of transliterations and translations to assist those without facility in Greek, necessary corrections, and some updates in relation to my own subsequent work (marked with square brackets and this year's date [2021:]), this book is basically the publication of the MTh as submitted.

Whereas an undergraduate degree is meant to familiarize a student with the classic discussions of the broad disciplines of their field of study, a master's degree takes them to the leading-edge discussions in a narrower area of inquiry chosen according to their interests. Unlike doctoral research, a master's degree is not required to show an exhaustive grasp of the relevant literature, nor is it required to contribute something new to the body of existing scholarship.

In my final year of undergraduate studies, Moore College permitted students to pursue a project (10,000 words, if I recall) that formed a piece of preliminary work towards the Australian College of Theology Master of Theology award. Having been alerted earlier to a minority view on the interpretation of the coming of the Son of Man in Mark 13:24–27, and then becoming fascinated with the newer literary studies of the Gospels

PREFACE

emerging during my undergraduate years (1982-85), when the final year opportunity presented itself, I decided to use these newer approaches to explore that minority view.

Because the world of literary studies was only just beginning to be applied to the Gospels, I had the opportunity to explore that world for myself as I sought to formulate an appropriate method (especially Booth, Iser, Chatman), following up leads suggested by those Gospels scholars who had begun to dabble themselves (especially Fowler, Dewey, Boomershine). The seminal ideas in an article by R.H. Lightfoot—brilliant, brief, and mostly ignored—suggested the way forward, and I was set to explore the central verses of Mark 13 (vv.24-27) in their "narrative integrity". Consistent with the brief of a master's degree, my research was not exhaustive. However, the resultant thesis accidentally made a new contribution by arguing Lightfoot's suggestions more carefully to give what seemed to be a much more coherent view of that difficult chapter than the prevailing views at the time.

Once I joined the faculty of Moore College in 1990, my explorations of Mark 13 began to be inflicted upon the students in my New Testament 1 class, and successive generations would be so inflicted for the next twenty-six years. I am grateful for the many fruitful interactions and oppositions that have enabled me to hone these ideas and to learn to better express them for an audience that was usually taken by surprise, to say the least.

After the thesis was awarded, I had the opportunity to present it in a summary paper presented to the SBL International Meeting, held in Melbourne in 1992. I then published a version of this paper a few years later in the *Reformed Theological Review*, under the title "Mark 13: An Apocalyptic Precursor to the Passion Narrative".[1] Despite this article being published in what might be regarded as "a rather obscure journal from the Antipodes", it was gratifying that it was occasionally noticed, even if—perhaps corresponding to its size—it received but little interaction![2]

---

1. Bolt, "Mark 13".

2. Reacting initially to the *RefThR* article, fellow Aussie, Keith Dyer applauded the bravery of my attempt, but found it "rather forced"; Dyer, "'But Concerning *that* Day'", 104 n.1. Subsequently, Keith interacted further with the article in *The Prophecy on the Mount*, 174 n.40, 219 n.16, 247 n.30, 260 n.45. Brower, "'Let the Reader Understand'", 124 n.15, declared me "correct" that Mark is anti-religious authorities, not anti-temple, but felt the latter was implicit, asserting that I minimized "the importance of the setting and 13:2" (cf. n.65). He also felt I was "probably right" to see "this generation" (13:30) "as pointing to events in the narrative itself", but felt there was nevertheless a future element pointing beyond the narrative (n.72). My colleague, Graeme Goldsworthy was affirmative, finding support in John 2:17-22: "the destruction of this temple is

Nevertheless, my research on Mark 13 went with me into my later work,³ even protruding into my King's College, London, doctoral thesis, published in 2003 as *Jesus' Defeat of Death. Persuading Mark's Early Readers*.⁴ That same year, I had the privilege of delivering the Moore College Annual Lectures, in which I explored Mark's presentation of the atonement. The conclusions of my MTh were most apparent in the third lecture, entitled "The Cross as the End of the World".⁵ When these lectures were published in 2004 as *The Cross from a Distance. Atonement in Mark's Gospel*, what was by then my long-held view on Mark 13 became more widely known. Even if still regarded as unusual, it began to be received at least as worthy of more consideration than the earlier quick interactions.

Over the years, narrative-reader studies on Mark have become an industry in their own right, and I could certainly use much of this scholarship to further bolster the arguments made in the MTh.⁶ The difficulties and fascinations of Mark 13 and its central figure, the Son of Man, have also continued to inspire further inquiries and publications, upon which I have kept a quiet but interested eye. Some of this work could also be used to strengthen the position argued for here. See, for example, Geddert's work, which also drew upon Lightfoot with a similar aim to my own, shared some similar conclusions, but differed on others. Geddert published as my MTh research was about to be submitted, enabling only a little interaction.⁷ However, many of the subsequent publications simply plough time-honoured furrows. I have had more than enough to keep me far too busy in other areas to publish any kind of ongoing interaction with this literature. Neither

---

clearly the crucifixion, for its rebuilding is the bodily resurrection of Jesus"; *Preaching the Whole Bible*, 175. In order to critique my disavowal of the notion of imitation, Hood, "Evangelicals and the Imitation of the Cross", also touches on the article (and some of my other writings, but notably, not *Jesus' Defeat of Death*, which would have been to his advantage). Most recently spotted, N.T. Wright's discussion of "the End of the World" notes the article as a "fascinating suggestion that the chapter is replete with hints towards the coming passion narrative"; *History and Eschatology*, 307 n.62. So in its brief mentions the article seems to have moved from "forced" to "fascinating", which is at least in the right direction!

3. For my relevant articles published since 1991, see bibliography.

4. Bolt, *Jesus' Defeat of Death*, 252–53. Its influence is also apparent elsewhere in both the identification of Mark's narrative flow and in numerous questions of detail.

5. Bolt, *Cross from a Distance*, 85–115.

6. To say the least, my own narrative-reader approach has continued to be refined, as reflected, for example, in *Jesus' Defeat of Death*.

7. Geddert, *Watchwords*.

PREFACE

can I do this at this present stage of my life, and I am loath to promise any larger-scale publication for the future! But in view of the trickle (if only it were a flood!) of requests I have had over the last three decades to make my original thesis available to more people than the few who can find it on a dusty library shelf in Sydney, it seems to me to be entirely justified to publish it in more or less its submitted form, with some reference to my own further work where it has been built on in various ways. This publication might save some from the embarrassment of having to deal only with my conclusions without having had the opportunity to carefully consider the supporting evidence and argument. It may also assist others to gain a richer appreciation for the marvelous artistry of the Gospel of Mark. But, most importantly, in so doing it may help them to stand in greater awe of the work of the Lord Jesus Christ in enduring the greatest distress ever in order to deliver us a safe passage into the glorious kingdom of God.

Abbreviations

AJ   Josephus, *Antiquities of the Jews.*

AncSociety   *Ancient Society.*

Asyndeton   The lack of connection between two Greek sentences.

BAGD   Walter Bauer, William F. Arndt, F.W. Gingrich, and Frederick W. Danker, *A Greek-English Lexicon of the New Testament and Other Early Christian Literature.* Chicago and London: University of Chicago Press, 1957, ²1979.

BDBG   Francis Brown, S.R. Driver, & Charles A. Briggs, *The New Brown-Driver-Briggs-Gesenius Hebrew and English Lexicon with an appendix containing the Biblical Aramaic.* Lafayette: Associated Publishers, 1978.

BDF   F. Blass, A. Debrunner, and Robert W. Funk, *A Greek Grammar of the New Testament and other Early Christian Literature.* Chicago and London: University of Chicago Press, 1961.

BJ   Josephus, *Jewish War.*

BJRL   *Bulletin of the John Rylands Library.*

CBQ   *Catholic Biblical Quarterly.*

CD   Karl Barth, *Church Dogmatics.*

ABBREVIATIONS

ChrCent	*Christian Century.*
ExpT	*Expository Times.*
Hendiadys	A device where two Greek words are meant to be read together, signalled, e.g., by both being governed by the one article.
HTR	*Harvard Theological Review.*
IDB	*Interpreters Dictionary of the* Bible, edited by G.A. Buttrick. 4 Volumes. Nashville: Abingdon, 1962.
IDBSup	*Interpreters Dictionary of the Bible, Supplement,* edited K. Crim. Nashville: Abingdon, 1976.
Int	*Interpretation.*
JAAR	*Journal of the American Academy of Religion.*
JBL	*Journal of Biblical Literature.*
JLit & Theol	*Journal of Literature and Theology.*
JR	*Journal of Religion.*
JSNT	*Journal for the Study of the New Testament.*
JSNTSup	Journal for the Study of the New Testament Supplement.
JSOT	*Journal for the Study of the Old Testament.*
JTS	*Journal of Theological Studies.*
LSJ	Henry G. Liddell, Robert Scott, Henry S. Jones, Roderick McKenzie, *A Greek-English Lexicon.* Ninth edition. Oxford: Clarendon, 1940.
Neot	*Neotestamentica.*
NovT	*Novum Testamentum.*
NovTSup	Novum Testamentum Supplement.
ns	new series.
NTS	*New Testament Studies.*
RefThR	*Reformed Theological Review*

Rest Q	*Restoration Quarterly.*
Str–B	Hermann L. Strack and Paul Billerbeck, *Kommentar zum Neuen Testament aus Talmud und Midrasch*. 4 volumes. München, C. Beck, 1922–28.
TDNT	*Theological Dictionary of the New Testament*, edited by Gerhard Kittel and Gerhard Friedrich. Translated by Geoffrey W. Bromiley. Grand Rapids: Eerdmans, 1964–76.
TynBul	*Tyndale Bulletin.*
Zerwich	Max Zerwich and Mary Grosvenor, *A Grammatical Analysis of the Greek New Testament* (Rome: Biblical Institute Press, 1981).
ZNTW	*Zeitschrift für die Neutestamentliche Wissenschaft*
[2021:]	Additions made to the original thesis for this publication.

Introduction

THE INTERPRETIVE PROBLEMS OF Mark 13 revolve around verses 24–27 (Chapter 1). The referent to these verses is usually taken to be either the parousia or the fall of Jerusalem in AD 70. Both of these positions generate interpretive problems, not the least of which is that neither adequately explains the function of these verses within Mark's narrative. Alongside these majority positions, there is a minority reading that connects these verses with the passion narrative, which begins to overcome this major weakness. Following this lead, this book explores the narrative role of Mark 13 with special emphasis upon verses 24–27.

The approach adopted follows the trend in contemporary Gospel studies, being literary in general and reader-oriented in particular. After outlining the method (Chapter 2), it is then applied to an overview of Mark 1–12, the narrative which prepares for Mark 13 (Chapter 3). A first reading of Mark 13 (Chapter 4) addresses questions of form and function and concludes that the form of the chapter encourages it to be read as an integral part of Mark's narrative. A close reading (Chapter 5) examines the chapter in detail and identifies certain expectations that are erected for the reader. In particular, the expectation of the destructive sacrilege, the coming of the Son of Man, and the gathering of the elect are identified. Mark's passion narrative is then read against these expectations (Chapter 6) and it is demonstrated that the narrative encourages the crucifixion to be read as the horrendous sacrilege, the resurrection as the coming of the Son of Man,

INTRODUCTION

and the prospective meeting in Galilee as the launching of the Gentile mission (the gathering of the elect).

In conclusion (Chapter 7) this book proposes that Mark 13 is an apocalyptic precursor to the passion. In particular, the referent to Mark 13:24–27 is the resurrection. This reading not only provides the solution to the various difficulties, but, unlike other readings, it allows Mark 13:24–27 to be read as an integral part of the Gospel according to Mark.

For the sake of completion, the parallels are briefly discussed in Appendix 1, and are found to be supportive. Appendix 2 briefly discusses Timothy J. Geddert's, *Watchwords*.

I

The Referential Problem of Mark 13:24–27

The Problem

The Difficulties

THE INTERPRETIVE DIFFICULTIES OF Mark 13 are well known,[1] embracing questions concerning sources,[2] authenticity, historical background,[3] *Sitz im Leben* (both of the chapter itself, and for the Gospel as a whole),[4]

---

1. Hooker, "Trial," 78, has stated that few things can be said of this chapter without fear of contradiction. Carson, "Matthew," 488: "Few chapters of the Bible have called forth more disagreement among interpreters." Dewey, *Markan Public Debate*, 14, cites it as a section of the Gospels over which scholars are most divided.

2. Wenham, *Rediscovery*, and also Beasley-Murray, *Jesus and the Kingdom*, 322–37, show that the question of sources behind Mark 13 is still very much a live issue for some.

3. What are the external events referred to by the chapter? What is the relationship of this chapter to the fall of Jerusalem in AD 70? What is its relationship to the "oracle" referred to by Eusebius, and so to the post-AD 70 church? What is its relation to Jesus' second coming? Does it predict any historical signs premonitory to that event? What is its relation to the passion / resurrection events so central to the Christian message?

4. Chapter 13 is considered important for establishing the Gospel's *Sitz im Leben* by historical critics (e.g.,, Hooker, "Trial"; Hengel, *Studies*, 1–30; Brandon, "Date") and those advocating a Literary-Critical approach (e.g., Petersen, *Literary Criticism*, 68–73).

and questions of fundamental exegesis,[5] theological interpretation,[6] and application.[7]

The Cause

The various difficulties are created by the quest for the referent to vv.24–27.[8] R.T. France notes:

> The difficulties are created entirely by the assumption that vv.24–27 refer to the parousia, as an eschatological event which is still, for us, in the future. From this arise the awkward transitions in the chapter, and the embarrassment of vv.24a and 30, which leave no room for a time-lag of 2,000 years.[9]

Attempts to unravel the problems of Mark 13, therefore revolve around the reading of these key verses.[10]

Three Readings of Mark 13:24–27

Three Readings

There are three basic proposals for the referent of Mark 13:24–27. The first reads these verses of the parousia, the second of the destruction of Jerusalem in AD 70, and the third reading suggests a relationship with the events of the passion narrative.[11]

---

5. How do the different sections relate to each other internally, especially when some appear contradictory?

6. What does it mean that the Son does not know something (verse 32)? Was Jesus mistaken about the coming of the Son of Man? Who did he think this Son of Man was? Does the chapter teach a doctrine of the parousia, and, if so, to what extent?

7. Used in the sense of: What does it mean for the ordinary Christian reader in his or her modern world? What is its message for the faith community which regards this chapter as canon?

8. These verses are the central element of the discourse. See the analysis of Lambrecht, *Die Redaktion der Markus-Apokalypse*, as summarized by Wenham, "Recent Study (Part 1)," 14.

9. France, *Jesus*, 229.

10. For a survey of the literature see Beasley-Murray, *Jesus and the Future*. For a more recent survey Wenham, "Recent Study (Part 1)," and "Recent Study (Part 2)."

11. In what follows I mainly follow the convenient classification given by France, *Jesus*, 227–39, although he does not mention the third possibility.

The Parousia

Two Subgroups

Despite the interpretive difficulties it causes, two subgroups read verses 24–27 of the parousia.

The uncommon[12] "prima facie" subgroup is content to live with an abrupt transition between the fall of Jerusalem and the parousia at several points in the chapter.[13]

The second subgroup seeks to overcome the difficulties by asserting the chapter has a "prophetic perspective," in which the judgment on the Jewish nation (i.e., AD 70) is a foreshadowing of the final judgment (i.e., at the parousia), and the long ages between the two are prophetically telescoped.[14]

Some Difficulties

This "parousia" position recognizes that Mark 13 uses Old Testament "last day" language. However, it has some serious difficulties. It generates the problems alluded to above (awkward transitions and the christological problem of verse 32),[15] disregards the clear chronological connection in the

---

12. For a list of scholars who hold this view see France, *Jesus*, 28 nn. 4 & 5.

13. On this view, the chapter is interpreted as follows: vv.5–23 events up to AD 70; vv.24–27 parousia; vv.28–31 fall of Jerusalem; vv.32–37 parousia.

14. This is the most popular explanation, cf. France, *Jesus*, 228, n.6.

15. Wenham, "Recent Study (Part 1)," 7, classifies their proposed solutions into four groups:
   1. Jesus was mistaken, but this mistake is unimportant as it merely reflects Jesus' humanity.
   2. The parousia is not included in the ταῦτα πάντα *tauta panta* of v.30.
   3. The saying in v.30 does not go back to Jesus.
   4. The "Prophetic Perspective" view.

chapter,[16] and has the profound weakness of being largely unargued,[17] but simply assumed, perhaps due to its democratic majority.[18]

However, its major problem is that it fails to treat vv.24–27 in their narrative integrity.[19] There is no adequate explanation offered as to why Mark has a prophecy of the parousia at this point—especially given the disregard of the subject in the rest of the Gospel[20]—or how it functions in the narrative.

16. There is "a very definite temporal link [...] between the events of verses 5–22 [sic] and those of verses 24–27 [...] a connection not in principle only, but in time, which is only made more explicit by verse 30"; France, *Jesus*, 229. See below for the importance of this observation.

17. It is regularly introduced without major argument in the commentaries. Cf. Allen, *Mark*, 160; Barclay, *Mark*, 332; Bartlet, *Mark*, 362–63; Beasley-Murray, *Mark 13*, 89–90; Blunt, *Mark*, 241; Bowman, *Mark*, 250; Branscomb, *Mark*, 238; Cole, *Mark*, 204; Cranfield, *Mark*, 406; Crotty, *Mark*, 105–06; Earle, *Mark*, 101–02; Goodwin, *Mark*, 206 n.1; Lane, *Mark*, 474; Taylor, *Mark*, 517–18; Williamson, *Mark*, 240–41. Its opponents don't refute any arguments, which leaves the impression that there are none.

18. Some proponents put forward slight arguments. Alexander, *Mark*, 358–60, says the advantage of the parousia assumption is that "all believe it to be predicted elsewhere." This is hardly an argument based on an exegesis of Mark 13 itself. Anderson, *Mark*, 298, argues that "Mark's first readers would have identified the figure here with Jesus and would have thought of his parousia [...] v.26 has the clear imagery of the return of the Son of Man to judgment." However, the latter part of this quote begs the question, and the former makes assumptions about the readers. This may have been so, but why would they have so thought? Can we discern any exegetical foundation for what the first readers would have thought? These questions are suggestive of the approach taken below. A position without argument rests on a shaky foundation and demands further scrutiny. Carson, *Exegetical Fallacies*, 12–13: "The essence of critical thought [...] is the justification of opinions. A critical interpretation of Scripture is one that has adequate justification [...] provides sound reasons for the choices it makes [... and is] opposed to merely personal opinions, [and] appeals to blind authority" (see also p.125).

19. Pesch, *Naherwartungen*, criticizes all or most of his predecessors for failing to expound Mark 13 within its Markan context; as reported by Wenham, "Recent Study (Part 2)," 1. Any reference to Pesch, *Narherwartungen*, below will be taken from Wenham's two studies. The identified problem becomes most significant under an approach guided by the newer literary criticism (see Ch. 2), which is "concerned with interpreting the Gospel as an integral, literary whole"; Fowler, "Using Literary Criticism," 628, 629, thus the term "narrative integrity." The only sustained attempt to read Mark 13 in its narrative context that I am aware of is Geddert, *Watchwords*. Unfortunately this work came to my attention too late to fully interact with, although I have inserted a few comments in the notes, and a summary comparison in Appendix 2.

20. In each case where some would find the parousia, an argument can be mounted to the contrary. I would argue that there is no explicit reference to the parousia in Mark, although it is implicit to the Son of Man theology drawn from Daniel 7.

The Fall of Jerusalem

Two Subgroups

Two other subgroups "postulate that vv.24–27 do not refer to the parousia, but are in fact a symbolic description of the fall of Jerusalem and its implications."[21]

One group understands the chapter as referring entirely to the fall of Jerusalem in AD 70.[22] The other is a mediating position which reads the fall of Jerusalem as the referent for vv.5–31 and the parousia for vv.32–37.[23] This means that: "there is no time-lag to explain away, and v.30 loses its terror; the doctrine of 'prophetic perspective' becomes unnecessary as an apologetic device."[24]

Arguments and Difficulties

For convenience the arguments of France will be listed and critiqued. This is justified by the fact that he maintains they have not been refuted in twenty years.[25]

CONTEXT

In his major argument, France considers that the context demands vv.24–27 to be interpreted of AD 70. Vv.1–4 are solely about the Temple's destruction, and which leads us to expect a statement about the fall of the city. Vv.5–13 are about this fall (the second person indicates these people will see the events; vv.14–23, which are generally taken to refer to the events of AD 66–70, are closely linked). Vv.14–23 describe the events leading up to the siege but do not describe the fall. Thus we are left with the impression

---

21. France, *Jesus*, 230.

22. The most radical interpretation is that of J.S. Russell in which the events of AD 70 *were* the parousia and there is no New Testament warrant for any future coming of Jesus. Gould, *Mark*, and Feuillet, *Mark*, whilst agreeing that the whole chapter refers to AD 70, deny that this was the second coming, cf. France, *Jesus*, 229, 230 nn.10 & 11.

23. This represents France's position, held in company with others, *Jesus*, 231 n.13ff.

24. France, *Jesus*, 229.

25. Although he offered these arguments in 1971, in *Divine Government* (1990) he advanced substantially the same arguments, noting "I have not yet seen reason to change my views except in details" (p.78).

that we are about to get a scene of the catastrophe. Vv.28–30 confirm the impression by the repetition of the second person and the reintroduction of ταῦτα *tauta* and ταῦτα πάντα *tauta panta* from before.

Verse 32, however, begins a new section referring to the parousia, since:

a. This event is unknown by Jesus yet he did know the event of vv.5–31 was soon to come; and

b. περὶ δὲ τῆς ἡμέρας ἐκείνης *peri de tēs hēmeras ekeinēs* is a contrast to the preceding, being a new phrase in the chapter with clear Old Testament allusions referring to the last day.

These arguments fail to establish that the fall of Jerusalem is the subject of vv.5–31. The use of the second person in vv.5–13 to establish that the referent *will be seen* by the hearers does not in itself establish *what that event will be*. Likewise, the statement that vv.14–23 are "generally taken to refer to AD 66–70" begs the question of why they are so taken.[26]

France's admission of the parousia into vv.32–37 can also be questioned. To know something is 'soon' is not equivalent to knowing the precise date, so this argument does not require two separate events. Likewise, a new phrase does not demand that a new subject is being introduced, especially given that the language of vv.24–27 is often associated with this phrase in the Old Testament, and that the equivalent phrase in the plural is actually used in verse 24! That it refers to the last day in the Old Testament is no criterion for suggesting that vv.32–33 introduce a new subject unless it has been demonstrated that vv.24–27 have not already referred to the last day.

The most France can establish by these arguments is that the referent of vv.24–27, whatever it may prove to be, will take place "in this generation." The real strength of his position rests entirely on his interpretation of vv.1–4, taken as controlling the thought of the chapter. The interpretation and nature of the control exercised by these verses will therefore need to be examined below.[27]

---

26. France's exegesis of vv.28–30 depends on prior reasoning and adds nothing further.

27. Their function and the extent of their control is discussed below in chapters 4 and 5.

Verses 24–27

France firstly adopts the premise that it is more consistent to restrict Jesus' words to their Old Testament sphere of reference, i.e., to national disaster. He then infers that "if this is so, it is hard to see a more obvious reference than to the fall of Jerusalem and the eclipse of the Jewish state."[28] Feeling that the language is clearly suitable to the fall (with J.S. Russell), France therefore rejects other alternatives. However, this premise is questionable,[29] and the inference, that the fall is "obvious" or "suitable," is hardly solid argumentation.[30]

Secondly, France tackles "the crux of the question," that is, the use of Dan 7:13 in verse 26. He correctly observes that Daniel 7 concerns vindication and exaltation and that the coming of the Son of Man is a coming *to God to receive dominion* not a descent to earth. He shows that Jesus uses this verse the same way at all times and nowhere uses it of his return to earth. As in the close parallel in Mark 14:62, here we have a "prediction of Jesus' imminent exaltation to an authority which supersedes that of the earthly powers which have set themselves against God."[31] Elsewhere Jesus may apply this Dan 7:13 vindication in other ways, but here the context is "quite unambiguous, Jesus is speaking of the fall of Jerusalem."[32]

---

28. France, *Jesus*, 234.

29. This will be critiqued in chapter 4.

30. This is the "referential fallacy" in the area of history. Using historical events to interpret the text simply because a certain event seems to be parallel/similar is fraught with danger.

31. France, *Jesus*, 235.

32. According to France, Jesus applies Dan 7:13 to (i) his exaltation immediately post resurrection; (ii) manifestation of this authority in the lifetime of his contemporaries; and (iii) the culmination of this authority at the final judgment; France, *Jesus*, 236. Wenham, "Recent Study (Part 2)," 6, criticizes this on two points: i. He disputes that the coming is consistently to vindication in Jesus' teaching; ii. He argues that the parallels are consistently to the last day.

The "three stage application" theory also needs examination, with special reference to vv.24–27 in the framework of their Markan context. For the moment, it can be noted that application (ii) sounds strangely like the "prophetic perspective" view with which France disagrees. Carson, "Matthew," on Matthew 24, lists other applications of this "manifestation" to events besides the fall of Jerusalem: the Resurrection, Pentecost, the growth of the church. The underlying warrant for such interpretations needs justification. What controls this kind of application?

The third stage of his treatment of vv.24–27 deals with verse 27.[33] Favoring the primary meaning of ἄγγελοι *aggeloi*, namely, "messengers," France says verse 27 is

> describing the sequel to the fall of Jerusalem. The Jews are no longer the people of God; now the true people of God, chosen from all nations, 'from the four winds', will be brought in. The agents of this 'gathering of the elect' will be the preachers of the Gospel, God's messengers, his ἄγγελοι *aggeloi*.[34]

The Old Testament language of the latter part of the verse does not require any eschatological sense, but is "typically applied to the gathering of the Christian church."[35]

But if this is the meaning of ἄγγελοι *aggeloi* in view here, what is the evidence that this really describes the sequel to the AD 70 fall?[36] Leaving Mark aside for the moment, the New Testament evidence suggests that the gospel was taken to the nations in the immediate post-exaltation period, and that this mission was well-established some four decades before AD 70. Moreover, the fact that France is forced to abandon his previous "strict" reading of Old Testament allusions (i.e., to the political sphere) by denuding the eschatological overtones here, questions whether his exegesis is the "best fit."

Synoptic Parallels

His third main argument invokes the support of other synoptic parallels, especially Matthew 24. Although the parallels are invoked by every position, they should not supply determinative but merely supportive evidence.[37] Mark must be allowed to speak for himself. I deal briefly with the parallels in Appendix 1.

---

33. France, *Jesus*, 238–39.

34. France, *Jesus*, 238. He no longer holds to this view of the angels, although the position does not hang on this. See his *Government*, 78 n.20.

35. France, *Jesus*, 238.

36. France supplies no supporting evidence.

37. Carson, *Exegetical Fallacies*, 43, 136, refers to the fallacy "parallelomania." The interpretation of the various "eschatological discourses" affords ample evidence of what could be called "circular parallelomania," in which Mark is interpreted by the parallels and the parallels are interpreted by Mark! This fallacious method can be avoided by dealing with one Gospel at a time, in its own right.

The Significance of the Fall of Jerusalem

Given that AD 70 was "the eclipse of the Jewish state," "the end of an era," "a symbol, and more than a symbol, of the inauguration of the kingdom of the Son of Man,"[38] France considers the extravagant language of the verses completely warranted.

This historical event looms large in the arguments of many and France ascribes it tremendous significance. But this significance needs demonstration. It is not certain whether the collapse of Jerusalem was treated so importantly by either Judaism or early Christianity. In view of this, is it really so significant for our chapter?[39]

It is also a severe weakness for this view that its mooted historical fulfillment is a very poor fit. Martin Hengel can even say that the chapter, read in this way, "does not fit at all into the situation at or after the destruction of the Temple."[40]

---

38. France, *Jesus*, 231, 232, 233, 236–37, etc.

39. Brandon, *Fall of Jerusalem*, ix, mentions the enormous claims (e.g., B. H. Streeter, "It is impossible for us nowadays to realize the shock of AD 70 to a community in which Jewish and Gentile members alike had been reared in the profoundest veneration of the immemorial sanctity of the Holy City and the Temple." Brandon goes on to bewail the fact that Streeter unfortunately "never made a study" of the basis of such a claim, and was content with "*a priori* considerations") and the enormous counter claims (e.g., E. Meyer, "the Jewish catastrophe had really nothing more than academic interest for Christians") made for the Fall, as the incentive for his work. See also his catena of modern opinion in the appendix to chapter 1. He eventually sided with the majority that the Fall had a secondary importance for the rise of early Christianity. As far as New Testament reference to the event he says: "on their testimony alone nothing would be known of the disaster which overwhelmed Israel in AD 70" (p.163). Gaston, *No Stone on Another*, 5, notes that despite second century claims that the Fall was the rejection of Israel: "In view of the great importance of the fall of Jerusalem, it is strange how seldom it should be mentioned in the New Testament," and, with Moffat: "the catastrophe is practically ignored in the extant Christian literature of the first century." And again: "There is no unambiguous reference to the fall of Jerusalem any place outside the Gospels." It is questionable whether there is any "unambiguous" reference *inside* the Gospels either.

40. Hengel, *Studies*, 16–18. After listing the evidence, he states: "The description in vv.14–20 has to be forced if it is to be fitted into the picture which Josephus draws of the Jewish war, the sacking of the Temple and the 'pacification' of the country. We might be more inclined to think of the megalomaniac attempt of Caligula to set up his statue in the Temple in Jerusalem, but here too there are considerable tensions with the actual events"; rather, "v.14 has nothing to do with the siege or the capture of the Temple by Titus in AD 70" but verses 14–20 reproduce "earlier pictures of apocalyptic terror." Likewise, Colani's theory began with the fact that "the abomination of v.14 never took place"; Beasley-Murray, *Mark 13*, 1.

THE NARRATIVE INTEGRITY OF MARK 13:24-27

The Logic of the Chapter

Finally, France argues that this interpretation improves the logic of the chapter by smoothing out some of the "awkward transitions" that the parousia position has to live with. Despite this, however, his position still leaves one "abrupt transition" unexplained (between vv.5-31 and vv.32-37). Why is the parousia suddenly introduced at this stage?

Narrative Integrity

Having critiqued France's specific arguments, a final criticism can be offered. As for the parousia position above, an explanation needs to be supplied for the occurrence of a prophecy of Jerusalem's fall at this point in Mark's narrative.[41]

The Passion Narrative

The Connection Felt

While not specifically reading Mark 13:24-27 as referring to the passion narrative, several writers have felt this connection. For example, in the midst of an interpretation of Mark 13 which mingles the parousia and the fall of Jerusalem Karl Barth states:

> *The discourse of Mk. 13 is a repetition of the three prophecies of the passion and resurrection of Jesus elevated to a cosmic scale* [...]. The prophecy of what the present generation will experience supremely in the destruction of the Temple will begin to be fulfilled at once with the story of the passion (Mk 14:1ff) with which the life story of Jesus reaches its climax [...]. Hence Jesus is *primarily foretelling His own impending death* when He speaks of these imminent events, *and His resurrection* when to the comprehensive picture of

---

41. See the criticism of Pesch, *Naherwartungen*, n.19, above. Kelber, *Kingdom*, attempts to link this theme with the preceding, however, his view (in which Mark 13 figures little) still does not do justice to the wider concerns of Mark's story. Geddert's marvelous treatment of the context (*Watchwords*, Ch. 5) argues that the destruction of the Temple is implicit throughout, but not the main concern. In reply, I suggest that the explicit teaching of the texts concerned, i.e., that they are directed not against the Temple but against Israel's leadership (see my chapter 3), which is admitted by Geddert, is the only necessary reading of Mark and the "implications" are merely the suggestions of the interpreter, not the text.

man tormented by war, division, earthquake and famine, of the persecuted and tormented community, of Jerusalem standing under mortal threat, He opposes the imminent end of time, the great καὶ τότε *kai tote*, the coming of the Son of Man to gather His elect, and therefore His triumphant life as the Lord of His community. [. . .] Even now, as [his generation] *begins to experience the passion of Jesus,* it is about to take part in the opening of the series of events which will be immediately followed by the coming of the Son of Man.[42]

R.H. Lightfoot understood the apocalyptic discourse as the immediate introduction to the Passion narrative[43] and uncovered various links between the two.[44] These parallels make verse 30 less difficult for: "a first fulfillment at any rate was not far off, which was regarded as a sign, a seal or assurance, and a sacrament of the ultimate fulfillment."[45]

Culmann, also on verse 30 (and Mark 9:1; Matthew 10:23), ruminates along similar lines:

> we might even wonder if in the three verses we have just quoted [Jesus] was thinking equally *of the contemporary generation as the generation which was to witness the decisive event of his death* [. . .] *the decisive stage in the coming of the Kingdom of God.*[46]

It is also relevant that many scholars have read some verses concerning "the coming of the Son of Man" of Jesus enthronement/exaltation—whether in a "progressive"[47] or a "punctiliar" sense. Although it is by no means usual to read Mark 13:26 in this way, consistency justifies a consideration of such a reading.

The authors mentioned here find the "ultimate fulfillment" elsewhere, but their suggestive comments may be evidence of them reading beyond the consensual boundaries of their critical community.[48] In view of this possi-

---

42. Barth, *CD* III.2, 501 (my emphasis).

43. Lightfoot, "Connexion," 50.

44. Wenham, "Recent Study (Part 1)," 9, reveals that a similar connection has been felt by scholars since the 1930's who have stressed that in the eschatological discourse "Jesus was [. . .] concerned [. . .] to encourage his followers to see the eschatological significance of the present—of his life, death and resurrection."

45. Lightfoot, "Connexion," 54. Geddert, *Watchwords*, Ch. 4, provides a sustained argument supporting Lightfoot.

46. Cullmann, "Return," 152–54.

47. France, *Government*, 73.

48. The constraints imposed by the critical community is one of the reasons new

bility, the reading of the passion / resurrection as a fulfillment (preliminary or otherwise) of 13:24-27 needs to be considered in its own right.[49]

The Crucifixion

Although definitely in the minority—for the view has not been widely discussed at even a cursory level—,[50] some have made the link specifically. Two recent writers have boldly followed Lightfoot in this direction. In her structural analysis of Mark 11–16, Marion Smith considers Chapter 13

> as an apocalyptic-style version of the passion narrative [. . .] it is fitting that the account of the events of the passion should be immediately preceded by their expression in messianic and apocalyptic terms.[51]

In his deconstructionist approach,[52] Radcliffe links Chapter 13 with the passion narrative since this is entirely consistent with Mark's usual penchant for intratextual referents: "He is not pointing us outside the text to some redemptive event which is yet to come. His references are nearly always intratextual."[53] Of Mark 14:62 (which is linked to 13:24-27) he writes:

> Clearly it must refer to that coming in power which was *his enthronement on the cross,* ironically recognized as 'King of the Jews',

---

literary methods haven't been radically adopted in Biblical Studies. See Porter, "Why Hasn't Reader-Response Criticism Caught on?".

49. Hargreaves, *Guide*, 215, hints at this direction as well, arguing from the parallels and John. Fenton, *Preaching the Cross*, 71, links 13:24 with the darkness at the crucifixion. Lane, *Mark*, 461 n.59, also refers to E. Larsson who finds parallels between 13:9-13 and Mark 14-15. Personally, I was originally alerted to this third possibility through a sermon preached by Rev. Phillip D. Jensen in 1981.

50. Cranfield, *Mark*, 409, mentions it without comment; Lane, *Mark*, 483, mentions Lightfoot without comment, although he appears to endorse his proposal (p.24). Geddert, *Watchwords*, 95, comments that "few interpreters have attempted to draw implications from Lightfoot's suggestion, [. . .] still fewer have attempted to provide a secure footing for [the suggestion]." Geddert, *Watchwords*, has certainly filled the gap, as does this present work.

51. M. Smith, "Composition."

52. Radcliffe, "'The Coming of the Son of Man,'" 183, who argues that Chapter 13 is a "subversion of apocalyptic."

53. Radcliffe, "'The Coming of the Son of Man,'" 184. For a similar concern with Mark's intratextuality, see van Iersel, "He will Baptize you."

when, as prophesied, the sun was darkened between the sixth and the ninth hour.[54]

Others, following the arguments of Vielhauer,[55] also consider the cross as Jesus' enthronement. Jackson explains 14:61–62 as a promise that, as proof of Jesus messianic status, Jesus' Jewish detractors "are to have the Crucifixion itself, which for Mark represents Jesus' enthronement at God's right hand as his eschatological judge."[56]

Perrin, on the same verse, explains that "'sitting at the right hand of Power' views the crucifixion-burial-resurrection as one continuous event and interprets it as an enthronement."[57] By extending Jesus' enthronement to the resurrection, this comment hints at the position being argued here.

The Resurrection

The argument that follows will develop these suggestive comments to argue that the Coming of the Son of Man in Mark 13:24–27 refers to Jesus' enthronement begun with his resurrection. This position makes sense of the connection "felt" by several writers, and adds greater precision to the views of those who have specifically connected these verses to the passion narrative.

An Apocalyptic Preparation for the passion

The reading of Mark 13 in general, and its central verses in particular, as an apocalyptic preparation for the passion narrative, accords Mark 13:24–27 the narrative integrity sorely lacking in the other two positions. This reading fits Mark 13 comfortably into Mark's famous "passion narrative with an extended introduction."

---

54. Radcliffe, "'The Coming of the Son of Man,'" 184 (my emphasis).
55. Vielhauer, "Erwägungen zur Christologie."
56. Jackson, "Death," 25.
57. Perrin, "The High Priest's Question," 91–93. However, note that he considers the Son of Man quotation as an anticipation of the parousia.

Mark 13:24–27 as a Problem of Method

Problems and their solutions can be related to method, as M. D. Hooker observes:

> The ways in which the problems of Mark xiii have been formulated and approached have varied considerably over the years. As we might expect, they reflect in large measure the concerns and methods of the times.[58]

Gospel studies are presently undergoing a "paradigm shift,"[59] claimed to be "possibly the most significant change of paradigm in biblical studies since the adoption of the historical model sometime after the Middle Ages."[60] Whereas such studies were previously done within the paradigm of history,[61] the shift is currently towards the paradigm of literature.[62] A change in paradigm entails "a shift in criteria governing the type of problems

---

58. Hooker, "Trial," 78.

59. Talk of "paradigm shifts" has been popular since Kuhn, *Structure*. For an assessment of the impact of Kuhn's philosophy of science on a wide variety of disciplines see the symposium Gutting, *Paradigms and Revolution*. The theory has been attacked in Suppe, *Structure*.

60. Robertson, "Literature." He explains a paradigm as "any idea or set of ideas that provides the framework within which a given set of phenomena are understood."

61. For an historical survey of the study of the New Testament, see the articles in Marshall, *New Testament Interpretation*.

62. The relationship of the newer literary criticism to the old paradigm is disputed. Some would see it as yet another progression within the historical paradigm, e.g., Redaction critic N. Perrin, "High Priest's Question"; the 'rhetorical' critic Dewey, *Markan Public Debate*, 9. Others, however, have rightly perceived that the relationship is probably more disjunctive. Petersen, *Literary Criticism*, 19, shows how the historical paradigm simply cannot answer the questions it poses and so a decisive break is needed. Carson, "Recent Developments," 33, notes that the newer tools and the old may in fact be mutually exclusive. He cites as an example the fact that the old source criticism would argue for disunity (and therefore different sources) and 'Rhetorical' criticism for unity using exactly the same textual evidence. The balance is struck by Fowler, "Using Literary Criticism," 626–29. Moore, *Literary Criticism*, Barton, *Reading the Old Testament*, and Porter, "Why Hasn't Reader-Response Criticism Caught on?," all portray Biblical critics as children of the historical paradigm who tend to domesticate literary theory for their own use, rather than realizing the different methods may be incompatible. [2021: in *Jesus' Defeat of Death*, I proposed a model of compatibility, in terms of two readerly moves in Gospel analysis: narrative-reader analysis to expose its impact upon the "implied reader"; and social-historical analysis to recover its impact upon the Gospel's early flesh-and-blood readers. In order to stand at the point of maximal impact later flesh-and-blood readers need to enter the mind-set of the early readers and become the implied readers].

that are studied, the selection of methods used to solve these problems, and the legitimacy and adequacy of proposed solutions."[63] Under this paradigm the text is approached with literary concerns and methods, and it promises fresh insights to old and thorny textual problems.[64]

Reading Mark 13:24–27

In this thesis Mark 13 will be approached from the heuristic perspective of this recent "paradigm shift".[65] Rather than reading Mark 13:24–27 within the paradigm of "history," in the first instance these verses will be read within the paradigm of "literature" in a quest for their narrative integrity.

---

63. Robertson, "Literature," 548.

64. Thus Petersen's comments that the newer criticism answers the questions which Redaction criticism raised but could never answer, *Literary Criticism*, 19. Dewey, *Markan Public Debate*, 15, suggests that a method which begins from literary techniques may even prove useful in interpreting such controversial sections as Mark 13. Although the new methods promise much, some have expressed disappointment that the results have not lived up to the promises due to the domestication of the method within the old paradigm or due to the restraints of the interpretive community; cf. Moore, *Literary Criticism*, xxii.

65. Kuhn's philosophy of "paradigm shifts" is not without its critics. Amongst biblical scholars, for example, Carson, "Recent Developments," 14, n.41, is dismissive of theories that rely too heavily on Kuhn. In the same volume, Woodbridge, "Some Misconceptions," 419, n.136, adds the European Historians W. Schmidt-Biggemann and H. Blumenberg to those who have abandoned Kuhn's theory. However, without claiming anything absolute for Kuhn, his paradigm-thinking can still be adopted heuristically.

2

The Literary Method

The New Paradigm

OPERATING WITHIN THE PERIOD broadly labelled "post-structuralism," the current approach, which rejects the paradigm of "history" in favor of the paradigm of "literature," is called the "newer literary criticism."[1]

The "newer literary criticism"

The term "newer literary criticism" gathers together a variety of methods

> which usually share at least one common belief: the meaning of a text, resides neither in the author's intention (as in traditional historical and literary criticism) nor in the text studied autonomously (as in formalism and structuralism) but in the mind of the reader or, most commonly, in the product of the interaction of the text and the reader.[2]

This thesis adopts the less esoteric and more widespread arm of Post-structuralism, Reader-response criticism.[3]

---

1. Blomberg, "Synoptic Studies." The "newer" is to distinguish this discipline from the older literary (i.e., source) criticism. The two approaches are radically different.

2. Blomberg, "Synoptic Studies," 43.

3. For the rise of such approaches see Tompkins, *Reader-Response Criticism*, which traces it through Richards, Harding and Rosenblatt, Gibson, Prince, Rifaterre, Poulet, Iser, Fish (early), Culler, Holland, Bleich, Fish (later) and Michaels. See also Suleiman,

Reader-Response Criticism

Despite their united and now commonplace[4] concern with what the text does to the reader, there is a variety of Reader-Response Criticisms, each ascribing a different relation of text to reader.[5] Biblical critics importing literary methods have tended to adopt a text-controlled approach,[6] i.e., those "who eschew both the intentionalist [sic] and the affective fallacies[7] but offer a more holistic model, seeking the locus of meaning in a text."[8]

However, most Biblical critics employing literary methods have failed to give the reader full recognition. Some attempts to use literary methods (for example, N. R. Petersen on Mark 13)[9] are no more than cosmetic, since the methods are still directed towards historical critical concerns.[10] Others,

---

"Introduction"; Mailloux, *Interpretive Conventions*. The best analysis and critique of the influence of post-structural criticism on Gospel studies is by Moore, *Literary Criticism*.

4. In (non-biblical) literary circles reader-oriented approaches are now so much taken for granted that one author can discuss its "now hackneyed theses [...] of a commonplace nature," Slawinski, "Reading & Reader," 521.

5. See Resseguie, "Reader-Response Criticism," 307. Some approaches focus on the reader encoded within the text: Genette, *Narrative Discourse*; Prince, "Introduction to the Study of the Narratee"; some give the reader dominance over the text: Holland, *5 Readers Reading*; "UNITY IDENTITY TEXT SELF"; Bleich, *Readers and Feelings*; *Subjective Criticism*; some see the act of reading as a dialectical process: Iser, various works; Fish, various works; see Resseguie's bibliography.

6. As does Fowler, "Reader—Mark." On p.43 Fowler mentions Booth, *Rhetoric of Fiction* and the early Fish (*Self-consuming Artifacts*) as two text-controlled critics who believe in the "rhetorical power of the text." See Fowler's table classifying critics, p.35.

7. The intentional fallacy is: "The error of criticizing and judging a work of literature by attempting to assess what the writer's intention was and whether or not he has fulfilled it rather than concentrating on the work itself." The affective fallacy is defined as "a confusion between the poem and its results (what it is and what it does). A critical error of evaluating a work of art in terms of its results in the mind of the audience." Both terms were discussed by Wimsatt and Beardsley in 1946: "The Intentional Fallacy." My definitions were taken from Cuddon, *Dictionary of Literary Terms*, 20, 330–31.

8. Blomberg, "Synoptic Studies," 43. Notice that the assumption is that there is one meaning embedded in the text, an assumption peculiar to text-controlled critics which touches upon a hotly debated area that I will leave to one side. Biblical critics who have adopted newer literary methods tend to be text-controlled after the fashion of the New Criticism of the 40's and 50's which secular criticism now deems as obsolete; cf. Moore, *Literary Criticism*, 10–11.

9. Petersen, "When is the End?"; "Reader"; *Literary Criticism*, 68–73.

10. This is also recognized by Vorster, "Literary Reflections".

limiting their concerns merely to the analysis of the narrative itself, ought more properly to be described as "Narrative Critics."[11]

Although there is now a "torrent"[12] of Gospel studies from the newer critical perspectives, Mark 13 has so far largely been bypassed.[13] This present work therefore attempts to feel the full weight of a text-controlled reader-oriented perspective with respect to Mark 13.

Reader-Response Method

Reader-Response methods consider a narrative text as a having a *Story*, that is, "the *what* of a narrative," and a reader-oriented *Discourse*, which "works" through a complex of intratextual relationships, that is, "the *how* of a narrative."[14]

A Story

A narrative is not studied referentially, that is, for information about something else (either history or theology), but for its own story.[15] Rather than

---

11. Following Moore, *Literary Criticism*, Ch.2.

12. "In the last few years a torrent of poststructuralist studies of the Gospels has been unleashed and there are no signs of its diminution," Blomberg, "Synoptic Studies," 43.

13. "The Gospel of Mark has so far proved most conducive to reader-response criticism, with its abrupt transitions, apparent doublets, intercalations and uncertain ending"; Blomberg, "Synoptic Studies," 46 n.96.

Scholars from a similar perspective have looked at Mark 2–3, 11–12; Dewey, *Markan Public Debate*, Mark 6–8; Fowler, *Loaves*, 14–16. However, it has not yet been applied to the study of Mark 13. Petersen, "End," has come the closest but, as is commonly done, rather than rigorously applying literary techniques to Mark 13, he simply assumes the historical critical positions on this chapter. Radcliffe, "'The Coming of the Son of Man,'" and M. Smith, "Composition," argue for Mark 13's integrity within the Gospel's story, but their treatments are necessarily summary. Geddert's treatment of the context is masterly, but he too assumes too much from the usual interpretations when he turns to chapter 13; see my Appendix 2.

14. Although the elaborations quoted here are from Fowler, "Rhetoric of Direction," 116, the distinction is drawn by Chatman, *Story and Discourse*, 10, 19, who deals with Story in Chs. 2–3 and Discourse in Chs. 4–5. Although the distinction should be maintained, it must be noted that the Discourse-level also includes the Story-level, for everything has a reader-oriented function.

15. Frei, *Eclipse of Biblical Narrative*, points out that Biblical scholarship tends to read the Bible to extract historical or theological information from it. Frei's proposal is "that the correct way to read a narrative text is not as a source of information, but as a narrative."

THE LITERARY METHOD

"muffling" its voice, Reader-Response lays aside historical questions to confront, or, better, to be confronted by the concerns of the text.[16]

A narrative develops towards a climax, using the basics of plot,[17] characters and time. A plot begins by commissioning the characters for their roles and then moves towards the fulfillment or frustration of these commissioned roles.[18] The interaction between characters with protagonistic and antagonistic roles reveals and builds the tensions that develop the action of the story and engage the reader.[19] The expectation of the resolution

---

"Narration—story-telling—is a basic human activity, which cannot be reduced to anything else"; "The critic's task is to read [. . .] with understanding, not to rewrite"; quoted from Barton, *Reading the Old Testament*, 160–64. Cf. Fowler, "Reading Matthew."

16. Tannehill, "Tension," 138. Needless to say, the focus is on the final form of the text, "as an integral, literary whole," cf. Fowler, "Using Literary Criticism," 628, 629.

17. I.e. a narrative of events arranged in their time-sequence, the emphasis falling on causality. Cuddon, "Plot," 513–14 (quoting from E. M. Forster) states that in general a plot is: "The plan, design, scheme or pattern of events in a play, poem or work of fiction; and, further, the organization of incident and character in such a way as to induce curiosity and suspense in the spectator or reader. In the space/time continuum of plot the continual question operates in three tenses: Why did that happen? Why is this happening? What is going to happen next—and why? (To which may be added: And—is anything going to happen?) [. . .] a story (is) a narrative of events arranged in their time-sequence. A plot is also a narrative of events, the emphasis falling on causality. [. . .] The time sequence is preserved, but the sense of causality overshadows it."

18. Tannehill, "Gospel of Mark."

19. Licht, *Storytelling*, 25.

of such tensions, aided by various time manipulations[20] and redundancies,[21] helps move the plot towards the climax[22] and subsequent dénouement.[23]

A Reader-Oriented Discourse

Reader-Response goes beyond the *What* of the story to discuss the *How* of the discourse, since "[the Gospel writers] told stories; and if we wish to understand what the Gospels say, we should study how stories are told."[24]

---

20. Time is another extremely important element for moving a plot. "It is indeed possible to describe almost all technical features and devices of storytelling in terms of time manipulation"; Licht, *Storytelling*, 98. "All narrative is concerned with time of two kinds, the time of the action and the time of its telling." Manipulation of these two times will produce various effects in the reader, cf. Licht, *Storytelling*, 96–120. For the complex use of time in Mark see Dewey, "Point of View," 104–05. Cf. Petersen, *Literary Criticism*, 49–80.

21. Redundancies, which take various forms, are necessary for "readability". See Anderson, "Double and Triple Stories"; Burnett, "Prolegomenon," 95–98. Anderson and Burnett also refer to: Suleiman, "Redundancy and the 'Readable' Text"; Wittig, "Formulaic Style"; *Stylistic and Narrative Structures*.

22. The climax of a narrative is "that part of a story [. . .] at which a crisis is reached and resolution is achieved." The climax is the moment of resolution after the crisis, i.e., "that point in a story or play at which the tension reaches a maximum and a resolution is imminent," Cuddon, "Climax," "Crisis," 125, 166. It is commonly observed that Mark's climax occurs in the centurion's confession (15:39) (for an alternative view, see Johnson, "Is Mark 15:39 the Key?"), and the passion events from Gethsemane to the crucifixion could quite appropriately be called Mark's crisis.

23. A dénouement "may be the event or events following the major climax of a plot, or the unraveling of a plot's complications at the end," Cuddon, "Dénouement", 181. Note that another broader usage of the term is possible. Stock, *Method*, 288, for example, argues that "In a rhetorical discourse the dénouement is the consequence of and corollary (*lysis*) to the middle section." For Stock, Mark's dénouement consists of 10:53—15:47. However, adopting Cuddon's definition, I would argue that Mark's dénouement consists of the "sandwich" reporting the women watching the crucifixion (15:40–41), the burial of Jesus (15:42–47) and the events surrounding the discovery of the empty tomb by those same women (16:1–8). Mark 13:24–27 therefore appears just before the crisis, climax and the dénouement of Mark's story.

24. Fowler, "Using Literary Criticism," 629.

THE LITERARY METHOD

The Temporal Reading Process

Reader-Response theory's significant contribution to the world of criticism is its attention to "the richness and the dynamism of the temporal experience of reading,"[25] in which it seeks to

> assess the meaning of a text for a reader at various stages of the reading process. Instead of focusing only on the text as a whole, it stresses how the reader's perception of meaning changes depending on the amount of a text he has read, and depending on the nature of the sequence of that text's episodes.[26]

Self-conscious regard of this "diachronic dimension"[27] involves

> the rigorous and disinterested asking of the question, what does this word, phrase, sentence, paragraph, chapter, novel, play, poem, *do*? And the execution involves an analysis of the developing responses of the reader in relation to the words as they succeed one another in time.
>
> The basis of the method is a consideration of the temporal flow of the reading experience, and it is assumed that the reader responds in terms of that flow and not to the whole utterance. That is, in an utterance of any length, there is a point at which the reader has taken in only the first word, and then the second, and then the third, and so on, and the report of what happens to the reader is always a report of what has happened to that point.
>
> Essentially what the method does is slow down the reading experience so that "events" one does not notice in normal time, but which do occur, are brought before our analytical attention. It is as if a slow-motion camera with an automatic stop-action effect were recording our linguistic experiences and presenting them to us for viewing.[28]

---

25. Fowler, "Reader—Mark," 49.

26. Blomberg, "Synoptic Studies," 43. This is an offshoot of new criticism's insistence on "close reading," cf. Cuddon, "New Criticism," 422.

27. This term is used with the meaning drawn from structuralist critics. "The diachronic dimension of a narrative is the chronological order in which events occur"; Malbon, "Galilee and Jerusalem," 248. Note, however, that this term is used differently within historical criticism to talk of the historical processes through which a text passed to reach its final form.

28. Fish, *Is there a Text?*, 26–28; quoted from Fowler, "Reader—Mark," 50, to whom I am indebted throughout this section. This temporal treatment of the text is "uniquely suited" to oral literature such as the Gospels, in which "the world of orality lingers and is still so prominent in the biblical texts, especially Mark, the temporal model of reading

What follows will attempt to "slow down the text" of Mark 13 to analyze its effect on the reader.

The Education of the Reader

The temporal nature of the reading process implies that the text educates its reader. The earlier portion of a story sets up the parameters and conventions that enable the reader correctly to read the rest of the story, the later material is read against the background painted by the preceding material. "While we are dealing with the flow of language, we are actively involved in reviewing what has preceded and speculating about what lies ahead."[29] During this psychological phenomenon of *anticipation* and *retrospection*:[30]

> We look forward, we look back, we decide, we change our decisions, we form expectations, we are shocked by their nonfulfillment, we question, we muse, we accept, we reject; this is the dynamic process of recreation (i.e., of the original act of creating the text).[31]

One particular aspect of this phenomenon is what Iser calls "Indeterminacies" or "gaps" or "blanks."

> it is the gaps, the fundamental asymmetry between text and reader, that give rise to communication in the reading process. [...] Asymmetry [...] [is a form] of an indeterminate, constitutive blank, which underlies all processes of interaction.[32]

The gaps, which "function as a kind of pivot on which the whole text-reader relationship revolves,"[33] guide the reading process by stimulating the reader to

---

employed by reader-response critics is uniquely suited to the study of Mark's Gospel," Fowler, "Reader—Mark," 51–52. Note that this refutes Boomershine's criticism of Reader-Response (Boomershine, "Peter's Denial"; "Biblical Megatrends"). He criticizes Iser's method for being modelled on a "silent reading" media model. However, this is not a necessary element of Iser's model, and in fact, his method is reinforced if Boomershine's media criticism is taken seriously and the text is read aloud. Moore, *Literary Criticism*, 84–107, makes the same observation.

29. Fowler, "Reader—Mark," 50.

30. Malbon, "Galilee and Jerusalem," 248, uses the metaphors "foreshadowing" and "echoing."

31. Iser, "Reading Process," 293; quoted in Fowler, "Reader—Mark," 50.

32. Iser, "Interaction," 109.

33. Iser, "Interaction," 111.

[fill] the blanks with projections. He is drawn into the events and made to supply what is meant from what is not said. What is said only appears to take on significance as a reference to what is not said: it is the implication and not the statements that give shape and weight to the meaning. But as the unsaid comes to life in the reader's imagination, so the said "expands" to take on greater significance than might have been supposed: even trivial scenes can seem surprisingly profound.[34]

When an indeterminacy occurs, rather than give in to the temptation to explain it "on the spot," the reader needs to feel the intrigue of anticipation and await the retrospection that *the story itself will provide in due time*.[35]

Given that Mark 13 is in the middle of Mark's narrative, it ought to be read in an educated manner, that is, in the light of the parameters set up by the earlier story (see Chapter 3). Given that it is not the end of the story, it will likewise anticipate the reading of the remainder of Mark. The reading of Mark 13 will cause the reader to speculate about the future text and the subsequent story will refine/answer/correct those speculations. After examining the broader and more detailed elements of Mark 13 itself (Chapters 4 and 5), Chapter 6 will therefore examine the conclusion of the story in Mark 14–16, which ought to control the reading of Mark 13 in retrospect.

Intratextual Relationships

Who is "the Reader"?

Reader-Response critics answer this "deceptively simple question"[36] with a complex set of interrelationships between text and "reader," outlined in Table 1.

---

34. Iser, "Interaction," 110.

35. This phenomenon can be readily identified in Mark, including chapter 13—as will be shown below. However, traditional Biblical commentating has been unhappy with such gaps. Rather than feel their strength for engagement with the story, they are usually treated as exegetical cruxes to be explained. The proffered explanation is usually extra-textual, not within the story. To pick a random example, see Long, "Shaping Sermons," on Mark 11:13c.

36. Fowler, "Reader—Mark," 31.

Table 1: Interrelation of the Parties in a Narrative Transaction[37]

	Critic
	Critical Reader
Real Author	Real Reader
Implied Author	Implied Reader
Narrator (s)	Narratee (s)

In Table 1, the box represents the text, thereby delineating extra and intratextual relations. The bracketed plurals are due to the possibility of multi-level Narrators/ees, discussed below. Different scholars use different terms,[38] but they describe basically the same interrelationships.

> The real author and real reader are easy enough to grasp. They are living, flesh-and-blood persons who once produced the text and now read it. [. . .] The terms implied author and implied reader, [. . .] have gained wide currency in recognition of the fact that a text implies a role or a persona for both the author and reader. [. . .] Finally, Narrator and Narratee (or) storyteller and listener [. . . sometimes] only oblique, covert [. . . sometimes] overtly portrayed as a character in the narrative.[39]

In order to experience the narrative in its fullest measure, the critic must be prepared to become a reader, albeit a critical reader,[40] and any reader must be prepared to become, at least momentarily, the "implied

---

37. Fowler, "Reader—Mark," 39, using Chatman's title, but modifying his diagram to include the Critic. [2021: in Bolt, *Jesus' Defeat of Death*, 5, I added "characters" as vehicles that may serve both "author" and "reader" sides of the transaction.]

38. Fowler, "Reader—Reader Response Criticism."

39. Fowler, "Reader—Mark," 39; "Reader—Reader Response Criticism," 12, lists three ways in which this analysis is helpful:

> 1. It indicates that there are at least two major role models provided in the text for anyone reading it, i.e., that of implied reader and narratee.
>
> 2. It provides the language necessary to explore the degrees of distance between all of them, and moreover, between any of the four and the characters.
>
> 3. It allows the recognition and a way to talk of the dialogical process that is built into the text and is demanded by the reading experience.

40. Fowler, "Reader—Mark," 32–38; "Reader—Reader Response Criticism," 12, discusses the relationship between "critic" and "reader." See also Moore, *Literary Criticism*, 98–107.

reader."[41] The relationship between the implied reader and the narratee can vary from close and intimate, to ironic and distant.[42] The same goes for the implied reader's relationship with the various characters.

Further refinement can be given in terms of "Narrative Levels," explained as

> a means of describing the phenomenon of stories within stories. The initial or first-level narrator is outside of the narrative (extradigetic) and narrates the first-level narrative. A character within the first-level narrative relates the second-level narrative; a character within the second-level narrative relates the third level, and so forth, as needed. As one changes level, the narratee changes along with the narrator. The first-level narrator addresses the primary narratee—in the case of Mark, the implied reader. The second-level narrator, him/herself a character in the first-level narrative (i.e., an internal character), addresses the second-level narratee, also a character in the first-level narrative (i.e., an internal audience).[43]

The intratextual relationships of Mark 13 can be charted as follows:[44]

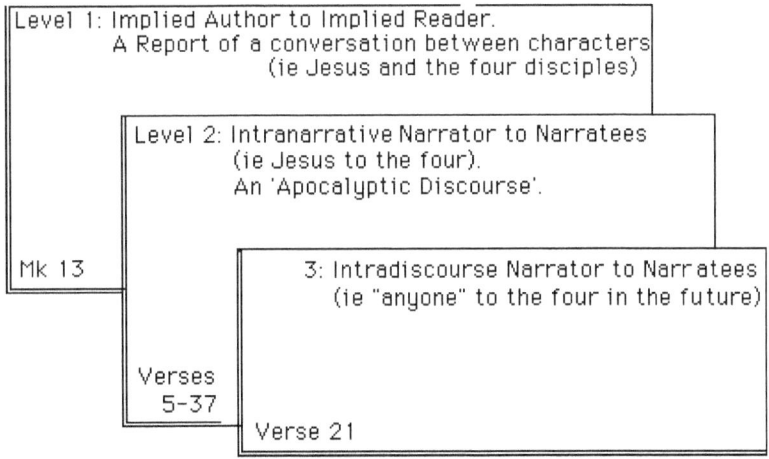

Intratextual Relationships & Narrative Levels in Mark 13

---

41. Fowler, "Reader—Reader Response Criticism," 12.

42. For the concept "distance", discussed and illustrated, see Booth, *Rhetoric of Fiction*, 155–58, 243–66. [2021: in Bolt, *Jesus' Defeat of Death*, I utilized Booth's "distance" analysis more fully.]

43. Dewey, "Point of View," 100, drawing on Genette.

44. Dewey, "Point of View," 102. The diagram is my own, however.

One of the highly unusual features of Mark 13 is that it contains the "famous apostrophe" which directly addresses the reader (verse 14).[45] This constitutes a "violation of narrative level," or, a "metalepsis."[46] The significance of this will be discussed below.

An awareness of such intratextual relationships will avoid their confusion or merging and enable more careful exegesis.[47] For example, the various imperatives of Mark 13 will not be automatically applied to the "flesh-and-blood" readers[48] but will be carefully analyzed through the matrix of intratextual relationships (see Chapter 5).

Who is the "Fit Reader"?

Discussion of the (implied) reader also involves the notion of a "fit," or "ideal," reader,[49] that is "a hypothetical reader with the general ability to comprehend literature."[50] Oversimplifying a rather thorny debate, this "fit reader" is one who is expected to share various assumptions with the implied author.[51]

---

45. Schneidau, "Let the Reader Understand." This fact alone perhaps justifies a reader-oriented approach to the chapter. It is this verse that gives Fowler the title for his forthcoming work [2021: i.e., at the time of the original thesis] *Let the Reader Understand*.

46. This is Genette's term; see Dewey, "Point of View," 103, n.29.

47. The analysis is not pointless, contra Dewey "Point of View." Her problem is that she adopts conventional interpretations for chapter 13 and so fails to see how such analysis points beyond the standard interpretive fare.

48. Which is the hip reaction of most interpreters, especially with verse 37.

49. Other terms used are: informed, optimal, superreader, competent, educated, and mature. Fowler, who thinks the ideal reader approximates the critic, also wants to distinguish between the individual ideal reader and the composite ideal reader. Fowler, "Reader—Mark," 46–49.

50. Mailloux, *Interpretive Conventions*, 203, quoted in Fowler, "Reader—Mark," 47. Biblical critics need to be warned against falling into the trap of trying to find an historical reader to match the implied reader. The implied reader is a textual construct, a "hypothetical reader" implied by the text itself (as if it was a mirror), not a flesh and blood reader that is discerned by looking through the text (as if it was a window).

51. "Every story assumes various norms. These are of two types, some are 'fixed'—the author implies their continuance into the 'real world'—and some of them 'nonce'—embraced only temporarily and applied only in the world of the story," Booth, *Company*, 422.

One of these assumptions for Mark's "fit reader" is the message of the Old Testament.[52] Through quotation, allusion and thematic dependence,[53] the Old Testament is introduced as an authoritative given, inviting the reader to understand Mark by reference to the "informing theology" erected by the Old Testament.[54]

The Method in Action

What follows is an attempt to apply these perspectives to the interpretation of Mark 13 and Reader-Response methods will be in action, even if not always made explicit. I begin with an examination of Mark 1–12, so that the reading of Mark 13 can be done in an educated fashion. A first reading of Mark 13 follows, and then a close reading. The anticipations raised by Mark 13 will then be tested against their retrospections in Mark 14–16, before conclusions are drawn.[55]

---

52. It could be argued that another is the basic gospel message itself, the "beginnings" of which (1:1) are now "fleshed out" for Mark's audience. Recall the observation of Dodd, *Apostolic Preaching*, that Mark's outline is the same as that found in the early Christian *kerygma*. [2021: Cf. Bolt, "What is the gospel?"].

53. That is, rather than a search for proof texts or an examination of only passages directly quoted or alluded to, a sensitivity to any broad Old Testament theological themes which may "inform" our text; cf. Dumbrell, *End*, introduction.

54. The term is Kaiser's describing the flow of biblical theology that precedes the text at hand; Kaiser, *Toward an Exegetical Theology*, ch. 6. Some Reader-Response critics (e.g., van Iersel, *Reading Mark*, 13) deliberately ignore the Old Testament in the interest of reading like a "first-time reader" (or, Moore's colorful term, "the virginal reader"; *Literary Criticism*, Ch.6). This is mistaken, as it overlooks the fact that the Old Testament is a fixed norm for Mark (i.e., part of the "real world" that exists and continues outside his narrative).

55. Despite the increasing tide of opinion, not everyone agrees that Mark is a coherent narrative, or that one can read it as such. See, for example, Meagher, "Die Form- und Redaktionsungeschickliche Methoden"; *Clumsy Construction*; and Räisänen, *The 'Messianic Secret' in Mark's Gospel*, who both argue for the pendulum to swing back to a halfway position between the Form and Redaction critical positions, namely that "the earliest evangelist [is] more of a bearer of tradition, and less of a theologian or interpreter, than recent research has generally assumed him," Räisänen; quoted from the English extract from his German edition: "The 'Messianic Secret' in Mark's Gospel." However, as Räisänen himself acknowledges (of Meagher), these two have "raised a lonely protest against the view of Mark as a great artist," "'Messianic Secret,'" 11.

3

Mark 13 in Anticipation (Mark 1–12)

The Narrative of Mark 1–12

THIS CHAPTER WILL BRIEFLY analyze the expectations raised for the reader by the preceding narrative to facilitate the reading of Mark 13 in its narrative integrity.[1] Different structures have been discerned in Mark's narrative, but it is beyond my scope to argue at length for the structure adopted here.[2] I will outline the contours of Mark's story in five main sections, including additional comments on the dynamics occurring at the discourse level.[3]

---

1. Tannehill, "Gospel of Mark," 77, affirms such integrity: "Mark is a single, unified story because of its progressive narrative lines. Events in the first thirteen chapters are necessary parts of the main lines of action, rather than being preliminary to them." However, in the usual manner, despite this affirmation, Mark thirteen figures minimally in his discussion.

2. For example: Tannehill, "Gospel of Mark" (1:1—8:26; 8:27—10:52; 11:1—16:8); and Butterworth, "Composition" (1:1–13; 1:14–45; 2:1—3:6; 6:1—8:26; 8:27—10:52; 11:1—12:44). My "structure" attempts to capture the flow of the story's movements.

3. My comments on both story and discourse will be necessarily partial and incomplete. It is beyond my scope to argue for all the exegetical conclusions in this chapter which is preparatory to my main concern. I have provided some argument in the footnotes when my exegesis differs from prevailing opinion.

MARK 13 IN ANTICIPATION (MARK 1–12)

The Commissioning Chapters (1:1—3:35)

In Mark's first three chapters all of the major characters are introduced and commissioned for their roles in the narrative.[4]

Jesus (and Disciples) Commissioned

Jesus is titled as "Christ, Son of God" (1:1),[5] heralded as the fulfillment of Isaiah's hopes for forgiveness and the stronger one who, in the Holy Spirit, will bring a baptism to Israel (vv.2–8),[6] and introduced by the heavenly voice as the Son of God who will act as the Servant of the Lord[7] (vv.9–11; cf. Ps 2:7, Isa 42:1).[8] He is tested by Satan (vv.12–13) before emerging with the announcement that the kingdom of God is near (1:14–15).[9]

---

4. That is, they are assigned a goal or task which they will then attempt to fulfil. The term is Tannehill's, "Gospel of Mark," who notes that structural analysis also uses the terms "mandate" and "contract." These commissionings generate the following narrative sequence which "will then relate the fulfilment or nonfulfilment of the commission." In this way "the commission provides an overarching purpose and goal which unifies the sequence and gives meaning to the parts."

5. Although the absence of the words "Son of God" in important elements of the textual tradition may show that they are not original (Head, "A Text-Critical Study of Mark 1.1"), their presence is entirely suitable to Mark's narrative concerns.

6. John is announced in terms of the fulfilment of Isaiah's promises. His ministry is exercised to the recipients of those promises (vv.5–6; cf. Isa 40:9), and his preaching concerns a baptism in anticipation of the promised forgiveness (εἰς *eis* v.4 should be taken in a purposive sense. [2021: Bolt, "'With a view to the forgiveness of sins'".] The forgiveness looked for is that promised by Isa 40:1–2). He promises the coming of "the stronger one" (ὁ ἰσχυρότερος *ho ischyroteros*, v.7, cf. Isa 49:25) who, with the authority of the Holy Spirit, will also have a baptism to perform on this same group (v.8). ἐν πνεύματι ἁγίῳ *en pneumati hagiō* is understood on analogy with similar phrases in Mark (cf. 3:22) which relate to the authority by which a person is operating. See Bolt, "Spirit," 46–48.

7. Not everyone agrees that either Mark or Jesus draws upon the Suffering Servant of Isaiah at this point or later in the Gospel. See, for example, Hooker, *Jesus the Servant*. For the contrary view, more in line with the position adopted here, see Cullmann, *Christology*, 51–82, and the literature cited therein.

8. The emphasis is on his role as Servant, cf. Bolt, "Spirit." For the link between the descent of the spirit and Isa 63:14 (LXX), and therefore between Jesus' baptism and his death via 10:38–39, see Buse, "Markan Account."

9. The "uncertain" (van Iersel, *Reading Mark*, 37) reference to "the beasts" is explained as an apocalyptic motif recalling Daniel (Boomershine, *Story Journey*, 48). These beasts were symbols of world kingdoms, opposed to God, who would be destroyed in the end time when the one like the Son of Man would receive the eternal kingdom of God (Dan 7:13–14). The temptation therefore implicitly prepares for the kingdom announcement

THE NARRATIVE INTEGRITY OF MARK 13:24-27

At the discourse level the prologue commissions Jesus for his role. This information is given to the reader and not the other characters.[10] This gap in the story creates the "opacity" that provides momentum for the reading experience,[11] for the reader now awaits the characters' discovery of what he already knows about Jesus.

Jesus gathers together some disciples and promises to make them into fishers of men (1:16-20; 2:13-14), and to act as an extension of his ministry (3:13-19). This represents the disciples' commissioning, although their prospective role is a subset of Jesus' commissioning.[12] His authority is openly recognized (1:21-45)[13] and eventually explained as that of the

---

in 1:15.

10. The title (v.1), and the scriptural explanation of John's ministry (vv.2-3) are for the reader's ears only. The commissioning scene (vv.9-11) is narrated as a private occurrence from Jesus' perspective, and its telling is therefore the impartation of privileged information. For the effect of privilege on the relationship between Implied Author and Implied Reader see Booth, *Rhetoric of Fiction*, 160-64.

11. Fowler, "Rhetoric of Direction," 125-26: "opacity occurs when either the story or the discourse halts and the other level proceeds by itself. Opacity occurs whenever the narrator introduces a gap into either the story or the discourse, thus excluding either the characters or the narratee from understanding a portion of the story. [... O]pacity is the ultimate strategy of indirection, since it is the outright denial, to either a character or a narratee, of the opportunity to experience and understand fully the story that is being told."

12. Tannehill, "Gospel of Mark," 62, identifies this as the disciples' commissioning "which will provide a norm by which the disciples' subsequent behaviour can be judged." He fails to observe that their commissioning is a subset of Jesus', since the narrative promises activity from Jesus ("I will make you become [...]").

13. For authority as the theme in this section see Gros Louis, "Mark," 300-09.

Son of Man who brings forgiveness to the earth (2:10),[14] which provides a retrospection for the reader (1:4).[15]

Opponents Commissioned

Although his popularity increases (1:33,37; 2:2,13; 3:7-9,20), Jesus also meets with opposition. He is opposed from the outset by the demonic world (1:12-13,24,34,39) and the religious authorities (1:22,45; 2:6-7,15-17), who quickly form an alliance with the political Herod party to work towards Jesus' destruction (3:6). This represents the commissioning of the last major character group so the contours of the story are now in place.[16] Before long the narrative at the discourse level clearly associates the human opposition to Jesus with the demonic opposition that has been there from the beginning (3:20-35).[17]

14. I take this as an explanatory comment by Jesus in the story level, and the narrator's commentary beginning with λέγει *legei*, "he says". Others suggest the whole verse is the narrator's "wink to the reader." To argue this from later material (i.e., that it is too early in Jesus' ministry for a revelation of his person as Son of Man; Lane, *Mark*, 96), ignores the dynamics of the reading experience. Also, if the Son of Man stands implicitly behind the beasts, the kingdom, and Jesus' ἐξουσία *exousia*, "authority", as I have suggested, then he is already part of Mark's presentation of Jesus. Fowler, "Rhetoric of Direction," 121-22, argues for a "wink to the reader" on the basis of the syntax and other parallel pieces of authorial commentary. The function of the narrator's intrusion, λέγει τῷ παραλυτικῷ *legei tō paralytikō*, "he says to the paralytic", for which Fowler asks an explanation, is simply to signal that Jesus then switched addressees from the scribes (vv.8b-10a) to the paralytic (NB v.8 λέγει αὐτοῖς *legei autois* [. . .] v.10b λέγει τῷ παραλυτικῷ *legei tō paralytikō*). The break from speech to the speech-act of healing portrays the same vividness as the drama of the occasion no doubt commanded.

15. It is usual to treat 2:1-12 as the beginning of the so-called controversy section (2:1—3:6). However, such a division ignores the function of the journey from Capernaum (1:21-34) to elsewhere in Galilee (1:34-44), to the desert again (1:45) and then "back home" (cf. ἐν οἴκῳ ἐστίν *en oikō estin*, 2:1) to complete the circle and focus on the end scene, as well as the new beginning in (2:13; cf. 1:16 and 3:7; 4:1,35) and so misses the climactic nature of the paralytic healing scene (2:1-12). There are also several clear links between the two scenes which reinforce them as counterparts: the crowd 2:2, cf. 1:32-34; the amazed response 2:12, cf. 1:27; the conflict with the scribes 1:22 implicit, 2:6-9 explicit; the authority question asked 1:(?24), 27, cf. 2:6-7, and answered 2:10.

16. Tannehill, "Gospel of Mark," 62, who also observes that "these three commissionings (i.e., Jesus, the disciples, the opponents) or tasks, then, have a scope which enables them to bind Mark together as a single narrative."

17. This is achieved by Mark's "sandwich" technique, which, by inserting one story into the middle of another, two stories must be read together. See Edwards, "Markan Sandwiches."

Jesus Accepts his Commission

The commissioning chapters end with Jesus clearly assuming his commissioned role (3:31-35), despite the temptation not to (3:20-21),[18] and the blatant opposition (3:22-30). He will continue to act as the Servant of the Lord amongst Israel.

Preparation in Parables (4:1-34)

The Parables Discourse

Once the commissioning chapters have set the expectations for the story, the middle section of Mark is introduced by the "Parables Discourse."[19] Aided by its concentric structure, this section focuses upon the coming harvest, which is a picture of the coming kingdom of God.[20] The sower is already at work and there is an abundant harvest in view (vv.3-9).[21] However, in the vein of Isaiah 6, parables are told to effect a temporary hardening of Israel,[22] who are nevertheless paradoxically prevented from

---

18. The focus of this section is about Jesus, rather than the crowd about him. The family plans to take charge of him, and presumably return him to Nazareth where it all began, constitute a potential reversal of his mission (3:20-21; cf. 1:9), and a denial of all that has taken place thus far. His decision to stay with those who do the will of God (3:31-35) is therefore a decision to embrace the will of God for him. See also Donahue, "Neglected Factor."

19. I have retained this usual descriptive term despite the potential confusion with Chatman's more specialized use of the word "discourse" (see above, pp. 18, 20). In length, the Parables Discourse it is second only to the Apocalyptic Discourse and in narrative position it mirrors Mark 13.

20. Donahue, *Gospel in Parable*, 28-52.

21. The sudden introduction of ὁ σπείρων *ho speirōn*, "the sower", draws upon the imagery of God's salvific activity through his word in Isa 55:8-13. Since Mark 1:14 Jesus has been proclaiming "the gospel of God" and this riddle now suggests that through this word God will inevitably work the harvest of salvation promised in Isaiah. Cf. Isa 55:10 LXX δῷ σπέρμα τῷ σπείροντι καὶ ἄρτον εἰς βρῶσιν *dō sperma tō speironti kai arton eis brōsin*, "to give seed to the sower and bread for food". The focus is on the inevitability of the harvest, which metaphor is then applied to the inevitability of God's promised salvation and the joy of those rescued. Jesus' reference to the sower catches up the whole picture, i.e. the reality through the figure. With this background it is misguided to allegorize Jesus as the sower. As in Mark 1:14 Jesus is proclaiming the gospel of God, and through this word the sower (God) will inevitably work his harvest.

22. Other explanations are given: 1. It is not a deterministic saying, but a mistranslation. a) of the Aramaic: ἵνα *hina* becomes a code word which introduces the Scripture

receiving forgiveness only by their lack of hearing with understanding (vv.10–12).²³ This underlines the necessity of receiving the word in such a way that it issues in harvest (vv.13–20), that is, through listening well (vv.21–25).²⁴ The secret of the kingdom (4:11) then begins to be explained by two parables which liken the kingdom to the harvest. Once the seed is scattered it will come suddenly, as an interruption to ordinary life (vv.26–29), and it will be a harvest that will encompass the world (vv.30–32).²⁵ What begins amongst hardened Israel will issue in the universal kingdom of God. Jesus' teaching is immediately realised in the story, for through his parabolic teaching people only received the word in proportion to their understanding (vv.33–34). Jesus' parabolic teaching method is part of his

---

quotation; μήποτε *mēpote* mistranslates the Aramaic for "unless." This is meant to describe the reaction to Jesus' ministry, and not just the parables. Jeremias, *Parables*, 13–18. The positive evidence is that the text is closest to the Aramaic Targum of Isaiah. b) Greek to modern language: ἵνα *hina* used for result (Moule, *Idiom Book*, 142–46), cf. Matt 13:13 changes to ὅτι *hoti*. (μήποτε *mēpote* still remains a mystery). 2. It is a deterministic saying of the early church about Israel. Its background would be in the OT hardening theme (Exod 4:21; 8:15,32; 9:34), and such teaching as found in Rom 9:16–19, 10:16–21, 11:7–10, John 12:37–41, and Acts 28:25–8. Donahue, *Gospel in Parable*, 28–52, feels that Mark 12:12 is against this opinion, for there the Jews do understand. However, in terms of Isaiah 6 they don't really see at all, for if they see and hear they would turn and be forgiven. Mark 12:12 underlines their rebelliousness by showing that, despite getting so far, they nevertheless did not turn to find forgiveness. 3. It is a deterministic saying that Mark has inserted, because it suits his theology. This is then linked to his secrecy theme. 4. It is ironical, Fowler, "Rhetoric of Direction," 124–32; and Hollenbach, "Lest they should turn," 319 n.8, who briefly surveys the variety of opinion.

23. The allusion to Isa 6:9–10 is not only "a statement about the people of Judah who are unwilling to turn and be healed" (Hollenbach, "Lest they should turn," 312), but reveals God's express purpose to temporarily harden Judah so that he can go through with his purposes of judgment (cf. Isa 6:11–13). Because the hardening theme appears inconsistent with other revelation of God's character in the narratives, both Fowler and Hollenbach argue that this statement is meant to read as "patent nonsense" (Fowler, "Rhetoric of Direction," 128) or "absurdity" (Hollenbach, "Lest they should turn," 313) and therefore as ironical. It is better to notice that such a statement, certainly shocking, is inconsistent and absurd *unless a good explanation is forthcoming*. In Isaiah such an explanation is given in terms of a temporary hardening, which is recognized by Hollenbach in a footnote (p.313 n.4, citing Isa 29:13–14,23–24), but not taken seriously in his text.

24. The promise of the disclosure of the secret (vv.21–22) makes listening all the more imperative (v.23). The imperative is given in terms of the earlier discourse (v.23 resumes v.9; v.24 resumes the vocabulary of v.12, βλέπετε τί ἀκούετε *blepete ti akouete*), as is the final promise and warning attached to it (vv.24b–25; cf. 4:11–12): "See what you are hearing," i.e., attend to the word from God that has arrived in Jesus!

25. The parable draws on Daniel's world tree, an image of a great world kingdom (Dan 4:10–12, 20–27; cf. Ezek 17:22–24 and Judg 9:7–15).

strategy to establish a remnant within hardened Israel (cf. Isa 6:13). Those who listen well become insiders, eager to do the will of God; those who do not, remain outside (cf. 3:31–35).

The Discourse of the Parables Discourse

In terms of its function for the reader this section opens up an opacity in both story and discourse (now used technically). Verse 11 creates gaps in the story concerning the identity of the insiders and outsiders,[26] and the nature of the secret given, since there is no indication that there was any uptake[27] by the characters of the content of this mystery.[28] Although the latter gap is soon closed (vv.26,30), it is immediately replaced with the expectation of the sudden kingdom of God harvest (4:26–32).[29] Verse 11

---

26. Like Isaiah's ministry established a remnant (Isa 6:13), so too has Jesus' ministry (3:31–35), and it will continue to do so. However, with Donahue, *Gospel in Parable*, 28–52, these groups are open-ended at this stage. See further Bowker, "Mystery and Parable."

27. Fowler, "Rhetoric of Direction," 118, drawing upon Austin's speech-act theory, indicates that "uptake" is when a character in the story-level demonstrates clear and unmistakable knowledge of the issue concerned.

28. In line with the usage elsewhere in the New Testament, where the context regularly shows that the mystery has been revealed, it is usual for commentators to talk of them receiving revelation, and then to embark upon a quest for the content of that revelation (See Kingsbury, *Conflict in Mark*, 135, n.15). However, the word itself need not contain this full revelatory significance here. The most that can be said from the word is that it is something that needs to be revealed if it is to be understood. Whether or not it is revealed is a question to be answered from context. In Mark 4 the usual understanding doesn't reckon with the strangeness of the combination τὸ μυστήριον δέδοται *to mystērion dedotai*, and hardly comports with the dullness of the twelve for at least four more chapters, if not longer! The Q saying (Matt 13:11=Luke 8:10) adds the infinitive γνῶναι *gnōnai* which reveals the intention but not the timing of the knowledge. This therefore reinforces the point being made here. Although Fowler majors upon the gap at discourse level, he leaves open the possibility of a story gap as well, "Rhetoric of Direction," 130.

29. Cf. Van Iersel, *Reading Mark*, 79–80, who argues that they

> have definitely been given a secret but do not know its content and so the reader awaits the report of their full understanding. As with a document enclosed in an envelope, they know that the secret exists, but not what it contains. Are they for this reason in a better position than the outsiders, who are unaware of the existence of a secret? Most certainly! To the outsiders everything comes in riddles, nothing is comprehensible. They do not even know that there is a key to the riddles. But those who have been given a secret know at least that there is a secret and that there are riddles (4:11). And riddles, they know, can be understood if one is in the possession of

also creates a gap in the discourse since the report that the mystery is given to some in the story has the effect of making the reader an outsider at this point.³⁰ This is sustained by the exclusion of the reader from Jesus' private explanations to his disciples (v.34). The prologue generated momentum through the expectation that the characters will gain the reader's privileged information. The Parables Discourse continues the momentum by making the reader curious to gain entry to the disciples' privilege.

The Unbelief of Israel (4:35—8:26)

The next section of the story is structured by a series of three sea crossings in which the reader shares the disciples' privilege.

Jesus and Israel's Political Leadership

The first sea crossing (4:35–41) reinforces the authority of Jesus (vv.39,41; cf. 1:27), reveals the unbelief of the disciples (v.40) and explicitly raises the question of Jesus' identity (v.41).³¹ The reader recognizes an answer in the next unit, which, through the narrator's retrospection to the riddle of the strong man (3:27), shows Jesus to be the stronger one promised by John

---

the key. For the time being they hear only that the secret refers to the kingdom of God. A key is not yet provided.

He cites 1 Enoch 68:1 as the only other example of the noun μυστήριον *mystērion* being the direct object of δίδωμι *didōmi*. He argues that the gap remains open unto the Last Supper, sacramentally understood (cf. also his technical treatment in "Reader of Mark as Operator."). Bassler, "The Parable of the Loaves," agrees the gap stays open until the Supper but interprets the closure in terms of the Crucifixion, of which the supper is a symbol. In actual fact, as argued below, the gap is closed within the parable discourse and then another gap is opened up in terms of the harvest.

30. "In 4:11 it would seem that Jesus' disciples are insiders, who possess the secret of the kingdom, while the narratee is an outsider, not possessing the secret. At this point in the passage the reader seems to stand on the outside of the privileged circle of insight and understanding, and laments that she or he has been so excluded," Fowler, "Rhetoric of Direction," 126.

31. The story has clearly been concerned about this question already, but it has done indirectly what a character now does with a direct question. For an example of how unanswered questions guide the reading process; see Fowler, "Rhetoric of Direction," 121.

(1:7; cf. Isa 49:24-25),³² and recognized as the Lord (5:19-20).³³ The "stronger one" begins to plunder Satan's domain in the next two sandwiched scenes in which he gives more than expected (5:21-43).³⁴ Jesus can be trusted to give salvation, and in the face of death this even means resurrection. The faith shown in these scenes is contrasted by the unbelief of Nazareth (6:1-6), and Herod (6:14-29), and yet this is the context in which Jesus' mission is taking place. As he promised (3:14-19) he now sends out his disciples (6:7-13), despite the opposition that lurks in the background from Herod's kingdom (6:14-29; cf. 3:6). When they return, Jesus performs a miracle which the narrator's commentary (v.34)³⁵ directs the reader to view as *an issue of the leadership of Israel* (cf. Num 27:17; Ezek 34:5). Israel's political shepherd Herod has let them down, and now the good shepherd feeds them (Ezek 34:11-16). The focus on cost (6:36-37) highlights that this bread was free, and so recalls the promises of Isa 55:2 and the need for Israel to listen with understanding (Mark 4:3-9; cf. Isa 55:10-12). The

---

32. By slowing the narrative down, the descriptive details focus the reader's attention on this man: he came from the tombs v.2; he had an unclean spirit v.2 (later we will learn that this is an understatement!); the repetition that he dwelt in the tombs v.3 raises the question why he adopted this abode. The reason follows: καὶ οὐδὲ ἁλύσει οὐκέτι οὐδεὶς ἐδύνατο αὐτὸν δῆσαι, *kai oude halysei ouketi oudeis edynato auton dēsai* ("and neither was anyone able to bind him with a chain") which is further emphasized by the graphic details of v.4. The real point of the description is then resumed in the final climactic description καὶ οὐδεὶς ἴσχυεν αὐτὸν δαμάσαι *kai oudeis ischyen auton damasai* ("and no-one was strong [enough] to subdue him") which is then linked to his abode in the tombs and tormented state, v.5. The verbal links with 3:27 are patent: ἀλλ' οὐ δύναται οὐδεὶς εἰς τὴν οἰκίαν τοῦ ἰσχυροῦ εἰσελθὼν τὰ σκεύη αὐτοῦ διαρπάσαι, ἐὰν μὴ πρῶτον τὸν ἰσχυρὸν δήσῃ, καὶ τότε τὴν οἰκίαν αὐτοῦ διαρπάσει *all' ou dynatai oudeis eis tēn oikian tou ischyrou eiselthōn ta skeuē autou diarpasai, ean mē prōton ton ischyron dēsē, kai tote tēn oikian autou diarpasei* (cf. also 1:7 ἔρχεται ὁ ἰσχυρότερός *erchetai ho ischyroteros*).

33. This fact is delightfully and subtly drawn to the reader's attention by the narrator's exact repetition of Jesus' direct speech with one crucial variation, highlighted by a change in word order: v.19 ὅσα ὁ κύριός σοι πεποίηκεν *hosa ho kyrios soi pepoiēken*, v.20 ὅσα ἐποίησεν αὐτῷ ὁ Ἰησοῦς *hosa epoiēsen autō ho Iēsous* ("the Lord" . . . "Jesus" . . .). The magnitude of his discovery is also reinforced by the changed sphere of proclamation (from the house to the ten cities!) and the generalized response of amazement.

34. The curious use of "twelve years" (vv.25,42) is intriguing, and perhaps by virtue of its curiosity simply functions to bind the two stories even closer together, so that their lessons are mutually reinforced. For a treatment of the term from an historical perspective see Moiser, "'She was twelve years old,'" although he fails to tie in the reference in 5:25.

35. It employs both an inside view and an explanation.

Jesus and Israel's Religious Leadership

In the next sea miracle (6:45–52) Jesus reveals his divinity,[37] but the disciples miss the point. The narrator, closing the gap left by the previous scene, explains to the reader that this was because they had not understood the miracle of the loaves and, in fact, their hearts were hardened (vv.51–52). This immediately causes the reader to associate them with Jesus' opponents (3:5) and the story goes on to make this association public. In 7:1–37 Jesus exposes the hard heartedness of his Pharisaic opponents (v.6; cf. Isa 29:13,19,21) who refuse to listen to the word (vv.8,13), and deliberately compares the disciples with this group (7:18).[38] Although Israel and the disciples are hard-hearted, there are some outside of Israel who readily recognize Jesus' identity (7:24–30,31–37).[39] Jesus repeats the feeding miracle (8:1–10) for the disciples, and although their response is not given, their dullness is obvious to the reader.[40]

---

36. They come, they suggest people ought to go for food, vv.35–36; he tells them to feed the crowd, v.37; they object, v.37; they are to investigate how many loaves, v.38; they sit them down, vv.39–40, feed them, v.42, and collect the pieces v.43. Presumably it is they who count the leftovers, and there is one basket for each of them, v.43.

37. Not only is walking on the sea a divine ability (Job 9:8–11), but ἤθελεν παρελθεῖν αὐτούς *ēthelen parelthein autous* (v.48) alludes to Exod 33:19,22; 34:6 and ἐγώ εἰμι *egō eimi* (v.50) alludes to Exod 3:14, cf. 34:6. Guelich, *Mark*, 350–51.

38. Not all English versions bring out the force of the Greek: Οὕτως καὶ ὑμεῖς ("you also") ἀσύνετοί ἐστε; οὐ νοεῖτε *houtōs kai hymeis asynetoi este? ou noeite* (cf. 4:12), although cf. KJV, NEB, NASB.

39. Both stories speak of the impossibility of keeping the news about Jesus quiet (vv.24,36). The people of the Decapolis, who have already heard of the strong man before (5:20), now proclaim the news that Israel's Messiah has arrived (v.37; cf. Isa 35:5–6).

40. Fowler, *Loaves*, examines the two stories exhaustively. With the memory of the other feeding fresh in mind, the disciples' question (v.4) makes the reader groan at their dullness, especially after the intervening events. "One can no longer dodge the admittedly distasteful conclusion that the author intends for the disciples to come off badly in this pair of stories. They look dumb because that is the way the author paints them," Fowler, "Using Literary Criticism," 629.

Jesus Warns against his Opponents

Their departure upon their third sea crossing raises the expectation of further revelation (v.10),[41] but this is delayed by the arrival of his opponents to test him through demanding a sign, which they do not receive (8:11–13). When it arrives, the expected revelation is a warning against the Pharisees and Herod (15).[42] This coalition against Jesus (cf. 3:6), already encountered in this section (Herod, ch. 6; Pharisees, ch. 7), constitutes a danger for the disciples too. The warning, however, is misunderstood (v.16). The section (4:35–8:26) ends with a series of incredulous questions in which Jesus stresses what the narrator previously revealed (cf. 6:52).[43] The disciples' failure to understand the miracles of the loaves is because they are hard hearted. Rather than being part of the remnant, they still appear to be part of hard-hearted Israel. However, Jesus' question also raises the expectation that their ignorance is not the last word (οὔπω oupō, v.21). The journey ends with the two-stage healing of a blind man, which reinforces this hope by acting as a picture of the disciples' partial sight.

The Discourse

After the "Parables Discourse" the reader looked for a mutual exchange of privilege with the disciples. In this section he has shared their private transactions with Jesus and discovered that the exchange has been one way. Although the revelations of Jesus' identity have reinforced the reader's privilege, there appears to be no uptake by the disciples. Their lack of understanding is such that Jesus tragically questions whether they are aligned more with his opponents than with him. These "blind men" need to be made to see.

---

41. Since this is now the third in the series, it also raises the expectation of a *climactic* revelation.

42. The genitives are epexegetic, "The yeast *which is* the Pharisees and Herod."

43. They allude very clearly to the "Parables Discourse" which preceded it, and the hard-heart theme that has recurred throughout:
   Don't you see or understand? (i.e., Isa 6, cf. Mk 4:12)
   Do you have ears/ eyes yet do not see (i.e., Jer 5:21, cf. Mk 4:23, 29)
   Cf. Geddert's treatment of this segment as contributing to Mark's epistemology, *Watchwords*, Ch 3.

MARK 13 IN ANTICIPATION (MARK 1–12)

The Necessity of the Passion (8:27—10:52)

This section revolves around three predictions of the passion and their accompanying teaching on discipleship.[44]

The Kingdom is Near (8:27—9:29)

The turning point of the story[45] arrives when the disciples begin[46] to answer their own question (4:41) by confessing Jesus as "the Christ" (8:27–30).[47] Jesus' first passion prediction (v.31) emphasizes the necessity of the Son of Man's suffering, rejection by Israel's leaders, death and resurrection.[48] Suffering is not integral to the Son of Man (cf. Daniel 7), but this expectation is drawn from the Servant motif. Jesus, who will be Son of Man, must firstly fulfill his role as the Servant who suffers as Israel and for Israel (Isaiah 53). This statement meets with resistance (v.32b),[49] but Jesus rebukes such human thinking (v.33). Despite the potential for danger (v.35) his followers—if they are to be the remnant of Israel—must be prepared to

---

44. My heading for these chapters is taken from Burkill, "Strain on the Secret," and reflects the fact that the dominant concern is the passion, not discipleship itself. Tannehill, "Gospel of Mark," 72, is a bit confusing when he names discipleship as "the dominant concern" and the passion predictions as "the key element in 8:27–10:52."

45. An "observable moment when, [...] there is a definite change in direction and one becomes aware that [...] the narrative is now about to move towards its end," Cuddon, "Turning Point," 727. It is commonly recognized that Mark 8:27–30 is such a moment.

46. It is not as fulsome a recognition as that of the reader nor the other characters (e.g., demons 1:24,34; 3:11; others in strange places 5:19–20; 7:37), nor as fulsome a view as that revealed by Jesus himself (2:10,28; 5:1–20; cf. 3:27; 6:31–44,45–52; 8:1–10).

47. This recognition is two staged, clearly paralleling the scene before, and indicating that their blindness has begun to be "healed": 1. Jesus asks them for the results of the opinion poll (vv.27–28, with the focus on himself, με *me*). 2. Jesus puts them on the spot (v.29, ὑμεῖς *hymeis*, "you", is emphatic in nature and position) and Peter answers v.29b.

48. Rather than giving new content to Jesus' commissioning (i.e. his suffering) (Tannehill, "Gospel of Mark," 72–73), this prediction merely draws out what is implicit in Jesus' designated role as Servant (1:9–11; cf. Isa 52:13—53:12).

49. Rather than reading this as a christological misunderstanding (which needs to be read into both Peter's mind and Mark's text), his action ought to be set against the backdrop of opposition from the already familiar opponents and extant plot (3:6). His rebuke occurs in direct connection (καί *kai*) with Jesus' open speech (παρρησίᾳ *parrēsia*). Given the insidious backdrop of Herod (3:6; 6:14–29), in whose territory they now stand (8:27), and the powerful religious authorities, it arises from his sense of danger at Jesus' public "slander" of the powers that be. Peter is ashamed of Jesus' word and so he tries to silence it. This then makes sense of the following rebuke by Jesus (vv.35,38).

die,⁵⁰ and ought not be ashamed of him or his words in the face of the pressure of "this sinful and adulterous generation" (v.38).⁵¹ There is an urgency about following him on his road to suffering, since the kingdom of God has a definite time frame: it is about to burst upon them in power (9:1; cf. 1:15).⁵²

The voice on the mountain reveals Jesus' commission to the three disciples (9:2-8 cf. 1:11),⁵³ but Jesus silences them until the Son of Man rises from the dead (9:9).⁵⁴ Their discussion about the resurrection day (v.10)⁵⁵ leads to an observation that Elijah must come first (v.11). Jesus

---

50. Tannehill, "Gospel of Mark," 73, is right that this is a "new statement of the disciples' commission," although it is merely the spelling out of the implications of following Jesus, now that he reveals that the outcome of his ministry will be death. The language is deliberately reminiscent of 1:16-20, and the focus is upon the act of following (twice). What is emphasised here is that this involves the preparedness to die (= the denial of self and taking up of the cross) for Jesus and his words/the gospel.

51. In New Testament usage ἐπαισχύνομαι *epaischynomai* suggests silence rather than speech. This then links directly with Peter's action in v.32. The reference to "this generation" (ἐν τῇ γενεᾷ ταύτῃ τῇ μοιχαλίδι καὶ ἁμαρτωλῷ *en tē genea tautē tē moichalidi kai hamartōlō*, v.38) in the context can only be the generation that kills Jesus (v.31), i.e., the opponents of the previous narrative who are paradigmatic for hardened Israel; cf. Jer 7:29.

52. France, *Government*, 64-84, discusses the history of interpretation of this verse.

53. Reading the transfiguration as the referent to the promise of 9:1 is misguided. Apart from proximity, which is not sufficient in itself, there are no closures in 9:2-13 suggesting that this is the fulfillment, but rather expectations are sustained, suggesting that closure is yet to come. The arguments of Nardoni, "A Redactional Interpretation of Mark 9:1," can all be pressed into service for a more literary interpretation in which the expectation of 9:1 is sustained *through* the transfiguration scene. The discussion about God's eschatological timetable (9:11-13) provides the reason for the kingdom's imminent arrival: Elijah has come; the Son of Man is about to suffer too, as the last event in the expected sequence.

54. Lane, *Mark*, 323: "The clear implication of the statement is that the period of concealment is to be followed by a time of open proclamation when his status as the transfigured Son and eschatological Judge is to be announced to all (cf. 13:10; 14:9)." It is the only instance where Jesus sets a limit to the silence he is so fond of imposing.

55. This discussion involved neither a general debate about resurrection nor an analysis of the Son of Man's coming resurrection, *pace* Lane, *Mark*, 324, and Taylor, *Mark*, 394, both based on the Western text (ὅταν ἐκ νεκρῶν ἀναστῇ *hotan ek nekrōn anastē*; D W et al) rather than the reading in the majority of manuscripts, including the older and better (τί ἐστιν τὸ ἐκ νεκρῶν ἀναστῆναι *ti estin to ek nekrōn anastēnai*). However, this text should not be accepted. It is the easier reading (*pace* Cranfield, *Mark*, 297), being a direct lift of a phrase from v.9. It also misunderstands the disciples' situation, since they would have had no concept of an individual resurrection, cf. John 11:23-24. On the other hand, the general resurrection was already linked to the Son of Man by the

agrees with the scribal exegesis,[56] before reinforcing and explaining the previous necessity (8:31): the Scriptures say that the Son of Man must suffer *before the resurrection day occurs* (v.12). Since the Elijah prophecy has been fulfilled already (v.13),[57] the only thing to occur before the resurrection day—and so the kingdom[58]—is his predicted suffering. This imminence is reinforced by the event at the foot of the mountain (9:14–29) which is cast as a resurrection scene.[59] Since resurrection has come amongst them, the end must be imminent indeed.

---

narrative flow of Daniel (7:13–14; 12:1–3). Lane commits an even worse anachronism by suggesting the disciples argued over the relationship between his resurrection and parousia, when they would have had absolutely no concept of such a separation until after Jesus' resurrection had occurred. Misunderstanding the force of the vocabulary and the connection between the several components of the sentence has also bedevilled translations. It is best rendered: "and they [the disciples] seized upon this statement, debating amongst themselves 'what it is to rise from the dead,'" —that is, they excitedly discussed the nature of the resurrection day which was already part of their own hope. The connection latent in Jesus' saying between the coming of the Son of Man (Dan 7:13–14) and the general resurrection (Daniel 12) began an excited discussion concerning what it would be like to rise from the dead when this great hope finally arrived. This understanding does justice both to the vocabulary and the syntax of the sentence and to the disciples' salvation-historical context.

56. Note that the disciples' reference to the scribes is simply a quotation of Mal 3:23 (LXX).

57. The reader recalls previous allusions to Elijah in the ministry of John the baptizer: in 1:2–8, both through his resemblances to Elijah, and the Malachi quotation, and also in 6:14–29 where he is harassed by a wicked woman and a weak king, cf. 1 Kgs 19:2,10 (Lane, *Mark*, 326).

58. Daniel expected the Son of Man to be given the kingdom of God (7:13–14) and then to share it with the saints (v.27). As his prophecy concludes it becomes clear that this sharing will be through resurrection (Daniel 12).

59. Verse 22 hints in this direction. He is referred to as dead twice (v.26 ὡσεὶ νεκρός, ὥστε τοὺς πολλοὺς λέγειν ὅτι ἀπέθανεν *hōsei nekros, hōste tous pollous legein hoti apethanen*), and twice as resurrected (v.27 ὁ δὲ Ἰησοῦς [. . .] ἤγειρεν αὐτόν, καὶ ἀνέστη *ho de Iēsous* [. . .] *ēgeiren auton, kai anestē*), cf. Lane, *Mark*, 334, "the accumulation of the vocabulary of death and resurrection in verses 26–27, and the parallelism with the narrative of the raising of Jairus' daughter, suggest that Mark wished to allude to a death and resurrection."

Entering the Kingdom (9:30—10:31)

Jesus' second passion prediction stresses the coming death and again mentions the resurrection, but its new feature is the note of betrayal (9:31).[60] The disciples' concern with greatness issues in the enigmatic sayings regarding service (v.35) and the reception of children (9:33–37). The former provides "service of all" as the criterion for greatness, and opens a gap concerning who will prove to be "the first."[61] The latter saying erects a gap requiring an explanation of why the receipt of a child in Jesus' name is the receipt of Jesus and his sender.[62] Nevertheless it means that care needs to be exercised towards others who side with Jesus (vv.38–41). Entry to the kingdom is so important that radical action needs to be taken against anything that causes the disciples to sin in this way (vv.42–50).[63] In the next scene the hard-hearted religious leaders (10:5; cf. 7:1–23; 8:11–14) continue their opposition.[64] The "great" of the land "test" Jesus, but the "small" are brought to him for blessing (10:13–16) and Jesus then provides the explanation lacking previously (v.15 cf. 9:37):[65] to receive a child is to receive a reminder of how anyone enters the kingdom, not through greatness but through dependent reception, "being blessed" by Jesus (v.16).[66] In contrast, the moral man who

---

60. This perhaps explains why Jesus was being secretive (v.31 is causally connected to v.30, γάρ *gar*).

61. The Greek is not usually well discussed; e.g., Lane, *Mark*, 339–340; Best, *Following Jesus*, 77–78; Cranfield, *Mark*, 307–08; Taylor, *Mark*, 404–05. Rather than treating the protasis as a general condition, and giving the future in the apodosis imperatival force, the construction appears to be an example of "εἴ *ei* with the indicative of reality" (BDF, #372), which can be taken as Jesus throwing down a challenge: "If anyone *really wishes* to be the first, he will (genuine future) be the servant of all," in other words, true greatness will be proved by the future course of events. This raises the question, who will this "first one" prove to be? Cf. 10:45.

62. This is reflected in the debate over the verse. The connection with 10:13–16, and 10:43–44 is often noticed, e.g., Fleddermann, "Discipleship Discourse," but their relationship ought to be explained as one of anticipation/retrospection.

63. Presumably in the context the sin is something that causes them to scandalize others. For example, the desire for greatness (vv.33–34) and exclusivity (v.38).

64. The reader enters into something of the frustration expressed by Jesus (10:5), since, after 9:42–50, he knows it is time for some radical choices, but instead they merely engage Jesus on a fine point of Jewish law!

65. A clear retrospection to 9:33–37. The reader is aware that the disciples still have not learned their lesson, since here Jesus must reinforce it.

66. With Best, *Following Jesus*, 107–08, ὡς παιδίον *hōs paidion* means not "as a child is received" but "as a child receives" namely, in trust. Cf. Lane, *Mark*, 360, "receive as gift [. . .] objective humbleness"; Taylor, *Mark*, 422, "not humility but receptiveness."

proves to be wealthy (vv.17–27)[67] is an example of the impossibility of any human "great one" entering the kingdom, and an opportunity for Jesus to teach that salvation is only possible with God (v.27). Jesus then reassures the disciples that their step of leaving everything to follow him will not go unrewarded (vv.28–30). The "great ones" who have everything are not as well off as these who have left it all behind, since a great reversal will take place, and many will find that first place ahead of the ones who appear to be first in this world (v.31).

The Means of Entering the Kingdom (10:32–52)

With Jerusalem in his sights, Jesus privately revealed to his disciples the things which were now imminent (τὰ μέλλοντα αὐτῷ συμβαίνειν *ta mellonta autō symbainein*). This third passion prediction gives the specific location and detailed processes by which the Son of Man will be condemned, handed over to the abuse of the Gentiles, and killed before rising (10:33–34).[68] The imminence of the suffering and therefore the kingdom (cf. v.37) prompts a request from James and John (v.35).[69] In reply to the Zebedees, and also to the resultant bickering over greatness, Jesus reveals why the Son of Man's death is necessary. It is the baptism of Jerusalem promised by John (v.38; cf. 1:8),[70] the removal of their cup of wrath (v.38; cf. Isa 51:17–23) and their ransom (v.45; cf. Isa 53:12). Jesus will die as the Suffering Servant. He is the one who becomes last of all, the servant of all (cf. 9:35). This is the means by which God achieves the impossible, for by the Servant's death his disciples will benefit (v.39),[71] and the many will enter the kingdom ahead of

67. No-one in the story demonstrates uptake of the fact that the man was wealthy, but v.22 is simply a word to the reader. "It is only at the level of discourse, and then only after the story itself has ceased, that the narrator informs *only* the narratee that the man has great wealth. Then, in retrospect, the narratee can think back through the episode and see the whole episode in a new light. [. . .] (i.e. [the man] as less of a seeker after truth and more of a self-aggrandizer)"; Fowler, "Rhetoric of Direction," 117–18.

68. The prediction is based upon Psalm 22 and Isa 50:4-7 (Lane, *Mark*, 375), which underlines that the coming suffering was according to the Scriptures (cf. 9:12).

69. Jesus' preliminary reply may be entirely appropriate to the situation in which he is just about to leave his disciples (cf. Elijah in 2 Kings 2:9–10), Boomershine, *Story Journey*, 127.

70. Bolt, "Spirit," 49–50. "Jerusalem," in terms of Isaiah, is, of course, metonymic for the people of Israel.

71. Jesus' answer is to "a question which the disciples had not put and which they had obviously not considered, namely, how a man is to enter at all into that glory. The

the "greats" of this world (v.45; cf. v.31). Bartimaeus completes the picture (vv.46-52)[72] by showing that sight is restored and salvation received, not through attaining human greatness, but through asking Jesus for mercy (vv.47-48,52; cf. 10:13-16).[73]

The Necessity of the Passion (8:27—10:52)

Despite the hard-heartedness of Israel and the disciples (4:35—8:26) the kingdom is imminent. The passion of the Son of Man is the only thing that must first occur, and it is about to happen. It is necessary because the Servant must die as a ransom to enable the many to enter the kingdom, for it is only through his mercy that the blind will see and be saved. It is through the betrayal of the Son of Man, that God will do the impossible for those who are following in his way.[74]

---

answer is that he enters into that glory, not as he 'can' participate in Jesus' baptism of death, but as his participation in it actually becomes an event. If in passing—but only in passing—there is here perhaps a hint at the martyrdom which the disciples should suffer, the decisive reference of the prophecy is to the death of Jesus Himself, in which it is ordained that the disciples should participate. Jesus does not drink that cup for Himself alone. He is not baptized with that baptism in isolation. [. . .] they too, will die in His death, and therewith their entry into glory will be secured (no matter what place they occupy)"; Barth, *CD* IV.4.16.

72. He recognizes the man from Nazareth as the Son of David. Jesus is only addressed by this title here (vv.47,48). It could be (Cranfield, *Mark*, 345): 1. Messianic: cf. Isa 11:1–11; Jer 23:5-8; Ezek 34:23-24; and is so used in later Judaism. However, only PsSol 17:23 (v.21) is pre-Christian, therefore perhaps it is not an unambiguous reference to Messiah. 2. An ambiguous reference, either a polite address or an expression that Jesus is a special Israelite, and yet messianic for Mark's reader; 3. A later gloss (cf. Matthew's frequent use of this title). At this point in the narrative it lacks clarity, but will clearly become messianic as the story proceeds.

73. Bartimaeus is asked the same question as were the Zebedees (vv.36,51), which Boomershine, *Story Journey*, 127, links with the transference of power when the prophet was about to leave his disciple (cf. 2 Kgs 2:9-10). Rather than power, Bartimaeus is granted sight—a far greater commodity in Mark's story.

74. There is no doubt that the Bartimaeus story also acts as a foil for the disciples (cf. 8:22-26). Cranfield, *Mark*, 346, need not be so tentative: "A literal following of Jesus along the road to Jerusalem is no doubt intended." He nevertheless allows for the possibility of a "deeper significance of ἀκολουθεῖν *akolouthein*, if Bartimaeus actually became a disciple, as seems likely from the fact that his name was remembered. The suggestiveness of the whole incident when thought of as a picture of the meaning of discipleship may well have struck Mark and those who related the story before him." The text emphasizes that he is called by Jesus (3 times in v.49; cf. 1:16-20 and 3:14-19)—the vocabulary is different (φωνεῖν *phōnein* here, cf. καλεῖν *kalein* previously) but the idea is

The Discourse

The disciples have partially entered the privilege shared by the reader. Their confession showed partial insight (8:29; cf. 1:1a), the three were granted exactly the same revelation as the reader (9:2–8; cf. 1:9–11), and they are more definitely following Jesus (10:32; cf. 8:32).[75] Their obsession with greatness maintains their distance from the reader,[76] but the reader's strong attraction to Bartimaeus encourages the expectation that Jesus will show them mercy too.[77]

The Provocation of the Passion (Mark 11–12)

In Mark 11–12 the action begins to rise towards the necessary passion.[78] Throughout the temporally and geographically structured story of events in Jerusalem,[79] Jesus is very clearly in charge and appears to provoke his own passion.[80]

---

the same. S.H. Smith, "Literary Structure," 108.

75. There appears to be a clear distinction between the twelve (the subject of ἐθαμβοῦντο *ethambounto*) and those who follow fearfully (οἱ ἀκολουθοῦντες *hoi akolouthountes*); Cranfield, *Mark*, 335.

76. In this scene the reader is at a distance from the twelve, since the request and response both betray an attitude that Jesus has corrected (9:34), and deny teaching he has previously given (9:35–50; 10:13–16). Although they are with Jesus, they still lack understanding.

77. It begins with an inside view (v.47) which creates very close identification with him (Boomershine, *Story Journey*, 126), and he is characterized positively. Rather than simply indicating that he is known to the church (Cranfield, *Mark*, 344), or providing contrast between honor and the shame of begging (Boomershine, *Story Journey*, 126), his naming creates intimacy with the reader. The retrospections to the positive characters of chapter 5 also help the readers' alignment with Bartimaeus and their warm appreciation of his story.

78. The rising action is "that part of a play which precedes the climax," Cuddon, "Rising Action," 575.

79. The reader is guided through these chapters by "temporal and geographical rubrics, especially the celebrated three day structure"; S.H. Smith, "Literary Structure," 105–06.

80. "In chapters 11–12 Jesus appears to be beyond [the opponent's] power"; Tannehill, "Gospel of Mark," 77.

THE NARRATIVE INTEGRITY OF MARK 13:24-27

The Kingdom is Near (11:1-11)

On the first of three successive days, Jesus' entry to Jerusalem continues the expectation of the imminent kingdom (11:1-10).[81] His arrival at the Temple is anticlimactic, and creates an expectation of later action (11:11).

The Leadership Attacked (11:12-19)

The events of the following day are enigmatic. Mark himself draws attention to the strangeness of the cursing of the figtree (vv.12-14), by underlining that it was not the season for fruit. This is a clue that the incident ought to be understood symbolically and the ready background for the symbol is Mic 7:1-7, in which Israel is in ruins due to the corruption of the leadership and there is not one godly man to be found.[82] The incident in the Temple (vv.15-18), although usually explained in terms of the Temple,[83] is directed against *the leadership*,[84] and appears to be in preparation for the eschatological inclusion of the Gentiles (v.17; cf. Isa 56:7).

---

81. Through prior preparation and detailed instructions to the disciples he deliberately fulfills messianic prophecy (Zech 9:9). The reference to the coming kingdom (v.10) coupled with Jesus' arrival at his goal (cf. 10:32) sustain the expectations of the imminent arrival of the kingdom. Cf. S.H. Smith, "Literary Structure," 112-13.

82. The prophet is in misery like one who searches for a harvest too early. The one who comes for the firstfruits (בִּכּוּרָה *bikkûrâ*; τὰ πρωτόγονα *ta prōtogona*) finds no grapes, no early figs. This is symbolic of the godly being swept from the land, and the rulers being corrupt. The day of the watchman has come, i.e., the day of God's visitation, God's salvation. It is a day when his enemy gloats (v.8) yet the Lord will vindicate and the enemy will be ashamed. It will be a day when the land (i.e. Israel) will be desolate because of its inhabitants, at the hands of Assyria and Egypt. And yet, on the other side of the judgment, God will show his wonders to the nations, namely his forgiveness of the remnant (v.18).

83. This takes two forms: either a "cleansing," arguing that the merchants shouldn't have been there, and so Jesus cast them out, or a "portent of destruction," arguing that the merchants were a normal part of the Temple's sacrificial system and so Jesus' attack is on the Temple practices themselves, and therefore a sign that the Temple's days are over. Cf. Evans, "Jesus' Action."

84. The story itself clearly indicates that Jesus' action was not directed against a structure but against his opponents (v.17b, ὑμεῖς *hymeis*). Mark reinforces this point by immediately reporting the reaction of this group (v.18). Jesus' activity in the Temple concerns the condemnation of the leadership, who have caused the barrenness of Israel. Geddert's exegesis of Mark 11-12 confirms that these chapters are not directed against the Temple, nor Israel as a whole, but the leadership; *Watchwords*, Ch. 5.

MARK 13 IN ANTICIPATION (MARK 1–12)

The Leadership Challenge (11:20—12:44)

The lengthy and climactic third day reflects upon the events of day two.[85] The cursed figtree is a sign that the end has arrived and Jesus encourages his disciples to keep on believing that their eschatological hopes are fulfilled in him (11:20–26).[86] The opponents still do not recognize this (cf. 3:22–30) and Jesus silences them by relating his authority with that of John (11:27–33), before using a parable to indict them for their murderous nature[87] and provoke them[88] to renew their plot to arrest and kill him (12:1–12; cf.

---

85. Although it is usual to consider chapter 12 as a summary of teaching spread over a number of days, Mark's arrangement forces it to be read as the events of the third day in this series, since the temporal and geographical end-point indicators (cf. 11:11,19) do not begin to occur until 13:1,3 and even then they are not completed (cf. 14:3).

86. The imminence of that day is grounded on the faithfulness of God (v.22, reading ἔχετε *echete* as indicative not imperative; Lane, *Mark*, 410). The prayer is specifically concerned with the coming of the kingdom, with a background in Zech 14:4,10, when the Mount of Olives ("this mountain") will be turned into a plain (Lane, *Mark*, 410). The reference in v.24 is likewise specific, not general (πάντα ὅσα *panta hosa* referring to actual requests "everything whatever," and the present tenses προσεύχεσθε καὶ αἰτεῖσθε *proseuchesthe kai aiteisthe* —taken together "asking in prayer"—suggest that Jesus is addressing the current Jewish hopes and prayers in which the disciples share. The aorist ἐλάβετε *elabete* therefore points to the fact that their hopes are fulfilled, namely, in Jesus), urging the disciples to continue to believe (present imperative πιστεύετε *pisteuete*) that the Jewish expectations are fulfilled in him, the kingdom of God has drawn near and forgiveness has come to the earth. It is as they believe this that they will find it to be true (cf. 4:25) and they will enter the kingdom when it comes. As they pray for the kingdom, they need to live out its characteristic forgiveness (v.25). [2021: cf. Bolt, "Faith of Jesus Christ".]

87. Through the allusion to Isaiah's parable of the barren vineyard (Isa 5:1–7), which symbolized Israel devastated by his leaders (Isa 3:14), this parable, like the figtree, is not about Israel *per se* but about the leadership.

88. By his action in the Temple and his parabolic attack on the leaders, Jesus has provided them with a motive to kill him. S.H. Smith, "Role of Jesus' Opponents," 175: "The purpose of (the judgment parable) and the Temple-cleansing narrative may be to specify a reason behind the machinations of the authorities in Mark 14, 15. The passion story itself describes *how* Jesus' crucifixion was secured, whereas 11:15–18; 12:1–12 explains *why*."

3:6).⁸⁹ This begins a series of three testings (12:13-34)⁹⁰ which ends in the defeat of his opponents' plans to test him (v.34).⁹¹

Jesus then turns on the offensive and launches a scathing attack on his opponents. He attacks their Christology (12:35-37) by proposing, but not answering, a riddle concerning the relationship between the Christ and David, using Ps 110:1. He warns people against them for they—and presumably those who associate with them—will receive a terrible judgment

---

89. Fowler, "Rhetoric of Direction," 119: "Jesus issues a patently indirect narrative puzzle within the story, but it is only the narrator at the discourse level who provides the crucial key for solving the puzzle." The parable is thoroughly metaphorical or figurative, i.e. it needs to be figured out. Although Jesus begins this in vv.10-11, his explanation is likewise figurative and is therefore of no help. "The substitution of one figurative riddle for another does not solve anything for us." What allows the narratee to solve the puzzle is the insight given by the narrator (12:12). Although the subject is ambiguous, the preceding context makes it clear that it is the priests, the scribes, and the elders (11:27; 12:1). As we read back "it will not be difficult to infer that the parable is a figurative attack upon the interlocutors introduced back in 11:27 and mentioned again in 12:1, namely, the chief priests, scribes and elders." Once the narrator provides the necessary information (12:12), the pieces of the puzzle are solved in retrospect.

90. All three are read as controversies. An insidious context is erected at the beginning which hangs over into the next two (12:12-13; cf. 3:6). The Sadducees attack the resurrection, i.e. the central element of Jesus' teaching (= kingdom of God). [2021: cf. Bolt, "What Were the Sadducees Reading?"] The scribe by his very designation is one of Jesus' opponents out to kill him (11:27). *Pace* S.H. Smith, "Role of Jesus' Opponents," 177, who does not treat the next two as controversies, following Daube, "Four Types."

91. It comes from a scribe, who is therefore automatically labelled by the reader as one of Jesus' enemies. It is a mistake to call him "friendly," as does Murray, "The Questioning of Jesus," 275, for there is nothing friendly about the scribes in Mark, and there is nothing friendly about this particular series of controversies. When no-one asks more questions (v.34), this represents the defeat of the opponents' plan to trap Jesus: "even a scribe finds it necessary to concede Jesus' unimpeachable claims. Here is another intriguing twist in the plot: surely Jesus has triumphed; the scribes have been defeated; it only remains to seal their condemnation—κρίμα *krima*"; S.H. Smith, "Role of Jesus' Opponents," 178. Tannehill, "Gospel of Mark," 66, also acknowledges the opponents' difficulty in fulfilling their task, until a new way is found in 14:10-11.

(vv.38–40).⁹² In the final scene Jesus sits over against the Temple⁹³ and points out a pathetic example of the ruin caused by Israel's religious shepherds. The widow, for whom they should have especially cared, has her "house devoured" as she is forced to give her last two cents to the Temple treasury, while the wealthy pass by untouched (vv.41–44).⁹⁴

Discourse

The end has come, the religious leaders have opposed Jesus and lost. However this is the same group which, according to his prediction, will kill Jesus (11:27; cf. 8:31; 10:33), so the reader expects that they will find another way (already hinted at in 3:19). Jesus' attack on the rulers throughout this section continues the theme that has been evident before, *that the shepherds of Israel have ruined Israel, and he has come as the alternative shepherd*. While it is clear that the Son will be killed by the wicked tenants (12:1–12), the gap erected by the riddle in Ps 110:1 also raises the expectation that his enemies will ultimately be defeated. The open-endedness of the third day leaves the reader still expecting a conclusion to this section.

The Anticipation of Mark 13

The characters have been commissioned and the conflict begun (Mark 1–3). The theological expectations were raised that the word sown amongst a blind Israel in order to establish a remnant amongst Israel would eventually issue in the universal kingdom of God (4:1–34). The stronger man then operated amongst a blind Israel, typified by his own disciples (4:35—8:26). A turning point was reached and Jesus outlined the necessity for the one

---

92. The warning is due to this coming judgment. The list of religious hypocrisy, in which there is the outward show combined with the destructiveness of the very ones the shepherds of Israel were meant to care for, is given by a series of articular participles in apposition to the scribes (τῶν θελόντων [. . .] οἱ κατεσθίοντες [. . .] προσευχόμενοι *tōn thelontōn* [. . .] *hoi katesthiontes* [. . .] *proseuchomenoi*). The basis of the warning is that this group will receive judgment (οὗτοι λήμψονται περισσότερον κρίμα *houtoi lēmpsontai perissoteron krima*) and, implicitly, "therefore do not associate with them"; cf. 8:11–15.

93. S.H. Smith, "Literary Structure," 110.

94. Wright, "The Widow's Mites"; Fleddermann, "Warning." In extending Wright by contrasting the widow's piety with the scribes' robbery of God, Geddert, *Watchwords*, 136, simply reinforces this point.

who would be Son of Man to suffer as the Servant (8:27—10:52), and then proceeded to provoke this passion with a clear demonstration that the end had come for Israel's shepherds (11–12).

At the end of Mark 1–12 the action is rising towards the climax. There is an imminent expectation of the kingdom of God, held back only by the imminent suffering of the Son of Man at the hands of his opponents. It is at this point in the narrative—after the turning point and as part of the rising action before the climax—that Mark 13 is situated.

4

Mark 13: A First Reading

THIS DESCRIPTION OF THE gross features of Mark 13 precedes the more detailed treatment to follow.

A Narrative Pause

The Narrative Position

JESUS' LAST GREAT SPEECH[1] occupies a narrative position that is after the turning point and before the climax. It is immediately after a crisis (11–12) in which the opponents' plotline was reissued (12:12–13; cf. 3:6) only to fail (12:28–34). The story expects its re-emergence, since it is also part of Jesus' plotline to be killed specifically by this group (8:31; 9:31; 10:33), and has provided a clue regarding the means by which it will re-emerge (3:19).

Despite being situated amongst the rising action, chapter 13 does not advance the plot at all. After the scribes are defeated (12:28–34), questioned (via a puzzle, which remains unresolved, 12:35–37), and indicted (12:38–44), the story's action has come to a standstill.

---

1. It has been called Jesus' Farewell Discourse, or his "last will and testament," and compared to similar speeches in the Old Testament.

THE NARRATIVE INTEGRITY OF MARK 13:24-27

The Narrative Pause

The pause in the story is reinforced by the chapter's form. The narrative has already been decelerating and the length of the discourse, its speech character, and its function as a monologue (see below)[2] delays things even further. The abrupt change of scene at the end and the resumption of the main plot (14:1) underline chapter 13's function as narrative pause.

A major contributor to this pause is the chronological patterning in which the chapter is embedded.[3] The chapter (13:1) is cast as a continuation of the preceding threefold temporal and spatial pattern in which there is a daily journey[4] to, and retirement from, the Temple and city (Day 1: 11:1-11; Day 2: 11:12-19; Day 3: 11:20—13:37).[5] An increasing amount of detail is provided as the days progress,[6] with a consequent slowing down of the readers' reading experience for day three. This reinforces the natural climactic function of day three.[7] Day one raised the expectation of action, day two delivered it, and day three reflected upon it. Day three introduces

---

2. For time manipulation in a narrative, see Licht, *Storytelling*, 96-120.

3. Deceleration is aided by Mark's increasingly specific chronology as the Gospel proceeds towards its climax. Time is reckoned by days in chapters 11-12, then hours in chapters 14-16. Chapter 13 sustains the time focus by being dominated by chronological concerns (the disciples ask a time-oriented question v.4; the discourse moves from the vague "not yet" vv.5-13; through the definite chronological sequencing of vv.14-27; and the delimitation of vv.28-31; before returning to the "ignorance of exact time" theme of vv.33-37).

4. Malbon, "Jesus of Mark"; Fowler, *Loaves*, 63-68, 235.

5. Chapter 12 reads as events of the one day, despite the fairly usual assertion that they were fashioned this way by Mark. If this were so it merely underlines the importance of reading them together, as Mark has fashioned them to be so read.

6. Day One: 11 verses; Day 2: 8 verses; Day 3: 97 verses (59 inside city, 38 for withdrawal).

7. A threefold pattern is especially powerful in arousing expectancy in the reader: "Two instances are sufficient to establish a pattern firmly. We then approach the third instance with a definite expectation that it will conform to this pattern. To be sure, we may expect the pattern will be twisted in the third instance, [...] but there is an element of suspense in this anticipation, which is the result of the pattern established by the first two instances." The third may be "a forceful example of this same pattern," or "it may contain an important difference. Then the difference stands out strongly. The first two instances serve as a foil for the third, our attention being attracted by the variation in the pattern. Contrast in a pattern is a way in which a skillful speaker points to what is crucial," Tannehill, *Sword*, 43-44. The threefold pattern is a common device in Mark: e.g., three sea journeys, three passion predictions, three mentions of miraculous feedings (including 8:14-21).

MARK 13: A FIRST READING

a further variation when Jesus' usual departure from the city commences (13:1), but his arrival at Bethany is delayed at the Mount of Olives (13:3).

This pause causes the reader to focus upon the Apocalyptic Discourse as a highly significant piece of the story. Because it is a pause *in the narrative,* the narrative can be expected to be resumed, after this "aside" is completed. In other words, the content of the pause is read as significant *for the story from which we have paused*. It encourages further reflection on the preceding so that what follows can be more clearly understood. It is natural, therefore, to read Jesus' final discourse as a further reflection upon the conflict over his authority, before the plot against him comes to completion.

The Narrated Speech

The Apocalyptic Discourse is a narrated speech,[8] although the significance of this fact has been almost entirely ignored. In narrative terms, his speech is a second level narrative,[9] since the main character of Mark's story is reported addressing four other characters within the story. This speech will therefore have a function *within the story, as part of the interaction between Jesus and his disciples in the context of the impending threat from his opponents.*

The Linking Scene (vv. 1–2)

The Form

Verses 1–2, consisting of a brief narrative[10] followed by a saying from Jesus, are an obvious pronouncement story.[11] The saying, which is considered the

---

8. The term is Vorster's, "Literary Reflections," although he does not capitalize on the observation.

9. Dewey, "Point of View," 100, although she downplays the significance of this observation. Perhaps through reading within the constraints of the community's conventional interpretations, she misses the potential of her own observations.

10. It follows the common pattern in reporting a change in location, and differences in focal characters and time compared with the scene before. Tannehill, "Introduction," 3.

11. So Bultmann, *History*, 36, 56, 60. Neither Dibelius, *From Tradition to Gospel*, nor Albertz, *Streitgespräche*, dealt specifically with the narrative; Taylor, *Mark*, 500. Blunt, *The Gospel and the Critic*, 58–59, defines them as: Short narratives which end with a striking saying which had reference to faith or practice. Called Paradigms by Dibelius, *From Tradition to Gospel*; Apothegms by Bultmann, "Study," 39; and Pronouncement

"whole point" in a pronouncement story,[12] is the prophetic / apocalyptic[13] "no stone" saying.[14]

Recent work on Pronouncement Stories[15] has sub-classified them,[16] and interpreted them holistically, that is, by analysing both the climactic saying *and* the narrative introduction which was previously ignored as mere "framework."[17] Analysis of the interaction between the two segments reveals that 13:1–2 is an example of a "correction story."

The Function

Such analysis is important for the function of the story in the narrative.

> A pronouncement story is a brief narrative which relates how someone responded to something said or observed on a particular occasion. The response is a pronouncement [. . .] and this pronouncement is the climactic element in the story. The story is told for the sake of the pronouncement, and the impact of Jesus'

Stories by Taylor, *Formation*, 63. Dibelius, *From Tradition to Gospel*, is a little more elaborate in his description, giving five characteristics: 1. a real rounding off (p.44); 2. Brevity and simplicity of narrative (p.53); 3. Coloring of narrative in a thoroughly religious, i.e. realistic unworldly manner (p.56); 4. Reaches its point in and concludes with a word of Jesus (p.56); 5. Ends with a thought useful for preaching purposes (p.58). Most of these are sound, although points three and five perhaps reflect Dibelius' assumptions about the use of the paradigm for preaching purposes, rather than being strictly descriptive.

12. Bultmann, *History*, 62; "Study," 40; Taylor, *Formation*, 63; Albertz, *Streitgesprache*, 6; references from Dewey, *Markan Public Debate*, 204, n.100.

13. Bultmann, *History*, 120.

14. Taylor, *Mark*, 500. This is not his term. He calls it "the prophecy of destruction." Such a description is too interpretation laden (i.e., AD 70) and it is better to use the actual words of the text at this stage.

15. Tannehill, "Attitudinal Shift"; "Synoptic Pronouncement Stories"; "Introduction,"; "Varieties"; Robbins, "Rhetorical Typology."

16. Dibelius had no sub-categories; Bultmann had three: i) Controversy Dialogues, ii) Scholastic Dialogues, iii) Biographical Apophthegms (which was, according to Tannehill, "a miscellaneous grouping without clear formal definition"). Tannehill, "Introduction," 6, has 6: i) Corrections, ii) Commendations, iii) Objections, iv) Quests, v) Inquiries, vi) Descriptions; Robbins, "Rhetorical Typology," reclassifies these six types.

17. Cf. Bultmann, "Study," 56; *History*, 55–65. He classified v.2 in the vague class "Biographical Apophthegms." This was separate from the pronouncement story class proper, of which he listed sixteen—fourteen of which were from Mark (2:3–3; 2:15–16; 2:18–19; 2:23–24; 3:1–2; 3:22–23; 7:5–6; 10:2–3; 10:13–14; 10:35–36; 11:27–28; 12:13–14; 12:18–19; 12:28–29). He had 20 biographical apothegms, including 3:31–35.

words is heightened by presenting him in interaction with other persons. [...] many of these narratives convey a sense of antithesis by presenting persons with contrasting attitudes in a situation of conflict.[18]

Pronouncement stories are shaped to have a particular impact upon the hearer, to affect attitudes and actions and move them into line with those expressed in the climactic response.[19] The attitudinal shift varies with the type of story, but in correction stories, the attitudinal shift is unexpected:

> In these stories [...] there is tension between Jesus and the one to whom he is responding, but here the tension appears as a surprise. The position corrected may appear to be reasonable or laudable, but Jesus does not praise or accept it. The corrective response of Jesus opens up a gap between himself and the position taken by another at the beginning of the story. The two positions define a decision for hearers and readers of such stories. They are faced with the question of whether they can negotiate this shift in position.[20]

The statement in verse 1 "appear(s) to be reasonable or laudable"[21] and it "contains no criticism of Jesus" (like the objection story), yet "Jesus does not praise or accept it." Jesus obviously disagrees with the disciple about the longevity of the stones and he "responds to what he sees or hears by correcting it."[22] The disciples' further question (vv.3–4) reveals their "surprise" at Jesus' reply.

The Function in the Narrative

The disciples' poverty of understanding and consequent need of correction is by now a familiar theme, and their surprised question (v.4), which provides the occasion for the Apocalyptic Discourse, is perfectly consistent behaviour for them. The corrective tone set by the opening pronouncement story suggests that, in what follows, Jesus will not simply impart the

---

18. Tannehill, "Tension," 144.
19. Tannehill, "Tension," 145.
20. Tannehill, "Tension," 146.
21. See chapter 5 for just how laudable this statement was.
22. This is quite consistent with the dynamics of their relationship portrayed in the preceding narrative. Jesus has corrected them previously.

information which the disciples request,[23] but he will continue to correct their faulty perceptions, so that their blindness will become sight.

The Apocalyptic *Discourse*

The Form and Function

In form, 13:5-37 consists entirely of connected sayings.[24] The lengthy discourse[25] begins as a dialogue (vv.1-4), but moves into the exalted planes of monologue, perhaps even soliloquy.[26] Whether technically a soliloquy or merely the more general "monologue" the function is the same:

> A soliloquy is a speech, often of some length, in which a character, alone on the stage, expresses his thoughts and feelings. [...] Its advantages are inestimable because it enables a dramatist to convey direct to an audience important information about a particular character: his state of mind and heart, his most intimate thoughts and feelings, his motives and intentions. [Soliloquies ...] are like prolonged asides and often take the form of a direct address to the audience. [Those using the soliloquy] are manipulators of the plot and commentators on the action.[27]

---

23. It is usual for commentators to speak as if he did this. However, Jesus is not in the habit of simply imparting information to the disciples in Mark. He constantly corrects them and stretches them beyond the limitations of their "human thinking" (cf. 8:33). Geddert rightly observes that: "Jesus was decidedly not in the habit of speaking with unmistakable clarity to one and all regardless of the true nature and the motivation of their enquiries," 83; "(Jesus) avoided answering inappropriate questions. He was more concerned to shape people's ways of looking than to describe the landscape for them," 179.

24. Earlier scholarship tended to treat the sayings individually, but the newer methods prefer to begin with the final form. In fact, the data previously used to divide the chapter (e.g., alleged "editorial additions") are now considered as indications of literary devices in operation.

25. A form found only here in the Gospel.

26. Given that there is absolutely no return to the disciples who provoked the discourse it merges into soliloquy: "A term used in a number of senses, with the basic meaning of a single person speaking alone—with or without an audience." Apart from prayers, much lyric verse, and all laments, there are four kinds: a) monodrama, an entertainment in which there is only one character, b) soliloquy, c) solo addresses to an audience in a play, d) dramatic monologue—a poem in which there is one imaginary speaker addressing an imaginary audience. Cuddon, "Monologue," 400.

27. Cuddon, "Soliloquy," 637.

MARK 13: A FIRST READING

Soliloquies, for example, are used in some plays to prepare us, with what we take as hard fact, for the ironic reconstruction of what characters later say and do. Speaking only to himself—and thus, by convention, conveying to us spectators some thoroughly reliable data about motives.[28]

By submerging the intranarrative characters, using speech,[29] and functioning as an extended "inside view,"[30] the form reduces the distance between the speaker and the reader. This powerfully engages the reader with the story, before imparting to him the "hard fact [. . .] thoroughly reliable data" that he will need to appreciate its remainder.

The monologue form of Mark 13 therefore justifies the expectation that this chapter will engage the reader, and provide some reliable information which will *powerfully prepare for what follows*.[31]

The Rhetorical Structure

Structure

We have seen that Mark 13 consists of a correction story which leads into a question, and then into Jesus' monologue (See Table 2).

---

28. Booth, *Rhetoric of Irony*, 63, (of Iago).

29. This reduces distance by "showing not telling," Dewey, "Point of View," 99. Licht, *Storytelling*, 25–27; Booth, *Rhetoric of Fiction*, 8, 211.

30. For "a character, alone on the stage, expresses his thoughts and feelings," "his state of mind and heart, his most intimate thoughts and feelings, his motives and intentions"; Booth, *Rhetoric of Fiction*, 163–65. Booth is particularly concerned with the device "inside view" which is an extremely powerful reducer of distance between story and reader.

31. Especially in view of the fact that the speaker, Jesus, is a thoroughly reliable character, who is closely aligned with the narrator of the story (Dewey, "Point of View," 103). Soliloquies do not always function this way, for example, if spoken by a villain (Booth, *Rhetoric of Fiction*, 316). For reliability in narration, see Booth, *Rhetoric of Fiction*, part II.

Table 2: The Forms of Mark 13

Introduction (vv.1-2):	"Correction" Story
Bridge Section (vv.3-4):	A Question
Discourse (vv.5-27):	Sayings—prophetic/apocalyptic
Discourse (vv.28-37):	Sayings—parabolic

Further structural subdivision[32] is possible after attending to other broad rhetorical structures, such as the "frame" (vv.5-6 and vv.21-23),[33] the imperatives and prohibitions[34] and other hook words;[35] "structurally significant" usages of ὅταν *hotan*,[36] Jesus' references to himself (vv.23,30,37), the alternation between second person exhortation and third person discourse,[37] the famous apostrophe (v.14), the clear hinge-point for the chapter (ἀλλά *alla* v.24), the chronological references

---

32. This breakdown, at the macro level at least, agrees with that of Pesch, *Naherwartungen*, as reported by Wenham, "Additional Notes," 1.

33. "A frame story is one which contains either another tale, a story within a story, or a series of stories," Cuddon, "Frame Story," 279; "something that frames another unit at its beginning and end, but which itself is not part of the unit framed," Dewey, *Markan Public Debate*, 34. Dewey isolates several frames in Mark. It is obviously related to the sandwich, intercalation, and concentric structure techniques used by Mark at several points, see Dewey, *Markan Public Debate*, 20-23; Edwards, "Markan Sandwiches." A frame interprets, in some way, the material it frames, therefore vv.7-20 need to be understood in the context of vv.5-6 / vv.21-23. Frames were called doublets by historical critics, usually implying different sources (See Taylor, *Mark*, 502, 515, 641).

34. βλέπετε *blepete* vv.5,9,23,33 (see below); μὴ θροεῖσθε *mē throeisthe* v.7; μὴ προμεριμνᾶτε *mē promerimnate* v.11; νοείτω *noeitō* v.14; φευγέτωσαν *pheugetōsan* v.14; μὴ καταβάτω μηδὲ εἰσελθάτω *mē katabatō mēde eiselthatō* v.15; μὴ ἐπιστρεψάτω *mē epistrepsatō* v.16; προσεύχεσθε *proseuchesthe* v.18; μὴ πιστεύετε *mē pisteuete* v.21; μάθετε *mathete* v.28; ?γινώσκετε *ginōskete* v.29; ἀγρυπνεῖτε *agrypneite* v.33; γρηγορεῖτε *grēgoreite* vv.35,37.

35. ταῦτα *tauta* / πάντα *panta* vv.4,23,29,30; παραδίδωμι *paradidōmi* vv.9,11,12; γρηγορέω *grēgoreō* vv.34,35,37; γινώσκω *ginōskō* / οἶδα *oida* vv.28,29,32,33,35.

36. As noted by Wenham with Pesch, *Naherwartungen*: vv.7, 11, 14, 28-29. Note its appearance also in v.4.

37. Pesch uses several of these devices to arrive at his structure, see Wenham, "Additional Notes," 1.

(vv.14,17,19,20,21,24–25,26,27,30,32,33), the explanatory γάρ *gar* clauses (vv.8,11,19–20,22,33,35) and Old Testament quotations.[38]

βλέπετε What?

The use of βλέπετε *blepete*, requires special comment. Although commentators usually notice its structural significance,[39] they also ignore the fact that the text gives *an object* to this imperative. When this is noticed, the imperative is clearly *not* an instruction for the disciples to watch *for future events*, but a warning for them to *watch out for themselves*.[40] This is reinforced by the second person address.[41] Jesus continues the correction begun with v.2, by warning them of a danger *to themselves*.

The outline structure of Mark 13 reveals its paraenetic nature (See Table 3).[42]

Table 3: Rhetorical Structure of Mark 13

Introduction:

vv.1–2 "Correction Story"

vv.3–4 Bridge Section (a question)

Discourse (vv.5–27) (Sayings—prophetic/apocalyptic)

vv.5–6 See to Yourselves, Lest you

vv.7–8 When you hear . . .

                              don't be troubled

                              for . . .

vv.9–10 See to yourselves!

vv.11–13 When they . . .

---

38. Vv.14a, 24–25, 26. For other quotations and allusions, see chapter 5.

39. Cf. vv.5,9,23,33. See, for example, the structural layout of France, *Government*, 128.

40. v.5 Βλέπετε μή τις ὑμᾶς πλανήσῃ *blepete mē tis hymas planēsē*, which is further clarified by its resumption in v.9 βλέπετε δὲ ὑμεῖς ἑαυτούς *blepete de hymeis heautous*; v.23 immediately follows the warning about the elects' potential demise; see chapter 5. Cf. Kilpatrick, "BLEPETE PHILIPPIANS 3₂."

41. V.12 is a general statement, v.13 makes it specific to the disciples.

42. This quality is often noticed and often wrongly set in opposition to "apocalyptic," see Torrance, "Olivet Discourse"; Wenham, "Additional Notes," 1.

	don't worry...
	for...
vv.14–23 When you see...	
	"quotation" (+ apostrophe)
	then...
	flee...
	don't come down... and enter
	don't turn back
	Pray!
	for...
	and then if they say...
	don't believe
vv.24–27 But in those days...	
	after...
	"quotation"
	and then you will see
	"quotation"
	and then...
Discourse (vv.28–37)	Sayings—Parabolic
vv.28–32 Learn...	
	when... you know...
	so also
	when... know...
	Truly I say
vv.33–37 See! Be alert!	
	for...
	as...
	Watch!
	for...
	I say... watch

The Language

In keeping with this paraenetic quality, the language of the discourse, with its rich, exaggerated,[43] apocalyptic imagery, and use of parable and metaphor, is almost entirely commissive,[44] whether "performative,"[45] "expressive"[46] or "cohesive."[47]

Unlike referential language, which aims at description and seeks to convey information,[48] commissive language also seeks to affect the recipient in some way. Rather than using the language of precision, it uses language more aptly described as "forceful and imaginative."[49] This audience-oriented language further engages the reader with the story.[50]

---

43. Stein, *Difficult Sayings*, cites as exaggerations: vv.2 (pp.23–24, 53, 65–68), v.8 (pp.79–80), v.13a (pp.65–68), vv.14–16 (pp.65–68), vv.24–25 (pp.65–68, 79–80), v.30 (p.82).

44. For what follows see, Stein, *Difficult Sayings*, ch. 3. Also Caird, *Language and Imagery*, 7–36.

45. "Performative" language "frequently makes use of commands or imperatival sentences [. . .] (and) carries with it a demand for decision and response. In seeking to achieve this aim, persuasive, emotional, and exaggerated language is frequently used, for such language has the capacity to stir the emotions," Stein, *Difficult Sayings*, 91. Cf. the paraenetic nature of Mark 13. The OT quotations can also have this function.

46. "Expressive" language seeks to "state certain facts in ways that will elicit specific feelings and attitudes." This type also uses language designed to make an impression, i.e., exaggerated, figurative, poetic or metaphorical language; Stein, *Difficult Sayings*, 91.

47. "Cohesive" language is "designed primarily to establish rapport, to set another person at his ease, to create a sense of mutual trust and common ethos," so Caird, *Language and Imagery*, 32, who refers to Malinowski's term "phatic communion." Much of the use of the Old Testament in the New is of this allusive kind, establishing rapport between author and reader and giving confidence in a background of shared assumptions. A quotation may be the basis of an appeal to authority, but an allusion is always a reminder of what is held in common," Caird, *Language and Imagery*, 33.

48. It seeks to "get rid of ambiguity and achieve semantic precision," Stein, *Difficult Sayings*, 90, quoting Wheelwright, *Metaphor and Reality*, 38.

49. The term is from Tannehill, *Sword*, 11–36.

50. Also note the links with the "inside view": Stein, *Difficult Sayings*, 100, "the expressive purpose of [attention getting exaggerations] is still very significant, for they reveal Jesus' innermost feelings on vital issues. [. . .] Jesus used exaggeration to highlight those [teachings] to which he wanted to give additional emphasis."

The Old Testament Tapestry

A major contributor to this commissive language is the plethora of Old Testament allusions and quotes woven into the fabric of the discourse.[51] The function of this rich tapestry varies depending on how it is imported.

Influence and Allusion

Influences, allusions, or comparisons,[52] merely convey the flavor or atmosphere of the Old Testament material. In Mark 13, the very multiplicity of possible allusions and influences militates against the reader drawing anything more explicit than an atmosphere or a "feel." Nevertheless the allusions and influences effectively import the flavor of Old Testament eschatology, evoking pictures of the Day of the Lord, the last judgment, final salvation and their associated cluster of ideas.[53]

Despite the fact that this language sometimes referred to political disasters in the original context, it is misguided to insist that these political connotations still cling to the allusion.[54] It is the theological dimension that abides beyond the original context in both Old[55] and New Testament[56]

---

51. "A perfect fog or mist of prophetic allusions," Derrett, *Making*, 219. In a canonical context these act as an authoritative model to guide the reading process. For the concept of guiding literature models see Rimmon-Kenan, *Narrative Fiction*, 124–27.

52. Kee, "Function," uses a tripartite classification (quote, allusion, influence). Others diminish the latter categories even more: Lane, *Mark*, 475, talks of "influence" rather than some of Kee's "quotes" and Cranfield, *Mark*, 405–06, merely "compares with." Needless to say, there is a high degree of subjectivity in the classification beyond direct quotations.

53. The cumulative effect of Old Testament eschatology gave its reader a multifaceted expectation. Thoughts of the Last Day would conjure up the whole package, a part would evoke the whole picture, if only to stand it in the background. Such ideas have been explored by the structuralist critics who would say that the surface structure evokes deeper structures in the mind. See, for example, Patte, *What is Structural Exegesis?*

54. Recall France's argument discussed above (p. 7).

55. E.g. Isaiah 13 (which lies behind Mark 13:24) is a prophecy concerning the "day of the Lord" (vv.6,9,13), which uses highly symbolic "eschatological language" (vv.10,13), and yet it refers to the coming Babylonian devastation (vv.1,19–21). However, the political destruction of Jerusalem by the Babylonians can be compared to the non-political overthrow of Sodom and Gomorrah since both were God's judgment (Isa 13:19; cf. vv.3,4,5,6,9,11,12,13,17).

56. The New Testament's use of the Old is a vast subject area and only cursorily dealt with here. See the literature cited in Silva, "New Testament Use"; Ellis, "How the New Testament uses the Old"; France, *Jesus*, 13 n.1.

allusion.[57] Against France's "Fall of Jerusalem" position, the pastiche of Old Testament allusion does not evoke politics *per se*, but eschatology. The historical referent to which the Old Testament eschatological language is applied still needs demonstration.

Quotations

Explicit quotations do more than create an atmosphere through evoking implicit clusters of ideas. Instead, unambiguous quotes ask readers to inform their reading by recollecting the explicit teaching of the quoted passage.

Mark 13:24–27 contains one such direct quotation. Through their various allusions, vv.24–25 and verse 27 convey a variety of impressions. However, since it can come only from Daniel 7:13, v.26 imports an explicit piece of Old Testament theology that will be vital to the reader's understanding of Mark's story. This explicit quotation at the centre of the discourse, invites the reader of the Apocalyptic Discourse to read against the backdrop of Daniel's apocalyptic vision.

---

57. See also Savran, *Telling and Retelling*, although his interest is somewhat tangential to mine.

The *Apocalyptic* Discourse

It is virtually undisputed[58] that Jesus' discourse belongs to the apocalyptic genre.[59]

The Usefulness of Genre

Some dispute the value of Genre as an interpretive guide,[60] but it usefully provides the interpreter with expectations and conventions.

> The new text evokes for the reader (listener) the horizon of expectations and 'rules of the game' familiar to him from earlier texts, which as such can then be varied, extended, corrected, but also transformed, crossed out, or simply reproduced. Variation, extension, and correction determine the latitude of a generic structure; a break with the convention on the one hand and mere reproduction on the other determines its boundaries.[61]

It is "a more institutionalised literary model" which guides the reading process:

---

58. The apocalyptic flavor of the sayings in vv.2, 5–8, 14–23, 24–27 is generally recognized although their authenticity may be debated. The older theory said Mark simply edited a "little apocalypse." When Taylor wrote his commentary he noticed that scholars were increasingly agreeing that Mark had before him a collection of sayings as well (Taylor, *Mark*, 499). Taylor's theory is that various groups of sayings were added to an original "apocalypse," with necessary editorial work being done along the way (pp.636–644). The original consisted of A [vv.5–8 & 24–27]. To this base was added B [vv.9–13] and C [vv.14–23]. D [vv.28–37] was appended and [vv.1–2 and 3–4] prefixed to give the entire narrative. Throughout this process various editorial additions had to be made. Taylor is confident that post-war scholarship has agreed that "with reasonable certainty the last Markan modifications can be determined." These he lists as: To Group A: v.5a Jesus began to say; ?v.6 in my name (p.40); v.8c These things are the beginning of travail; v.24a But in those days, after the tribulation (p. 639); To Group B: ?v.9a But take heed to yourselves; v.10. (Burney also includes v.9 "for a witness unto them"; v.12 "and father son" (p.640, n.1); To group C: ? vv.23; 21 (p.641); Group D he considers "somewhat artificially compiled" by Mark, consisting of sayings and parables, and now hard to discern how much modification has taken place (pp.519–20, 642).

59. Although perhaps apocalyptic with a difference. See Torrance, "Olivet Discourse", 908–09. However, differences within a genre are entirely legitimate, see the quotation from Jauss below.

60. See Cohen, "History." In support of its use Stein, *Difficult Sayings*, 13, "In communication of any kind one must be aware of genre."

61. Jauss, *Towards an Aesthetics of Reception*, 88, quoted in Cohen, "History," 210.

Its conventions establish a kind of contract between the text and the reader, so that some expectations are rendered plausible, others ruled out, and elements which would seem strange in another context are made intelligible within the genre.[62]

The recognition of a genre is only useful if it helps the reader read the text:

> discussing genre means discussing something to do with communication. [. . .] genre is a structure that functions within a communication between author and readers.[63]

Despite the broad consensus over the genre of Mark 13, the implications of this genre for its reading have not been fully explored. In part, this reflects the general difficulty of interpreting the apocalyptic genre.

The Apocalyptic Genre

Classification

Apocalyptic[64] should not be defined merely by the presence of certain characteristic features,[65] but rather by its' characteristic attitude to history.[66] In the prophetic world view, God's purposes would arise out of history, but in apocalyptic there is

> a highly developed sense that the present age will end and a new age will be introduced in which God's kingdom is established. The

---

62. Rimmon-Kenan, *Narrative Fiction*, 125.

63. Hartman, "Survey", 332.

64. Apocalyptic has been defined as: "a genre of revelatory literature with a narrative framework, in which a revelation is mediated by an otherworldly being to a human recipient, disclosing a transcendent reality which is both temporal, in so far as it envisages eschatological salvation, and spatial, in so far as it involves another, supernatural world," Collins, "Jewish Apocalypses," 22.

65. As is commonly done, see Rist, "Apocalypticism." See also the classification offered by Collins, "Towards a Morphology"; "Jewish Apocalypses"; Anderson, *Introduction*, 206–09; Morris, *Apocalyptic*. Such features would be: written (rather than spoken), pseudonymous, containing bizarre (although conventional) imagery; revelations, symbolism, pessimism, the shaking of the foundations, the triumph of God, determinism, dualism, pseudonymity, literary form, rewritten history, ethical teaching, prediction, historical perspective.

66. "It is perhaps in the attitude to history that the difference between prophecy and apocalyptic is most evident," Anderson, *Introduction*, 208.

kingdom is seen as God's new creation which cannot be brought about by reformation, but only by radical upheaval of the whole created order.⁶⁷

Or again:

Apocalyptic literature was not, as some have asserted, disinterested in history; it simply propounded the view that the solutions to the problems posed by the history of its times were not to be found within that history. God would bring an end to history whereby the everlasting kingdom of God would arise. [. . .] the evils of the age were so ingrained that nothing short of a new creation could provide the remedy.⁶⁸

Function

However, if genre functions as an act of communication it is not enough to simply classify apocalyptic, but questions of function must be addressed.⁶⁹ Hartman suggests that apocalypse tends to

[become] a means to join heaven and earth, so that divine secrets can be brought to human beings; further, [. . .] it anchors the authority of the message of the revelation with the divine Being Itself. [. . .] a typical message is one of comfort and exhortation to steadfastness.⁷⁰

If Mark 13 is read *as* apocalyptic then the peculiar perspective on history, and the illocutionary function⁷¹ of the genre will be taken into account.

---

67. Goldsworthy, *Gospel and Kingdom*, 82–83.

68. Dumbrell, *End*, 185. For further explication of the apocalyptic perspective on history, see Dumbrell, "Daniel 7." "In classical prophecy the realm of human history was the realm within which the covenant relationship between Yahweh and his people was being carried out; historical events were carriers of cosmic significance. [But in apocalyptic . . .] history is used as a timetable indicating how close men are to the ultimate event which would break the power which the inimical powers hold on the elect," Hanson, "Old Testament Apocalyptic Reexamined," 478, n.19; quotation taken from Morris, *Apocalyptic*, 66. This article is a convenient summary of Hanson's later book *Dawn of Apocalyptic*. See also his "Apocalypticism" and "Apocalypse, Genre."

69. This is the concern of Hartman, "Survey," although he is not satisfied that it has been addressed.

70. Hartman, "Survey," 334.

71. The "illocutionary force" of a sentence is "the purpose for which the sentence is used," Walhout, "Texts and Actions," 45. The same could be said of a genre.

MARK 13: A FIRST READING

The Apocalyptic Genre and the Reading of Mark 13

It is commonly assumed that the discourse is "predictive" in some way.[72] However, the distinctive view of history in apocalyptic writings essentially alters the flavor of their "prediction" in comparison to that of the prophets.[73]

> Speaking generally, the prophets foretold the future that should arise out of the present, while the apocalyptists foretold the future that should break into the present.[74]
>
> The apocalyptists had their eyes fixed on a more remote future. They were interested in the way God would break into this world of time and sense and bring an end to this whole present system.[75]

Rather than predicting things to arise within history, the apocalyptic perspective spoke of the end—eschatology in its ultimate sense.[76] Unless the events of AD 70 are considered in some "end of the world" sense, this observation immediately seems to prejudice the case for the Fall of Jerusalem position. However, it also needs to be noted that the end awaited by the Old Testament may not be necessarily equivalent to the end expected by modern readers. Old Testament language of the last day can be—and is—transformed in its New Testament context.[77]

This therefore raises the question once again of the context in which the apocalyptic material is found.

---

72. Torrance, "Olivet Discourse," 908–09, argues that the discourse is entirely predictive. He considers that this removes it from the realm of true apocalyptic.

73. How much prediction was essential to the prophets is a debated subject and need not concern us here (Morris, *Apocalyptic*, 61–63, has a brief treatment, with references). However, it is important to note briefly that biblical "prediction" is far from a "straightforward propositional prediction and fulfillment," or a system of "proof-texting" and requires a sensitivity to typology, theological motifs and themes, and the flow of Biblical Salvation-History; Dumbrell, *End*, introduction; cf. Moo, "Problem," 175–212.

74. Rowley, *The Relevance of Apocalyptic*, 38; cited from Morris, *Apocalyptic*, 62.

75. Morris, *Apocalyptic*, 62.

76. Cf. the warning against applying "the canons of historical precision" to the symbolic portrayal of the beasts in the first half of Daniel 7 in Dumbrell, *End*, 186.

77. So, for example, Peter in Acts 2 can use an Old Testament "last days" passage to refer to Jesus' exaltation.

Vision and Narrative in Apocalyptic Literature

In the two clear canonical representatives of apocalyptic (Daniel and Zechariah) the meaning is yielded by an interaction between the apocalyptic visions and their narrative contexts. In Zechariah, "[i]t seems clear that the second half of Zechariah forms a theological commentary on the first" as a "symbolic re-interpretation of history."[78] Likewise, in Daniel, "our chief canonical representative" of apocalyptic literature,[79] the probability is that "the Hebrew (1:1—2:4a; 8–12) interprets the content of the Aramaic (2:4b—7:28),"[80] and the "universal truths conveyed by Daniel 7" are applied by chapters 8–12 to the particular Israelite situation under review.

This apocalyptic pattern of a visionary portion commentating upon a narrative/more historical portion could very well be operative in Mark's Gospel. In this case the meaning of the discourse and the narrative will be mutually illumined.

The Three Readings: A Preliminary Assessment

The features discussed in this preliminary reading indicate that any view failing to assess Mark 13 in its narrative context is seriously flawed. On the other hand, the observations of this chapter lend impetus to the attempt to understand Mark 13 in its narrative integrity. Chapter 5 will now examine the details of the discourse in the context of their narrative setting.

---

78. Dumbrell, *Covenant and Creation*, 203.
79. Dumbrell, *End*, 185.
80. Dumbrell, *Faith*, 258.

5

Mark 13: A Close Reading

A Misguided Attitude (vv.1–4)

The Shift Begins (vv.1–2)

THE INTRODUCTORY "CORRECTION" STORY (vv.1-2) seeks to effect a shift in attitude. It consists of a statement from a disciple (v.1) which is then corrected by Jesus (v.2).

Jesus is the first subject encountered in verse 1, which encourages the adoption of his point of view.[1] Focalizing the scene in this way through Jesus prepares the reader to adopt the attitudinal shift that he will recommend.

The genitive absolute refers to Jesus' departure from the Temple, introducing movement. After an intense period of controversy in the Temple, which anticipated his death, Jesus begins his usual withdrawal (cf. 11:11,19). Since the readers are focalized through Jesus, this movement very simply engages them in a shift away from the Temple, although the end point of the shift is not yet revealed.

---

1. Although not named as yet, the preceding scene establishes him as the subject of the initial genitive absolute. The reader is already aligned with Jesus' point of view, given that Jesus is the character closely aligned with our "reliable narrator" and with whom the reader has enjoyed a privileged relationship since the prologue. For reliable narration see Booth, *Rhetoric of Fiction*, 75, ch. 7, 290, 293.

During the withdrawal, "one of his disciples" speaks to him. This anonymity reduces him to the status of a non-character, and makes the group from which he comes more prominent.[2]

Mark's narrative has shown a special interest in the education of the disciples for their special role.[3] They have been slow to understand, despite being privileged with Jesus' didactic efforts. The tension so integral to the correction story has existed between Jesus and his disciples almost from the beginning.[4]

This group also functions in the education of the reader of Mark's Gospel, but not through "identification."[5] Rather than promoting identification, the previous narrative has put distance between the reader and the disciples.[6] Neither does this verse encourage identification with the disciple. The anonymous "one" is dropped into the background and the scene is focalized through Jesus. The word order continues this trend by giving Jesus—who is the person addressed (αὐτῷ *autō*)—front position above the speaker, who is revealed last and who is quite clearly less important than his statement.[7] The distance between the reader and the disciple is further increased when the reader, already engaged with the move away from the Temple, feels the interruption posed by the question. The reader stands as an observer of this interaction with Jesus, with whom he is closer,

---

2. Pronouncement stories commonly depersonalize characters, Dibelius, *From Tradition to Gospel*, 57. See Rimmon-Kenan, *Narrative Fiction*, 39, for the importance of a name to character. Cf. Burnett, "Prolegomenon," 95–98.

3. Cf. 1:17; 3:14; 6:12. Unfortunately, chapter 13 is usually ignored in surveys of the disciples' role.

4. It will increase: "[t]his tension receives its greatest power and depth in the half of the Gospel dominated by the passion"; Tannehill, "Tension," 150.

5. Identification between reader and disciple is proposed at either a literary (Tannehill, "Tension," 149) or an historical level (Tannehill, "Tension," 150; Best, "The Role of the Disciples in Mark").

6. See chapter 3. Although this distance varies from both sides, the reader is never fully aligned with the disciples. He is more closely aligned with the narrator and Jesus, and, on the whole, has so far enjoyed a superiority over the disciples.

7. Word order is significant in the reading process, since the diachronic dimension of reading involves "the rigorous and disinterested asking of the question, what does this word, phrase, sentence, paragraph, chapter, novel, play, poem, *do*? And the execution involves an analysis of the developing responses of the reader in relation to the words as they succeed one another in time"; Fish, *Is there a Text?*, 26–28, quoted from Fowler, "Reader—Mark," 50.

and awaits the reason why Jesus' departure from the scene of controversy has been punctuated.[8]

Jesus has previously been presented as a teacher,[9] especially in chapter 12 where his wise teachings silenced his opponents. Now the silence is broken by this disciple's address (Διδάσκαλε *Didaskale*). This vocative has previously been used only by those who have prejudged an issue, and it has therefore always led to correction.[10]

In this case also, the following statement is in tension with the initial vocative and reveals that this disciple has also prejudged an issue. For it begins, not with a question appropriate to a willing learner, but with ἴδε *ide*, an imperative which places the speaker and the teacher on the same level.[11] Jesus is commanded to this activity, as if the "disciple" at this point has no need of being taught by the one he addresses as Διδάσκαλε *Didaskale*.

The disciple directs Jesus towards the quality of the stones and buildings in view, no doubt those of the Temple.[12] If his ejaculation is merely the expression of a simple awestruck Galilean, then it seems either inappropriate or far too facile.[13] Instead, his statement draws on the Old Tes-

---

8. The use of the historical present may also transport the reader into the scene. "The historical present can replace the aorist indicative in a vivid narrative at the events of which the narrator imagines himself to be present," a usage especially common in Mark; cf. BDF, 167. However, for a possible correction of this view, see also Osburn, "Historical Present."

9. The theme of Jesus as teacher is in fact more prominent than is sometimes allowed, cf. Best, "Jesus as the one who cares," 62–64. He is called ῥαββί *rhabbi* (9:5; 11:21; 14:45), ῥαββουνί *rhabbouni* (10:51) and διδάσκαλος *didaskalos* (4:38; 5:35; 9:17,38; 10:17,20,35; 12:14,19,32; 13:1; 14:14). It is also the obverse of the prominent discipleship theme. Dewey, *Markan Public Debate*, 153, feels the usage in 13:1 emphasizes the connection with chapter 12 in which Jesus' teaching activity is stressed.

10. 4:38; 9:17,38; 10:17,20,35; 12:14,19, cf. also 5:35. 12:32 may be an exception, but the identification of this man as one of Jesus' opponents gives his question negative overtones as well, see above, chapter 3.

11. Some have even called it a word of rebuke (for previous words of judgment against the Temple uttered by Jesus); Cranfield, *Mark*, 391; cf. Matt 23:38.

12. Ποταποί *potapoi* twice shows us that quality is the issue. It is a little-used word (other uses: Sus 54; Matt 8:27; Luke 1:29; 7:39; 2 Pet 3:11; 1 John 3:1). It matters little whether Jerusalem or the Temple is in view, for both could be spoken of synonymously by the devout Jew; Dumbrell, *End*, 37–38.

13. This is a common explanation, e.g., Lane, *Mark*, 451; Taylor, *Mark*, 500. It would be more appropriate at the first visit if it is an expression of awe; Beasley-Murray, *Mark 13*, 19; Dewey, *Markan Public Debate*, 153. Nineham, *Mark*, 344, following Bultmann, considers it too facile to be authentic. Jesus has just been through the final time of controversy before his crucifixion and, on this interpretation, all this disciple can do is act

tament's "inviolability of Zion" motif.[14] Yahweh's choice (2 Samuel 7; 1 Kings 8) had so endorsed Zion with his presence and his promises that the language of faith claimed Zion's impregnability.[15] When given a guided tour of Jerusalem's ramparts and walls, the pilgrim could see for himself the magnificence and permanence of God's earthly dwelling place (cf. Ps 48:12-14). Although the motif had to be reassessed after the shock of the city's destruction in 587 BC, it was used in magnificent proportions in the eschatological hopes of later Israel.[16] In the last days the pilgrims would again look at Zion and gasp at her wonders. Never again would she suffer under the judgment of her God, but her salvation would last forever and she would truly be inviolate.[17]

The disciple, informed with such theology, proclaims the glories of the stones and buildings of Zion. This expression of faith in the impregnability of God's earthly dwelling is an expression of faith in God and his protection. Indeed, all faithful Israelites could be exhorted to: "Walk about Zion, go round her, count her towers, consider well her ramparts, view her citadels, that you may tell of them to the next generation. For this God is our God for ever and ever; he will be our guide even to the end" (Ps 48:12-13 NIV).

Rather than a facile and insensitive comment from an awestruck Galilean tourist, this exhortation would provide theological encouragement from one Jew to another. It is therefore entirely appropriate for Jesus at this time, as he leaves a situation of controversy and opposition.

When Jesus spoke[18] to the unnamed disciple (v.2), the first part of his reply recalls the disciple's laudable Jewish statement. Βλέπεις *blepeis*, whether as a question or a statement, confirms that the disciple's vision, like that of any faithful Jew in such a situation, is focused upon the great

---

like a tourist!

14. For this motif, without connection to Mark 13:1, see Dumbrell, *End*, 5-27; von Rad, "City on the Hill"; Barrois, "Zion"; Roberts, "Zion Tradition." Beasley-Murray, *Mark 13*, 20, recognizes this motif lies behind this section.

15. In such language Zion could be described in terms that far outweighed the real size and strength of Jerusalem, e.g., Pss 48; 125.

16. In the rethink caused by the exile the magnificence of the Solomonic era began to inform the exalted imagery of the prophetic dream, even coupled with Edenic imagery. Dumbrell, "Some Observations."

17. Dumbrell, *Covenant and Creation*, 153-56, 190-200.

18. The aorist, after the historical present of verse 1, perhaps pointing to Jesus giving a definitive answer which deals with this statement once and for all.

buildings around them,¹⁹ and μεγάλας *megalas* reinforces the Zion theme raised by the disciple. However, as Jesus' reply proceeds the irony in this word becomes apparent. For he emphatically states that even these great buildings most certainly will not last,²⁰ but their future is one of total disintegration (καταλυθῇ *katalythē*).²¹ Rather than calling this "a prediction of the destruction of the Temple *in* AD 70," which illegitimately reads subsequent history back into the text,²² in accord with my chosen method it is preferable to use more cautious language that is simply descriptive of the text, i.e., here Jesus talks of the disintegration of these magnificent buildings, stone by stone!²³

In view of the Zion theme, this is an absolutely unexpected response which inserts a note of discord into the narrative, for it not only fails to affirm Jerusalem's eternal status, but even dismisses such a notion emphatically. This suggests that the physical Zion is not the last days' Zion of which the prophets dreamed. If this is all that occupies the disciple's sight, then he needs a new vision, for he is concerned with the perishable rather than the imperishable, the "things of man" not the "things of God" (8:33).²⁴

In this way Jesus' reply continues the movement away from the Jerusalem Temple, although the destination of the shift remains unknown. The dismissal of the disciple's eschatology raises the expectation that the

---

19. The verb may be unstressed, the equivalent of a gesture, or stressed, warning the disciple that he was preoccupied (so Cranfield, *Mark*, 391). Either way the effect is the same: the disciple's sights are on the buildings and his vision needs correction. Geddert, *Watchwords*, 86, endorses the point.

20. Note the emphatic negative future used twice. "Mark 13:2 is an impressionistic saying which uses exaggeration in order to depict in a vivid manner the temporalness of all human monuments," Stein, *Difficult Sayings*, 24, who nevertheless considers that it refers to AD 70.

21. Hengel, *Studies*, 14–16 nn.86–97, uses the phrases "complete annihilation," "complete destruction." Cf. LSJ lists one meaning (of governments, admittedly) as "to dissolve, break up."

22. Cranfield, *Mark*, 391, states: "That Jesus did predict the destruction of the Temple is hardly to be doubted." However, the verses he cites (Mark 14:58; 15:29; John 2:19; Matt 23:38) are far from clear. These references are all reports from people other than Jesus (and in Mark 14:58 false witnesses at that!) and John 2:19 explains that they represent a misunderstanding of Jesus.

23. The phrase λίθος ἐπὶ λίθον *lithos epi lithon* only occurs in LXX Hag 2:15, although Hengel, *Studies*, 128 n.88, finds an analogy in 2 Sam 17:13, a metaphor of complete destruction.

24. "The fascination of mere size, the external glory of Judaism, is corrected"; Beasley-Murray, *Mark 13*, 22.

positive alternative will soon follow. It is appropriate that Jesus' discourse is held together by verbs of seeing,[25] since it appears that he aims to fill the disciples' vision with an alternative to earthly Zion hopes. But, rather than jumping ahead, the narrative ought to be allowed to unfold in its own time.

The Shift Continues (vv. 3–4)

The "no stone on another" statement is followed by an introductory circumstantial statement (v.3) and a question (v.4) reported in direct speech.[26]

In the introductory genitive absolute Jesus is maintained as the focalizer. His seated posture ceases the movement, adding to the narrative pause and raising an expectation that the reason for the pause will now be revealed.

This verb may also evoke other connotations. It had a prominent position in Jesus' christological puzzle (12:35–38) which expected the Christ to be seated until his enemies are firmly defeated. This riddle opened a "gap" that was sustained by the use of the verb in 12:41–44 and remains unclosed. Although his enemies are still at large when Jesus moves away from the scene of controversy, the use of καθημένου *kathēmenou* in 13:3, being a partial closure of the gap, keeps alive the expectations that he will "rule in the midst of his enemies" (Ps 110:2).[27]

His location (εἰς τὸ Ὄρος τῶν Ἐλαιῶν *eis to Oros tōn Elaiōn*) represents a return to the beginning of this narrative section (11:1). This retrospection recalls the intervening narrative which has already raised the overtones of apocalyptic judgment attached to this mountain (cf. Zech 14:4) and increasingly reinforced the imminence of the End.[28] While geographically quite

---

25. See vv.2,5,9,23,33; cf. vv.4,7,14,21,22,26,29,33,34,35,37.

26. Perhaps in the form of a quest story. See Tannehill, "Varieties," 101–19.

27. Schneider, "κάθημαι κτλ," 442, mentions the association of sitting with ruling, adding that Dan 7:13 has influenced this association. Beasley-Murray, *Mark* 13, 25, refers to K.L. Schmidt's reading: "as he sat enthroned." This verse implicitly acts as a redundancy, keeping these Psalm 110 associated ideas alive on the way towards its further quote in 14:62.

28. Note allusions to Zechariah (11:1–9; "this mountain" into the sea, 11:23; cf. Zech 14:4,10, with Lane, *Mark*, 410; cf. Lightfoot, "Connexion", 49); the scribes were to receive tremendous judgment 12:1–12,40; the enemies (Ps 110) were to be overthrown on the "day of God's wrath," 12:35–37; and the certainty of the resurrection was discussed 12:23–27.

accurate, "opposite the Temple" also has ominous overtones.[29] Already the Judgment Day lurks in the background of this deliberate pause in the story.

The temporary delay of the subject leaves ἐπηρώτα *epērōta* indefinite, creating a resumptive link with the conversation of vv.1–2 and allowing Jesus' focalizing role to be maintained (through αὐτόν *auton* preceding the subject). The privacy of the question (κατ' ἰδίαν *kat idian*) raises an expectation of further revelation in which the reader will also be involved.[30]

The question is asked by two sets of brothers, who are named. Giving a character a proper name recalls their total portrayal in the narrative.[31] Thus, the mention of these four can recall not only the story's initial commissioning of the twelve, from amongst whom they come (3:17,18), but also all of the incidents in which this group have appeared together.[32]

Peter, James and John, have been the only disciples since the initial naming of the twelve (3:13–19) who have been mentioned again.[33] Their mention here recalls the questions they asked in the most recent references, and that they all required correction.[34] These recollections add to the expectation of correction here.

---

29. Nineham, *Mark*, 342, observes that the spot commanded a view of the Temple over the Kidron valley. Lane, *Mark*, 454, draws attention to Ezek 9:3; 10:18–19; 11:23; Zech 14:23. Κατέναντι *katenanti* is used in Ezekiel 11:1, a passage which has a clear tone of opposition, BAGD, 421. Cf. Geddert, *Watchwords*, 149.

30. Observed by Taylor, *Mark*, 501–02; see 4:10; 7:17; 9:28; 10:10.

31. Rimmon-Kenan, *Narrative Fiction*, 33, 36–40; Burnett, "Prolegomenon," 95–98.

32. Amongst this group, Peter plays the largest character role being mentioned by name (either Simon or Peter) twenty-four times in at least twelve separate pericopes, most of which are highly significant for Mark's story (1:16,29–30,36; 3:16; 5:37; 8:29,32; 9:2,5; 10:28; 11:21; 13:3; 14:29,33,37,54,66–67,70,72; 16:7). He has "acted" as a representative figure on a number of occasions (1:29–39; 8:31–9:1; 9:2–13 and 10:24–31), as well as in a solitary role (11:20–25) and of course his famous role at the time of the crucifixion is yet to be played out, as is his being specially mentioned by the young man in 16:7. The sons of Zebedee are also named on several occasions, although with a less prominent role (1:19,29; 3:17; 5:37; 9:2; 9:38; 10:35,41; 13:3; 14:33). They act with Peter mostly, although John has a solitary speech (9:38) and they act as a subgroup from out of the twelve in 10:35–45 (although Peter is not too far away, see 10:28). These appearances act as "redundancies" which keep their commissioning before the reader, cf. Anderson, "Double and Triple Stories," 71–89.

33. Judas Iscariot still has his role to play, anticipated by 3:19 (14:10,43, but even then it is rather downplayed), but the Gospel will close with the middle seven (in terms of the list in 3:13–19) never being mentioned by name again.

34. Peter (9:5–7, corrected straight from heaven!), John (9:38ff.) and James and John (10:35–45).

THE NARRATIVE INTEGRITY OF MARK 13:24-27

However, the familiar threesome is joined by Andrew, who is given some prominence by virtue of his novelty and his final position.[35] His mention recalls the only other occasion upon which he accompanied the other three, when Jesus promised to make them into fishers of men (1:16–20) in the initial period of his ministry. They immediately followed Jesus and played a prominent role in the subsequent narrative (1:16–39). This retrospection to the disciples' commissioning keeps the story on track, as well as introducing a partial closure to the narrative. The disciples have been following Jesus and have learned about his mission, but the expectation that they will be made into fishers of men is still outstanding.

Their question (v.4) not only reveals their lack of understanding, but it also represents an obstruction to their commission. They, too (cf. v.1), begin with an imperative (Εἰπὸν ἡμῖν *Eipon hēmin*), perhaps making it more like a demand than a question and leaving themselves wide open to being corrected.[36] They inquire about ταῦτα *tauta*, most naturally referring[37] to the event of no stone being left on another,[38] couched in Old Testament apocalyptic language of the End.[39] The disciples appear to assume that the only thing that will result in the end of the Temple will be that final destruction of all things. However, they do not ask for clarification of *what* this end will be, merely *when* (πότε *pote*) it will be. The two formal parts of

---

35. Novelty, because he is a break from the familiar threesome, who have by now become a redundancy, and finality because of the rule of end-stress.

36. They could have merely asked πότε *pote*.

37. Lane, *Mark*, 454; Taylor, *Mark*, 501–02; Cranfield, *Mark*, 393; recognize this is the natural sense. However, Taylor claims that the ταῦτα πάντα *tauta panta* has some forward-looking sense as well, as the chapter now stands. He admits this point has been debated "since earliest times." To give these words a forward sense is to commit the error of applying the effect of the whole to a part. What gives the forward sense is that it is a question that has been asked and questions await answers. ταῦτα πάντα *tauta panta* only looks back to whatever it was Jesus referred to. However, as soon as someone asks for greater specificity the question itself awaits that specificity being given. We should also note that the specificity that is asked for is *not* so much clarification of ταῦτα *tauta* / ταῦτα πάντα *tauta panta*, as they seem to assume common ground here, but *when* this "end" will occur.

38. Despite the assertion by Cranfield, *Mark*, 393, that it would be natural for disciples to assume the destruction of the Temple would be part of the complex of events leading to the End, with Schrenk, "ἱερός κτλ," the fall of Jerusalem or the same as a prophetic perspective foretaste of the end (as Lane, *Mark*, 454; Lagrange; Cranfield, *Mark*, 393) should not be read into the text.

39. Verse 4a quotes Dan 12:7 LXX and alludes to Dan 12:6, 8:19; Verse 4b quotes Dan 12:8 (LXX); Kee, "Function," 168.

the question are, for them, parallel in intent.[40] The simple question πότε ταῦτα ἔσται *pote tauta estai* defines what the disciples desired to know, and the second part shows how they immediately translate their desire: καὶ τί τὸ σημεῖον ὅταν μέλλῃ ταῦτα συντελεῖσθαι πάντα; *kai ti to sēmeion hotan mellē tauta synteleisthai panta?* ("What is the sign whenever these things are *about to be completed*?"). Although the issue is still the "when," their focus is on the request for a sign.[41]

However, from the reader's privileged point of view, the two parts are not parallel. The first part is the readers' question too, since they are already expecting the End (see chapter 3). However, the translated question is not shared by the reader at all, since, at the discourse level, this question has previously been outlawed. In asking for a sign the four disciples reveal an attitude that Jesus has specifically condemned (8:11–13; perhaps also 9:19) and warned his disciples against (8:14–21), and show that they have ignored his warnings (8:15; 12:38).[42] This means they are still aligned with Jesus' opponents and are part of hard–hearted Israel (cf. 7:18).[43] Their question reveals that their preparation to be "fishers of men" is incomplete, for they still do not share Jesus' perspective. The shift is not yet completed.

---

40. The single question is recognized by Lane, *Mark*, 454, as is the parallel nature of the clauses. Parallelism does not necessarily mean that the meanings are equivalent (cf. Carson's comments on "parallelomania," *Exegetical Fallacies*, 43, 136; Sandmel, "Parallelomania"). However, to the disciples, the intent of the question is the same in both cases. Beasley-Murray, *Mark 13*, 27, agrees that the question is twofold in form not content: "The second question brings out what is latent in the first, but with an added sense of climax throughout." Others read as two questions, see Beasley-Murray, 28.

41. Note the ὅταν *hotan* clause. The ταῦτα *tauta* and ταῦτα πάντα *tauta panta* are equivalents. Cranfield, *Mark*, 393, points out that this second question pervades all Biblical and extra-Biblical apocalyptic. He argues that a sign relieves people from the necessity to watch.

42. Geddert, *Watchwords*, Ch 2, agrees that the disciples' question imports negative connotations from 8:11–14.

43. Fowler, *Loaves*, 167–68, the rhetorical questions of 8:17–21 are answered "No, they still don't!" Mark 13:4 reveals this answer, if the reader has not guessed at it before. Beasley-Murray, *Mark 13*, 27–28, recognizes that the question ought not to be asked, but excuses the disciples due to the nature of the calamity: "we must not rob them of their right to behave as men of flesh and blood, possessed of a normal emotional life."

An Attitude Awaiting Correction

Although the question (v.4) bridges Jesus' saying (v.1) and his discourse, in itself it does not control the chapter.[44] Whether the disciples were thinking of the destruction of the Temple in an historical disaster, or as part of the advent of the end, matters little. The reader, who at this point in the story is closer to Jesus than the disciples, expects that the disciples will be corrected and so their understanding is irrelevant. Jesus is moving away from the Temple and its ideology, and so it is far more significant to discover *where he is moving them to*. Their question is therefore merely preparatory for his positive teaching.

By the same token, the saying in verse 2 does not control the chapter. It is part of the introductory complex (vv.1–4), in which vv.1–2 effects an attitudinal shift away from the Temple towards something else, and vv.3–4 continue the shift by raising a question which underlines the disciples' need for correction. Vv.1–4 do not control the chapter, instead they prepare the ground for the reception of Jesus' further teaching.

This analysis already raises questions about an interpretation that is preoccupied with the Temple, albeit with its destruction. Firstly, the complex works by moving the attention from the Temple to something else, which suggests that the positive end of the shift is more significant than what becomes Jesus' "passing remark" in verse 2. Secondly, the shift is not concerned with structures but *attitudes in the disciples,* which again suggests that a focus upon the actual Jerusalem Temple is misguided.[45]

A Warning for the Time of Distress (vv.5–23)

Jesus' responds with his Apocalyptic Discourse, in which we can expect him to complete the attitudinal shift that the disciples need.[46]

---

44. My argument therefore refutes France's claim that vv.1–4 control the chapter, see above pp. 5–6. Geddert, *Watchwords,* also rejects this view. In Mark, a disciple's question often introduces a section of teaching: 4:10, 7:17, 9:22, 10:10; cf. Lane, *Mark,* 454.

45. Such a focus means that the interpreter has not been effected by the shift at all, but is still saying "What massive stones! What magnificent buildings!"

46. The relationship of question to discourse is variously given. Nineham, *Mark,* 345, believes the question is not answered at all; Taylor, *Mark,* 504, sees a discrepency between sources (about the parousia) and the final text (about the fall of Jerusalem); Cranfield, *Mark,* 394, divides the discourse into various stages of the answer to the question(s) of v.4.

The Warning (vv.5–13)

Verses 5–6 form a frame with vv.21–23, which will guide the interpretation of the intervening material (vv.7–20).[47]

The Initial Warning (vv.5–6)

Jesus, still as the focalizer,[48] delivers the speech for which the hearer has been well prepared. ἤρξατο λέγειν *ērxato legein* introduces not only an air of formality, but also an expectancy that there will be more to come once his preliminaries are over.[49]

He begins with a warning, using the present imperative (Βλέπετε *Blepete*, See! Look out!) which implies the danger is current.[50] The warning safeguards against being led astray (μή τις ὑμᾶς πλανήσῃ *mē tis hymas planēsē*).[51] Although the dangerous persons are undefined (τις *tis*), Jesus has used this same imperative to warn the disciples against the scribes (12:38), and against the sign seeking attitude of the Pharisees (8:15). The only other use of this imperative encourages careful listening to the gospel of God (4:24), which is linked with the failure of Israel to listen and the warning to the disciples not to be like them.[52] The only other usage of πλανάω *planaō* is also associated with the opponents' failure to listen to God's word (12:24,27). These previous associations, linking the undefined τις *tis* with Jesus' already

---

47. For the function of a frame, see pp. 57–59. In vv.5–6, "the Old Testament furnishes parallels to nearly every phrase"; Lane, *Mark*, 456, with Hartman, "Survey," 147–50. Kee, "Function," 168, identifies a quotation from Isa 45:18 LXX; allusions to Dan 7:8, 11, 20, 25; influences from Isa 14:13, Dan 8:10, 11:36. Cf. Dan 8:25 (Lane, *Mark*, 456), ?Exod 3:14, Isa 43:10–11, 52:6–7 (Taylor, *Mark*, 504). As elsewhere in the discourse this means Jesus is speaking generally, not giving specific predictions. He warns rather than foretells.

48. Note the use of his proper name, in first-heard position, and the mere αὐτοῖς *autois*, "to them", trailing along.

49. "Jesus began by saying"; Taylor, *Mark*, 502–05: ἤρξατο *ērxato*—characteristic usage of Mark, a "quasi-auxiliary" sense (p.48), listed as an "Aramaism" (p.63). Nineham, *Mark*, 344 n*, notes that ἤρξατο λέγειν *ērxato legein* elsewhere in Mark is a formula used to begin a speech rather than answer a question, for which Mark has other formulas. Cf. Manson, *Teaching of Jesus*, 262, n.1.

50. BDF, 172. Βλέπετε *blepete* is discussed in Kilpatrick, "BLEPETE PHILIPPIANS 3_2," and Geddert, *Watchwords*, Ch. 3.

51. Πλανάω *planaō* has appeared in only one pericope so far. In 12:18–27 Jesus used it twice to say that the Sadducees were seriously misled by denying the last day resurrection, and these overtones may be in the background here. Its fourth and final use is 13:6.

52. 4:12 through to 8:15–18 and 8:23–24, in which βλέπω *blepō* is used.

familiar opponents, add an immediacy to Jesus' warning. Instead of being preoccupied with a city that will not last forever (cf. vv.1–2, βλέπετε *blepete*), Jesus turns their eyes on themselves and *warns them against being led astray by his opponents*.[53] This warning to the disciples is the theme of the discourse, for which βλέπετε *blepete* acts as both a key and a hook word.[54]

The pause created by the asyndeton of verse 6 allows the seriousness of the imperative to sink in. Verse 6 reveals that the threat will be from a large group (πολλοί *polloi*), expected anytime,[55] who will come ἐπὶ τῷ ὀνόματί μου *epi tō onomati mou*. This is immediately explained by the participial clause in terms of a claim to exercise an authority which Jesus considers properly to belong to him.[56] This need not be linked with a titular claim, nor with the first century messianic movements referred to in extrabiblical sources.[57] The Old Testament prophets contained examples of those exercising leadership over Israel "in God's name" when the reality was otherwise, and, in effect, these took the place of their God.[58] Such cor-

---

53. On this understanding the imperative is not unexpected (cf. Victor's famous comment "They asked one question, he answered another"), but is most necessary in view of the disciples dabbling in Jewish nationalistic eschatology; cf. Beasley-Murray, *Mark 13*, 30.

54. The former is thematic, the latter structural, Dewey, *Markan Public Debate*, 31–32. Βλέπετε *blepete* appears in vv.5,9,23,33; cf. v.2. Beasley-Murray, *Mark 13*, 30, comments that this warning "is the first, and most needed, word spoken to them. It is also the last (v.37), and it is dominant through all that lies between (vv.7,9,11,23,33,35,37)."

55. The simple future tense doesn't pinpoint the timing, for it simply refers to any time after the speaker has finished the sentence.

56. I.e. the two phrases are co-ordinate and explicative: "in my name, namely, saying 'I am'." (cf. 6:14; 9:37,38,39,41; 11:9 [Ps 118:25]). This 'name theme' has its climax in 13:13.

The phrase ἐγώ εἰμι *egō eimi* appeared in Mark 6:50, where it was informed by the exalted theology of Exodus 3:14 (cf. Mark 14:62). Given the importance of names to a narrative (Burnett, "Prolegomenon"), this marks out Jesus as the one on the side of the divine and οἱ πολλοί *hoi polloi* as usurpers of his position.

57. *Pace* Cranfield, *Mark*, 395; Lane, *Mark*, 457; Taylor, *Mark*, 504; Robinson, *Jesus and His Coming*, 113. Actually the latter entails the denial of the former. Popular messianism hardly ever produced a messianic claimant and so this statement needs to be broadly interpreted of pretenders who "assume messianic functions," Beasley-Murray, *Mark 13*, 31. However, once this broad understanding is adopted, there is a more readily identifiable group already within Mark's story itself.

58. This is clearly the case for those prophets who spoke in God's name but were not authorized by him to do so (e.g., Jer 5:31; 6:13; 14:14–15; 23:13 [LXX Aq],25–32; 26:7–9; 27:14; 29:9,13; Zech 5:4; 13:3) and for the priests (e.g., Jer 5:31; 6:13; 14:18; 23:33–39; Mal 1:6,11,14; 2:2; 3:5 LXX), and the scribes (e.g., Jer 8:8). The nation itself was meant

rupt leadership increasingly dissatisfied their Lord God. In response to the corrupt shepherds of Israel, God promised to send/to be his own shepherd (e.g., Jer 3:15; Ezekiel 34:11ff.). Thus the Messiah would be in continuity with Israel's leadership, but with a qualitative discontinuity. It is readily understandable, therefore, to have many who occupy the position within Israel that properly belongs to the Messiah.[59]

In Mark's story, those holding such positions, the religious leaders and Herod, have already been contrasted with the leadership of Jesus.[60] Once again Jesus refers to his opponents when he talks of those who occupy the role that only the Messiah will ultimately fulfill.[61] These de facto Christs will be a force which threatens to lead many astray and so Jesus warns his disciples to look out.[62]

The impending danger is appended as a consequence of the coming of the many: καὶ πολλοὺς πλανήσουσιν *kai pollous planēsousin*. The verb forms an inclusio with verse 5, linking this consequence tightly with the warning, and its object gives an aural repetition with verse 6a (πολλοί [. . .] πολλούς *polloi* [. . .] *pollous*). All of this underlines the simple consequential connection between many coming and many being led astray. Since, as I have

---

to bear God's name (Jer 14:9; Amos 9:12; Mic 4:5) and the kings were meant to rule in God's name (Deut 17:14–20). When they failed, they were indicted along with the corrupt prophets and priests (Jer 1:18; 2:8,26; 4:9; 5:4–5; 10:21; 13:13–14,18; 15:4; 17:19–27; 19:3–15; 23; Ezek 34, etc). The future ruler from Bethlehem will shepherd his flock in God's name (Mic 5:4; Jer 23:5–6).

59. Cf. Isa 47:8,10, where, in a chapter which rebukes the city of Babylon for thinking it is inviolate, the prophet says she has in effect taken on a divine prerogative, using as her self-title an ascription repeatedly used by God of himself: Ἐγώ εἰμι, καὶ οὐκ ἔστιν ἑτέρα *Egō eimi, kai ouk estin hetera*; cf. Mark 13:6. The religious leaders' clash with Jesus, and their debate over authority, assumes that "there is no other," apart from their own. The tragic irony is that they are claiming exactly what their ancient enemy Babylon had claimed, whose arrogant self-assertion was paradigmatic of the beastly powers of Daniel 7 that would be stripped away by the coming of the one like a son of man. Now that this event is looming on the horizon, their time is up, no matter how much their position may be buttressed by an inviolate Zion theology.

60. Explicitly (1:21–29; 2:1–12,13–17,23–28; 3:1–6,22–30; 6:14–56; 7:1–22, cf. 2:18–22; 8:1–21,31; 9:31; 10:33–34,42–45; 11:17–18,27–33; 12:1–12,13–44) and implicitly, by virtue of Jesus' designation as Son of Man, since Daniel promised that this figure would supersede any previous human power (Dan 7:12,26).

61. Cranfield, *Mark*, 395, gives for ἐπὶ τῷ ὀνόματί μου *epi tō onomati mou* the alternatives: 1. "sent by me," "appealing to me as their authority"; 2. "arrogating to themselves the title of Messiah, which by right belongs to me." My alternative is a variation of the latter: "exercising the role that only the Messiah will ultimately fulfill."

62. Opposition to Jesus has been expressed against the disciples previously (2:13–27).

suggested, οἱ πολλοί *hoi polloi* are those in high places, then this consequence can be readily understood, as can the need for stern warning.[63]

The point of verse 6 is now clear. The fact is that many will be led astray by those who abuse the role of Israel's shepherds. Jesus warns his disciples to watch themselves, lest they join the ranks of τοὺς πολλούς *tous pollous*.

Don't Get Agitated! (vv.7-8)

In vv.7-8, since he draws upon Old Testament allusions, it is likely that Jesus is speaking in a generalized way, rather than "predicting" specific historical events.[64] He projects a future situation (ὅταν δὲ ἀκούσητε *hotan de akousēte*) in which an imperative needs to be followed (μὴ θροεῖσθε *mē throeisthe*). Whenever the disciples hear of cosmic upheavals, they are not to be agitated![65] In the context, it is a fair assumption that such agitation will open them up to being led astray (vv.5-6).

The next statement, isolated by the asyndeton of v.7b,[66] describes the inevitability of hearing of such turmoil (δεῖ γενέσθαι *dei genesthai*)[67] and introduces the negative point:– ἀλλ' οὔπω τὸ τέλος *all' oupō to telos*. When unmodified τὸ τέλος *to telos* sounds ultimate (cf. 3:26) and, since Jesus offers no alternative, it is a fair assumption that he means the End *as defined by the Old Testament*. Jesus declares that these cosmic disturbances, which

---

63. Although Hengel, *Studies*, 21, mistakenly talks about this within the Christian community, his quote is apposite if we read it of the disciples within their Jewish community: "the danger from within of being led astray is even greater than persecution and physical distress from outside the community." The warning is analogous to 8:33.

64. For the expectations and language common to Jewish apocalyptic and the Old Testament, cf. Taylor, *Mark*, 505; Nineham, *Mark*, 344; Kee, "Function," 168. Taylor tentatively suggests this general interpretation. Cranfield, *Mark*, 396, treats the section as general suffering for all people. Klostermann says it is "simply following a schema," as quoted in Hengel, *Studies*, 22, who himself argues for historical referents *ca* AD 69, despite his recognition of "stereotyped apocalyptic themes [. . .] from apocalyptic horror literature."

65. The present imperative refers to the projected time of hearing. Warfare is a common OT and apocalyptic motif (cf. Isa 19:2; Jer 4:19-31; 6:22-30; 49; Dan 7:21-27; Joel 3:9-16; 2 Chron 15:6; Zech 14:2; Dan 11:44 Θ); Beasley-Murray, *Mark 13*, 34. The phrase is characteristic of apocalyptic, cf. Dan 2:28,29,45; Cranfield, *Mark*, 396.

66. Rather than evidence of an Aramaic source (Taylor, *Mark*, 505), or a gloss (Nineham, *Mark*, 346), it is very much a part of the rhetorical structure of the chapter. Early textual variants attempted to smooth it out by the addition of γάρ *gar*.

67. Δεῖ *dei*, used of "divine necessity," occurs only in the second half of the Gospel and always in significant contexts pointing towards Jesus' crucifixion (8:31; 9:11; 13:7,10,14; 14:31); cf. Donahue, "Neglected Factor."

must be capable of agitating and misleading the disciples, do not signal τὸ τέλος *to telos*.

Verse 8 explains (γάρ *gar*) verse 7—explicitly δεῖ γενέσθαι *dei genesthai*, implicitly οὔπω τὸ τέλος *oupō to telos*. The three future indicatives are not specific predictions of the End,[68] but merely the natural course of events to come. This is all exaggerated, general language drawn from the common stock of Old Testament tradition, "the dramatic language of judgment."[69] These things are part of the fabric of human history which stands under God's judgment and, in line with the apocalyptic view of history, Jesus disassociates these calamitous events from τὸ τέλος *to telos*. The kingdom of God will not emerge from within such history, but it will burst in upon this world of human turmoil (cf. Daniel 7).

Another asyndeton and the lack of an explicit verb give the last clause a starkness that enhances its climactic function.[70] This clause both describes what these things properly are and precludes them from consideration as signs of the end: ἀρχὴ ὠδίνων ταῦτα *archē ōdinōn tauta*.[71] ἀρχή *archē* implies there is plenty more to follow, and things will get worse and the eschatologically flavored ὠδίνων *ōdinōn* likewise points forward.[72] This cosmic turmoil is not the end, this is merely the beginning.

This has all been part of the explanation of the necessity of the disasters which will arise as surely as the beginning of birth pangs. The actual events to which all this disastrous OT language is to be applied remain to be seen. However, this apocalyptic language of "cosmic disturbance," suggests a world in turmoil and in need of salvific divine intervention. The reader is well aware that Jesus has just left such a world, in so much turmoil that the leaders of Israel can plot to destroy the Son of David (Mark 11–12).

Although the events await clearer definition within the story, at the discourse level this section clearly keeps the reader progressing towards the

---

68. *Pace*, Cranfield, *Mark*, 396; Lane, *Mark*, 458. This interpretation actually negates what Jesus says in v.7!

69. Stein, *Difficult Sayings*, 79. The Old Testament flavor of v.8 is pungent; cf. Beasley-Murray, *Mark 13*, 36. There is therefore no need to read-in the events of AD 70 here, *pace* Lane, *Mark*, 458.

70. Εἰσιν *eisin* needs to be supplied and the phrase interrupts the poetry; Beasley-Murray, *Mark 13*, 37.

71. Given Jesus' specific denials, it is surprising that Mark 13 is so often referred to in terms of "the Signs of the End".

72. For discussion: Cranfield, *Mark*, 396; Nineham, *Mark*, 346; Lane, *Mark*, 458; Taylor, *Mark*, 505; Kee, "Function," 169.

positive side of the shift. For in learning that "this is not yet the End," the reader keeps looking for the End yet to come to take on clearer definition.

The Top Priority (vv.9-11)

Verse 9 resumes the imperative of verse 5, reiterating the need to avoid going astray (βλέπετε δὲ ὑμεῖς ἑαυτούς *blepete de hymeis heautous*). Jesus uses the emphatic pronoun (ὑμεῖς *hymeis*) to contrast the four disciples with those who will be led astray (πολλούς *pollous*, v.6) and those who get agitated by connecting the world's turmoil with the end (v.7). The reflexive pronoun (ἑαυτούς *heautous*), which must not be ignored, makes the imperative of this section explicit: "rather than looking for signs, look out for *yourselves*, you are the ones in danger!".

The asyndeton once again isolates the imperative, adding solemnity to it. The impending danger is given by the verb παραδώσουσιν *paradōsousin*, a hook word for this section (vv.9,11,12) and a key word for the Markan story whose usage is predominantly oriented towards the coming passion.[73] Like John the Baptist and Jesus himself, the four disciples need to be prepared to be betrayed (cf. 8:34). When the indefinite subject of the verb is supplied by the preceding context, the warning is clear: the disciples, too, need to beware of betrayal by Jesus' opponents.

Rather than the following three clauses being parallel,[74] παραδώσουσιν ὑμᾶς *paradōsousin humas* stands apart as a topic sentence followed by two formally parallel clauses, *viz*:

εἰς συνέδρια καὶ εἰς συναγωγὰς	δαρήσεσθε
eis synedria kai eis synagōgas	*darēsesthe*
καὶ ἐπὶ ἡγεμόνων καὶ βασιλέων	σταθήσεσθε.
kai epi hēgemonōn kai basileōn	*stathēsesthe*.

73. 1:14; 3:19; 9:31; 10:33 (2x). The only exceptions are 4:29 and 7:13 (although even these may be more related to the passion than at first glance). The references after Mark 13 simply function as closure to these expectations (14:10,11,18,21,41,42,44; 15:1,10,15). Cf. Cranfield, *Mark*, 61-67, 306.

74. *Pace* Taylor, *Mark*, 506, whose second clause sounds strange. My reading removes this strangeness. I also differ from the structure proposed by Kilpatrick, "Gentile Mission." Nineham, *Mark*, 347, notes that εἰς συναγωγάς *eis synagōgas* goes not with παραδώσουσιν *paradōsousin* but with δαρήσεσθε *darēsesthe*. I am arguing that εἰς συνέδρια *eis synedria* does also (εἰς *eis* is equivalent to ἐν *en*; Taylor, *Mark*, 506).

The first clause has a thoroughly Jewish and religious flavor, with overtones of opposition to the cause of Jesus.[75] There is no need to prematurely search for "a fulfillment" of this "prediction,"[76] but instead its character *as warning* needs to be recognized. The subsequent course of events will fill out the details for the four.

By hendiadys, the second clause links two groups of secular figures ἐπὶ ἡγεμόνων καὶ βασιλέων *epi hēgemonōn kai basileōn*.[77] Βασιλεύς *basileus* has only appeared so far of King Herod (6:14,22,25,26,27) and will recur in the subsequent narrative only of Jesus (15:2,9,12,18,26,32). The reader also naturally associates this word with its cognate βασιλεία *basileia*, "kingdom", which occurs in Mark's central theme.[78]

The previous narrative has already set the kingdom represented by the religious and political leaders in opposition to the kingdom of God represented by Jesus. This "clash of kingdoms" has already been felt by the disciples (2:17,18,23–24; 6:14–29; 7:2–5) and Jesus has warned them on one prior occasion against both religious and political opponents (8:15). Now the warning is reissued in more detail.

Once again there is no need to immediately search for an historical "fulfillment." Rather than being a specific "prediction," this is a warning issued from reflection on the general teaching of the Old Testament and circumstances of the time. Like the godly Psalmist (Ps 119:46 is alluded to here),[79] the disciples will stand against various leadership figures, both religious and secular, in a clash of kingdoms.[80] Although the actual course

---

75. The synagogue has already appeared in Mark as a place in which Jesus taught with astonishing effects (1:21–28; 1:39); and in which increasingly hostile reactions were experienced (3:1–6; 6:1–6). It was the place in which the Jewish leadership displayed their hypocrisy (12:39). It doesn't appear again in Mark. The συνέδρια *synedria* make their first appearance here and their remaining two in the context of Jesus' betrayal (14:55; 15:1).

76. For συνέδρια *synedria*, most look ahead to beyond the crucifixion and refer to local Jewish councils, as in 2 Cor 11:23–24 (Nineham, *Mark*, 347, 349; Taylor, *Mark*, 506) or the several references in Acts (Hengel, *Studies*, 23).

77. Note the single preposition governing both plural nouns. This then clarifies the meaning of ἡγεμόνων *hēgemonōn*—only here in Mark.

78. 1:15; 4:11,26,30; 9:1,47; 10:14,15,23,24,25; 11:10; 12:24. I will argue below that the references after Mark 13 (14:23; 15:43) point ahead to the closure of this kingdom theme in the events surrounding the empty tomb. The kingdom of God and that of Satan are opposed to each other, in true apocalyptic style (3:22–30). Earthly kings and kingdoms stand in beastly array against the kingdom of God (King Herod and the Jerusalem leaders), cf. 13:8.

79. Nineham, *Mark*, 350.

80. Although ἡγεμών *hēgemōn* used of Roman officials in Matt 27:7 and Acts 23:24,

of events is yet to reveal what particular shape this opposition will take, the disciples are warned that they too are at odds with Jesus' opponents because of their involvement with his mission (ἕνεκεν ἐμοῦ *heneken emou*, "for my sake").[81] Nevertheless, there is a purpose to this clash for whenever the leaders oppose the disciples, there will be some kind of "witness (taking place) against them" (εἰς μαρτύριον αὐτοῖς *eis martyrion autois*).[82]

Reading καί *kai* in a co-ordinate rather than adversative sense,[83] verse 10 more closely defines this witness as gospel preaching.[84] This gospel activity is with a view to πάντα τὰ ἔθνη *panta ta ethnē*,[85] those involved in the cosmic turmoil (13:8), who have been let down by the Jewish leadership (11:17) and who will share in the world harvest of the kingdom

---

there is no need to demand that this clause refers to *Gentile* rulers; cf. Mark 6:14.

81. This gives the reason for both the beating and the standing, Beasley-Murray, *Mark 13*, 40, "on account of their attachment to Jesus and their proclamation of his evangel" (cf. 8:35; 10:29).

82. The meanings canvassed are:

   1. for a witness to (i.e., to give opportunity to believe), cf. RSV, Nineham, *Mark*, 349;

   2. for an evidence against (i.e. at the final judgment they will be incriminated by their condemnation of the disciples), cf. Matt 10:18, 24:14, Strathmann, "μάρτυς κτλ";

   3. allow for the various ideas in the witness terminology rather than choose i or ii. Cranfield, *Mark*, 397, suggests a threefold meaning: 1. disciples' profession is evidence of truth of gospel to themselves (Calvin). 2. to their persecutors. 3. if this evidence is not accepted by the persecutors it will be evidence against them at the judgment.

   4. the suffering of the disciples, as part of the final woes will give testimony that the end is near, Nineham, *Mark*, 349, following Kilpatrick.

Mark's use of the witness vocabulary gives it overtones of opposition (μαρτυρέω *martyreō*: not used; μαρτύριον *martyrion*: 1:44; 6:11; 13:9; μαρτυρία *martyria*: 14:55,56,59; μάρτυς *martys*: 14:63).

83. Hengel, *Studies*, 24: "However, the gospel must first be preached"; cf. 12:12,17,40.

84. Notice the overlap effect created by the prepositional phrases: εἰς μαρτύριον αὐτοῖς *eis martyrion autois* / καὶ εἰς πάντα τὰ ἔθνη *kai eis panta ta ethnē*, which may therefore add a purposive sense to v.10 as well.

85. Cranfield, *Mark*, 399, gives three interpretations of εἰς *eis*: i) = unto, as far as: i.e., extent of preaching—most probable; ii) = ἐν *en* amongst—next likely; iii) κηρυσσεῖν + εἰς *kēryssein + eis* = to preach unto someone—there is no clear example of this usage in the New Testament; cf. Kilpatrick, "Gentile Mission," 146-49. However, coming first in the sentence there is no way of knowing what sense it has at this stage, and the purposive use of εἰς *eis* is immediately fresh in the reader's mind so it is likely that, at least temporarily, this semi-purposive sense is read.

of God (4:30–32). The disciples are told to look out for themselves with an eye on the nations.[86]

The lack of precision with regard to the causal connection between the two verses (i.e., how does the situation of mutual opposition relate to the preaching of the gospel?) creates a "gap" which looks for closure.[87] This begins to be supplied by the verse's statement of priority, conveyed by πρῶτον *prōton*[88] in combination with the following δεῖ *dei*, which repeats what Mark's story has already established.[89] How this priority relates to the situation of opposition is explained in the following verses.

Verse 11 can be considered as a neatly balanced section consisting of a time reference and an imperative on both sides of the ἀλλά *alla*, focusing on the content of the troubled disciples' speech[90] and followed by an explanatory clause.[91] (see Table 4). This reading does not follow the normal procedure of construing the phrase ἐν ἐκείνῃ τῇ ὥρᾳ *en ekeinē tē hōra* with

---

86. It is the nations to whom the Jewish leadership will betray Jesus (10:33), over whom their rulers lord it (10:42). The preaching to the nations was a last days' activity promised in apocalyptic thought; cf. Zech 2:10; 14:16, which is alluded to in v.10 (Kee, "Function," 169). Jesus' arrival in Jerusalem prepared for this eschatological event, cf. 11:17.

87. For filling in the gaps in the reading process, see Iser, "Interaction", "Reading Process", pre-eminently, or Rimmon-Kenan, *Narrative Fiction*, 127–29.

88. I.e. read in a non-temporal sense ("above all"), cf. Hengel, *Studies*, 25. Surprisingly, Beasley-Murray, *Mark 13*, 41, gives two senses for δεῖ *dei*, both conveying priority (1. The persecutions are not to stop the gospel: "The gospel must be preached at all costs," 2. Must—the divine purpose declared in the prophets will be fulfilled) and then he desires a temporal usage for πρῶτον *prōton*. The temporal sense (Nineham, *Mark*, 347; Kilpatrick, "Gentile Mission") begs the question: "before what?" (Cranfield, *Mark*, 272, says before the end and compares Rom 11:25f.), requires reading-in other material and assumes that Jesus is actually giving some indicators of the program towards the end, a view rejected by the prevailing note on timing in this section (v.7).

89. The overtones of divine necessity (δεῖ *dei*) further reinforce the sense of priority. Cranfield, *Mark*, 272: δεῖ *dei* "referring to a necessity beyond human comprehension grounded in the will of God, a use highly characteristic of the NT." In Mark δεῖ *dei* focuses especially on the passion (Donahue, "Neglected Factor"). Hengel, *Studies*, 24, has recognized the links between vv.9–11 and the crucifixion.

90. The utterance (ὃ ἐὰν δοθῇ ὑμῖν *ho ean dothē hymin*, "whatever might be given to you"), being the significant point of the saying, occupies central position.

91. See Bolt, "Spirit," 50–53, for the advantages of this reading and for the discussion here.

the preceding subjunctive clause ὃ ἐὰν δοθῇ ὑμῖν *ho ean dothē hymin* taken in a future sense, but with the following imperative: "in that hour, say this."

Table 4: The Syntactical Structure of Mark 13:11

Time:	ὅταν ἄγωσιν ὑμᾶς παραδιδόντες *hotan agōsin hymas paradidontes*
	whenever they lead you, arresting,
Imperative:	μὴ προμεριμνᾶτε τί λαλήσητε *mē promerimnate ti lalēsēte*
	Don't worry what you might say
	ἀλλ' ὃ ἐὰν δοθῇ ὑμῖν, *all' ho ean dothē hymin*
	But whatever might be given to you
Time:	ἐν ἐκείνῃ τῇ ὥρᾳ *en ekeinē tē hōra*
	In that hour
Imperative:	τοῦτο λαλεῖτε *touto laleite*
	This, you keep saying.
Explanation:	οὐ γάρ ἐστε ὑμεῖς οἱ λαλοῦντες *ou gar este hymeis hoi lalountes*
	For you are not the ones speaking
	ἀλλὰ τὸ πνεῦμα τὸ ἅγιον *alla to pneuma to hagion*
	But the Holy Spirit

After the statement on priority, the participle (παραδιδόντες *paradidontes*) resumes the thought of verse 9 and provides an imperative for that situation (μὴ προμεριμνᾶτε *mē promerimnate*). They should stop being concerned beforehand about τί λαλήσητε *ti lalēsēte*.[92] Since evangelizing the nations is to be the top priority, then it is natural that the disciples are worried about what to say. However, when they are led before the authorities, they shouldn't have this worry, for they are to say what they have been given. Rather than this being a promise that the disciples will receive illumination from the Holy Spirit at the time of their need, supplying the words needed for their witness or defense,[93] it is more natural to expect that

92. This is a deliberative subjunctive, Taylor, *Mark*, 508.

93. This would be a new departure for the narrative which has so far linked the Holy Spirit only to Jesus as the Servant. Although this interpretation may well make sense to a post-resurrection perspective, it is difficult to see what the disciples would have made of it at the time of their first hearing.

the preparation would be done before the hour of need. In fact, the story so far shows that the disciples have already been adequately prepared, for they have already been given what to say, which basically amounts to the gospel (1:15,16–20; 3:14; 4:11; 6:7–13; cf. 13:10).

Jesus, who operates by the Holy Spirit (1:10,12; 3:29–30) and whose message is the message of the Holy Spirit,[94] gave them the words to say. Although the time of their speaking is future, the time when the utterance is given is during Jesus' ministry to the disciples. They will be tempted to be ashamed of Jesus and his words in the face of suffering (8:31–9:1), but they have already been given[95] the words to say. In that hour, they simply need to "keep on saying this" (τοῦτο λαλεῖτε *touto laleite*, present imperative).

The explanatory clause reinforces this interpretation by reminding the disciples of a fact that ought to be clear by this stage: they are not the speakers—in the sense of the authors of their speech. They have been drafted into Jesus' mission (1:16–20). They need to stick with him and his words, the gospel (8:35,38; 10:29). They are not to worry about what to say, for it is not their responsibility to invent the content. The true speaker is the Holy Spirit in the ministry of Jesus Christ. They are to say the message that the Spirit-anointed one has given them already. They are to stand firm in that future hour, and keep on speaking the gospel of the kingdom that they have been authorized to speak.[96] This is the alternative to preparatory worry.

Thus the gap of vv.9–10 is now closed, for it has been revealed that the situation of opposition will give an opportunity for the proclamation of the gospel, the top priority activity for which Jesus has already prepared them well.

---

94. Cf. the implicit assumption behind 12:36. Note too the readers' awareness that Jesus had been divinely given wisdom in 6:2 and 12:28–34; Dewey, *Markan Public Debate*, 157.

95. The aorist tense can now be treated significantly, indicating the action as global and completed.

96. In other words, they need to be true to their calling. Any pre-thinking is unnecessary because the message remains the same, no matter what the circumstances. This phrase may still perhaps reflect a "divine passive", as this is entirely appropriate to Mark's presentation of Jesus. Cranfield, *Mark*, 400, finds a parallel in Exod 4:12 and Jer 1:9. Taylor, *Mark*, 508, adds Num 22:35 and Exodus 4; cf. Kee, "Function," 169.

The State of the Nation (vv.12-13)

The key word παραδώσει *paradōsei* resumes the thought of vv.9-11, in preparation for more detail.[97] What follows is a disclosure that the betrayal comes from those closest[98] and it is unto death.[99] Since the verse is an explicit quote, the reader is invited to read in the light of the informing theology drawn from Mic 7.2,6 (Targum),[100] where the mention of family members is actually metonymic for *the apostate people of Israel*, especially the leadership (7:3). Mark's story has already drawn on Micah 7 to portray the corruption of Israel, especially the leaders (11:12-14) who were hardened against Jesus (11:27-12:12). Jesus now warns his disciples that if apostate Israel[101] and its leadership opposed him, they would also oppose the disciples. Verse 12 therefore reinforces what vv.5-11 have established.

By mentioning both the terrible opposition that these disciples (note the second person address) will endure (καὶ ἔσεσθε μισούμενοι ὑπὸ πάντων *kai esesthe misoumenoi hypo pantōn*)[102] and the reason for their opponents' hatred, i.e., διὰ τὸ ὄνομά μου *dia to onoma mou*, verse 13a continues familiar themes. As the ones who have been authorised to go out in Jesus' name (cf. 3:14-19; 6:7-13) and to be involved in Jesus' mission (cf. vv.9-11), they will suffer at the hands of those within Israel who falsely occupy the position belonging to the Christ (vv.5-6).

Following this resumption, the section is brought to a close with a promise of salvation to the one who has endured (v.13b). In the context, this enduring would mean saying what has been given, even in the face of the incredible, life-threatening betrayal, before such ominous opponents in high places. The limit to this endurance is εἰς τέλος *eis telos*. The ambiguous τέλος *telos* could, in the immediate sense, be adverbial, i.e., lasting through

---

97. Rather than being an intensification of the distress (Hengel, *Studies*, 24), vv.12-13 continue the same theme, but disclose the identity of the betrayers.

98. This is not only a feature of the last days in apocalyptic material (Nineham, *Mark*, 349; Cranfield, *Mark*, 400), but also entirely suitable to the lips of Jesus in the shadow of the cross (Beasley-Murray, *Mark 13*, 50).

99. A fact stressed by virtue of its repetition. The aim is probably to bring about their death, rather than kill them (Cranfield, *Mark*, 400).

100. Kee, "Function," 169.

101. Jesus was well-aware of being misunderstood by those closest to him: 3:20-21,31-35; 6:1-6.

102. I.e. ὑπὸ πάντων *hypo pantōn* does not further extend those hating the disciples (*pace* Beasley-Murray, *Mark 13*, 51, who expands to all the unbelieving world), but stands for those already mentioned. For the periphrastic future, see BDF, 203-04; cf. 13:25.

this coming betrayal. However, τέλος *telos* also has connotations, freshly raised for the reader (v.7)[103] and reinforced by allusions to Daniel,[104] of the End expected by the Old Testament. This ambiguity is maintained by the use of σωθήσεται *sōthēsetai*.[105] Thus the betrayal of the disciples has strong links with the end, but the resolution of the various ambiguities and what this end will be, awaits further information.[106] This promise of "eschatological" salvation forms an entirely fitting ending to this hortatory paragraph which stressed the need for the disciples to *watch themselves* (vv.5,9).

Conclusion to vv.5–13

Verses 5–13 can be linked in with Mark's plot and so contribute to the movement towards the climax. The events of a world in turmoil do not have any significance as pointers to the end, but are merely part of the general context in which Jesus and his disciples operate. Jesus warns the disciples that their involvement in Jesus' mission and the top priority task of proclaiming the gospel to the nations will bring hard times from the opponents in the last days crisis that his coming had brought to Israel. From this moment on (if not before, cf. 8:15), they must look out for themselves (vv.5,9), resolving to endure through to the ultimate.[107] Only the one who has not

---

103. This τέλος *telos* is exactly that one of v.7, *pace* Cranfield, *Mark*, 401; Taylor, *Mark*, 510, who appear to overlook the eschatological nature of τέλος *telos* due to an apologetic concern (*viz.* to allow for the fact that the first disciples died without the End coming). The adverbial sense can be catered for by recognising the ambiguity of the text. Jesus' words have the effect of filling the disciples' vision with the last day. Rather than defining when it is or what it is, Jesus gives his disciples the task of watching themselves/ enduring right until the ultimate. With their sights on the last day, they will also endure until their own death, if that comes along first.

104. Cf. 11:32, Kee, "Function," 169. Beasley-Murray, *Mark 13*, 52, cites Dalman recognising a quotation of Dan 12:13 here.

105. Mark's usage of σωζεῖν *sōzein* is ambiguous. Although the early references to σώζω *sōzō* appear to be non-eschatological (3:4; 5:23,28,34; 6:56) the reader's awareness of Jesus bringing in the kingdom raises the suspicion that this word means more, and this is clarified as the narrative moves forward and utilizes the word in a clearly eschatological sense (8:35; 10:26; [16:16]), which then maintains an eschatological loading for other more ambiguous usages (8:35; 10:52; 13:13,20; 15:30–31).

106. Cf Beasley-Murray, *Mark 13*, 53, "there is little need to differentiate between the two meanings; they have a similar force, since the end is looked for 'soon.'"

107. It is usual for commentators to read this section as immediately addressing the post-resurrection situation. However, in Mark's story it is a warning addressed to the four, presumably with immediate applicability from that moment on. This dimension is

been led astray (vv.5–6) will endure to find salvation. This warning gains added relevance, given that they have betrayed an attitude more in line with Jesus' opponents than their teacher (vv.1–4). Having described the general context of their mission, Jesus begins to tell them about the specific events that should dominate their vision. It is these events that have a definite chronological sequencing.

The Time of Distress (vv.14–23)

Verses 14–23 are filled with the exaggerated language of apocalyptic and are a single unit of thought ending with the tail-end of the frame begun in vv.5–6. Because it is linked with verse 4 by the recurrence of πάντα *panta* (v.23) some consider this section as the "most direct answer to the disciples' question."[108] However, although commentators find many exegetical difficulties here, they generally admit that this section prepares for vv.24–27. Its function is not to provide answers, but to prepare for things to come.

The Signal and the Reader's Entrapment

THE SIGNAL

Verse 14 opens with another example of an imperative to be carried out in the face of the events of an undefined future time (cf. vv.7,11). It will be time to act when they see τὸ βδέλυγμα τῆς ἐρημώσεως *to bdelygma tēs erēmōseōs*.

By quoting this phrase, which translates שִׁקּוּץ שֹׁמֵם *šiqqûṣ šōmēm* (Dan 12:11; cf. 9:27; 11:31), Jesus invites his hearers to understand what he is saying against the theology of Daniel.[109] In the Hebrew, שִׁקּוּץ *šiqqûṣ* is something detestable to, and rejected by God,[110] and the accompanying

---

consistently ignored.

108. Lane, *Mark*, 466.

109. Cranfield, *Mark*, 402; the phrase itself occurs in LXX Dan 12:11 (cf. Dan 9:27; 11:31; 1 Macc 1:54). Commentators take Dan 12:11 as referring to Antiochus Epiphanes in 167–164 BC, cf. Bruce, *New Testament History*, 4, although Jesus' use of the phrase forces them to admit that the meaning cannot be exhausted in this event. Cranfield, *Mark*, 402.

110. It is mainly used of idols, although is used once as an epithet for rebellious Israel (Hos 9:10). "Detested thing," BDBG, 1055. It appears, apart from the three Daniel references, in Deut 29:17(16); 1 Kgs 11:5,7,7; 2 Kgs 23:13,13,24; 2 Chron 15:8; Isa 66:3; Jer

participle שֹׁמֵם *šōmēm*[111] means "appalling, causing horror."[112] The emphasis is not on the desolation (i.e., the participle) but on the detestable/rejected thing (i.e., the substantive).[113] In other words, by the use of this phrase Jesus is referring to some frightful act of sacrilege, that causes great horror.[114] In the midst of a world in apocalyptic turmoil, an horrendous abomination will arise.

The significance of the masculine gender of the participle ἑστηκότα *hestēkota* is debatable.[115] It is misguided to call it a personification of τὸ βδέλυγμα *to bdelygma* if a figure is turned into a reality by saying it is referring to a person.[116] It is a good observation if personification is meant in the literary sense[117] as a device that vividly presents the "subject" to engage the hearer.

4:1; 7:30; 13:27; 16:18; 32:34; Ezek 5:11; 7:20; 11:18,21; 20:7,8,30; 37:23; Nah 3:6 (of filth); Zech 9:7.

111. Root meaning "be desolated, appalled," BDBG, 1030. The kal participle appears at 2 Sam 13:20; Isa 49:8,19; 54:1; 61:4,4; Lam 1:4,13,16; 3:11; Ezek 36:4; Dan 8:13; 9:18,26,27; 12:11. Cf. 9:17 as an adjective meaning devastated.

112. BDBG, 1031.

113. Nineham, *Mark*, 354. The emphasis falls on the detestable thing even more if BDBG, 1055, is correct that Dan 11:31 and 12:11 translate the name of Zeus Olympios = (lord of heaven).

114. Lane, *Mark*, 467, talks of "an act of profanation so appalling that the Temple would be rejected by God as the locus of his glory (cf. Ezek 7:14)." Cranfield, *Mark*, 402: "The Temple of God must yet suffer a fearful profanation by which its whole glory will perish." Beasley-Murray, *Mark 13*, 54, translates "Abomination that causes horror," cf. Jer 2:12, and adds that "the expression has by itself no thought of the Temple's destruction but purely its desecration." The suggestions offered are: Either Antichrist (Cranfield, *Mark*, 403; Nineham, *Mark*, 352); or Caligula in AD 40 (Taylor, *Mark*, 641–642, identifies this as the majority position; see *AJ* II, 184ff.); some say Rome (on analogy with Revelation 18:2; 1 Pet 5:13; man of lawlessness 2 Thess 2:3); or the events of AD 66–70 (some say that Luke is the first to take this view) even though no actual profanation occurred then (Taylor, *Mark*, 641–642; Lane, *Mark*, 469, points to the "profanation" of the farcical induction of Phanni as High Priest [Josephus, *BJ* 4.155], but this is not an obvious fulfilment).

115. The masculine participle for a neuter noun is quite common in the book of Revelation and in fact the masculine participle was increasingly preferred as the language developed; BDF, 75.

116. This is done by Lane, *Mark*, 467; Cranfield, *Mark*, 403; Nineham, *Mark*, 352; Hengel, *Studies*, 19.

117. That is, as a figure of speech. "The impersonation or embodiment of some quality or abstraction; the attribution of human qualities to inanimate objects. Personification is inherent in many languages *through the use of gender*"; Cuddon, "Personification," 501–02.

By the time the disciples see this horrifying thing it will be as a completed event, for "he" has taken "his" stand (ἑστηκότα *hestēkota*, perfect tense) ὅπου οὐ δεῖ *hopou ou dei*.[118] The location of this horrifying sacrilege seems to be unimportant for, despite commentators' eagerness to talk of the Temple, the text is indefinite.[119] In the context of the discourse the only analogous thing to "one standing where he ought not be" is those who stand in the place of the Christ (vv.5–6). However, here the undefined phrase is rather mysterious and provokes the question: and where exactly is that? As is common in apocalyptic writing, it is a mystery which needs to be disclosed.

The Entrapment of the Reader

This puzzling effect is intensified by the addition of ὁ ἀναγινώσκων νοείτω *ho anaginōskōn noeitō*, the famous apostrophe.[120] However this comment is understood,[121] in its present context it sounds like a violation of narrative level (since the reader is addressed by name),[122] and, as such, it has the same effect on the reader, either directly[123] or indirectly.[124] In this apostrophe readers hears the implied author speaking to them directly, which, while

118. Hengel, *Studies*, 19, "the place which is not his due."

119. This is observed by most with no real change in their exposition. Taylor, *Mark*, 641–642, offers the explanation that either i. the Roman situation prevented specificity; or ii. the Temple had already been destroyed so the prophesy was generalized. Since the text offers no specific warrant for Temple profanation, Hengel, *Studies*, 25, prefers to talk of "the eschatological enemy of God," by whom he means the Antichrist figure.

120. "A figure of speech in which a thing, a place, an abstract quality, an idea, a dead or absent person, is addressed as if present and capable of understanding"; Cuddon, "Apostrophe," 53.

121. i) An unknown apocalyptic writer has nodded (Colani); ii) Advice to the reader in the community to explain to his hearers (Wizsacher, Wellhausen, Bruce); iii) Jesus' advice to read Daniel carefully (J. Schmid); iv) A parenthesis of the evangelist highlighting either a fresh insight into the Daniel phrase (Cranfield, *Mark*, 403; Lane, *Mark*, 467; Hengel, *Studies*, 19), or appealing to look beneath the surface for a puzzle (cf. Rev 13:18, Beasley-Murray).

122. See Dewey, "Point of View," 103, citing Genette's term for this phenomenon: "metalepsis." If it is Mark's comment it is clearly such a violation.

123. In which case he is shocked by Mark's violent address towards him and is "hit between the eyes."

124. In which case he hears his name and is drawn into what Jesus says, even though technically the text is not addressing him. This causes him to identify with the reader and to hear Jesus' command as his own.

building upon their previous relationship,[125] draws them into the story and applies the puzzle to them for a solution. A mystery is a powerful device for engaging the reader:

> we are pulled forward by the desire to discover the truth about the world of the book. [...] we know that the book is completed when we once see the complete picture.[126]

This famous apostrophe therefore creates the desire to understand the significance of what has just been read.[127]

An important difference to the Daniel context needs to be noticed. The Daniel vision could not be understood (Dan 12:8) because it concerned the time a long way hence, namely, the end (12:4,9). The assumption of verse 14, however, is that the hearers/readers are *now in the time when these things can be understood*, in fact, *must* be understood. In terms of Daniel, this must mean that they are near τὸ τέλος *to telos*. Rather than this indicating that flesh-and-blood Mark saw the fulfillment of this word in the historical circumstances of his own day,[128] this must be understood in terms of its function within the narrative. Mark has propounded a puzzle by which the readers are intrigued.[129] Since there are no obvious answers in the text as yet, this increases the tension as they await the unfolding of the answer.

This represents a new stage in the intra-textual dynamics at the discourse level and is also a brilliant example of Mark's use of irony. By addressing the reader by name, this verse assumes the intimate relationship with the implied author which the reader has previously enjoyed. This position of privilege has entailed a fair degree of distance from the disciples, who continue to struggle towards what the reader is privileged to know. On the other hand, there have been occasions when the distance was created from the opposite direction, when the disciples were privileged against the reader. The text has exaggerated the distance by encouraging the reader to identify with Jesus' exasperation over the disciples' lack of perceptiveness and their hard-hearted inability to understand. However, this verse changes these dynamics.

---

125. See Dewey, "Point of View," 103.
126. Booth, *Rhetoric of Fiction*, 125.
127. Lane, *Mark*, 467, cf. Dan 1:17; 2:21,23; 9:25; 12:13.
128. Lane, *Mark*, 467, who sees it in terms of the fall of Jerusalem.
129. Authors have noticed the puzzle (Lane, *Mark*, 466, calls it "cryptic") without exploring its reader-oriented function. Hengel, *Studies*, 28, talks of "enciphered" due to alleged political situation. This recognizes both the puzzle and implicitly that it has a reader-oriented function, although attempting to understand it historically.

The form of the discourse has already brought the disciples towards the readers, by permitting the reader to overhear their intimate conversation with Jesus (contrast 4:34b). Now, in verse 14, Mark decreases the distance all the more by destroying the readers' position of superiority and bringing them towards the disciples. This is achieved as follows. The text suddenly addresses the readers, telling them it is now their turn to understand. Since it assumes understanding is possible, the imperative implies that the age of fulfillment has dawned for Daniel's vision. The apostrophe underlines that this is the issue that should be understood by the hearers (and readers)—if nothing else! This is when the irony dawns. The fact is that it cannot be understood—yet. For the text has not given enough information. In this way the "parenthesis" makes the readers feel their own ignorance, which strips away their position of superiority over the disciples. Like them, the readers are forced into the realization that they too "do not yet understand" (cf. 8:21) and this verse leaves them standing exactly where the disciples stand—ignorant of the End, which has now all but come upon them!

Thus the overall function of this verse is to increase the distance between reader and implied author, and to decrease the distance between the reader and the disciples. The net result is to disalign the readers from the implied author and to realign them with the ignorant disciples. Previously the narrator has brought the story to the reader, but now he has brought the reader to the story.[130] The readers have lost their autonomy and have been taken captive in the story![131]

Mark has now thoroughly engaged his reader, ready for the story's climax. Both the disciples and the readers now stand in a "gap" which generates an intense expectation that this "gap" will be filled. They are both immersed in hearing Jesus' discourse, and they both cry out for the revelation of τὸ βδέλυγμα τῆς ἐρημώσεως ἑστηκότα ὅπου οὐ δεῖ to bdelygma tēs erēmōseōs *hestēkota hopou ou dei*. What and when will this signal be?

---

130. This is a significant difference. The first allows the reader to "apply" the story to himself from his position of autonomy, the second engages him with the story and he is then subject to be moved wherever it wishes to take him.

131. Entrapment of the reader is when the work seeks to "assault, perplex, beguile, seduce, irritate, or 'con' the reader into a response." Such a work "seems to read [the reader]. The tables are turned; he himself becomes its subject"; Vieth, "Entrapment," 230, 231. Fish, *Surprised by Sin*, in discussing Milton's great work of entrapment (which is "not so much a teaching, as an intangling"), shows that Milton consciously imitated this method from Jesus' teaching (pp.21,45). Resseguie, "Reader-Response Criticism," 314, cites Mark 3:22–26 as a rare instance of entrapment in the synoptic Gospels. Mark 13:14 is another.

The Imperative

Whenever it may be, at the very time (τότε *tote*) the disciples see the horrifying sacrilege, they have an imperative to perform. Those disciples in Judea are to flee into the mountains. Ordinarily the Jew considered Jerusalem a place of refuge,[132] yet the impregnable walls will offer no refuge,[133] for Judea will be the arena of trouble.

This is not at all surprising. Although there were early positive signs amongst the Judeans (1:5,8; 3:8), Judea has developed into the centre of opposition to Jesus (e.g., 3:22–30; 7:1–23; 10:1–12) from which they have just emerged (chs. 11–12). Jesus doesn't share the disciples' optimism (cf. vv.1–2), but predicts that, as in the days prior to the great fall of Jerusalem (cf. Jeremiah 6), Judea will be the place of strife, and safety will be found only in flight.

The Old Testament links the flight motif to judgment, especially that from Sodom (Gen 19:17) and the end-time judgment of Zech 14:5,[134] and the hills to refuge.[135] This use of allusion once again suggests that Jesus is speaking very generally. Rather than being a command to actually flee, this flight motif is used to stress the suddenness and severity of the judgment,[136] which is further developed by vv.15–18.

---

132. Isa 16:3; Jer 4:6; Zech 2:11.

133. Lane, *Mark*, 467.

134. Cf. Isa 15:5; Jer 4:29; 16:16; 49:8; Ezek 7:14,16; Amos 5:19; cf. 1 Macc 1:54–59; 6:7. 1 Macc 2:28 similarly talks of a distress severe enough to cause the abandonment of worldly possessions. Lane, *Mark*, 467; Beasley-Murray, *Mark 13*, 57; Cranfield, *Mark*, 403.

135. Cf. Gen 14:10; 1 Kgs 22:17; Jer 16:16; Nahum 3:18; Zech 14:5; Heb 11:38. The hills are also part of the inviolability of Zion theme, e.g., Ps 125.

136. This lessens the power of the argument which says that if this was the End then flight would be useless; see also Hos 10:8. Such a symbolic interpretation is even needed for some historical options. If v.14 is referring to Caligula in AD 40 it can hardly be expected that the disciples urgently fled to the hills and stayed there for another 26 years. Surely this would remove any need for urgency. Nineham, *Mark*, 351, therefore opts that this flight theme is not an historical feature. Other proposals include that it alludes to 1 Macc 2:28 at the time of Antiochus, or is a reminiscence of the prophetic oracle of Eusebius, *HE* III 5.3. Some think Eusebius' oracle refers to this verse (Lane, *Mark*, 467), others deprecate the historicity of the Pella flight (Brandon, *Fall of Jerusalem*, 168–73), whereas Hengel, *Studies*, 27, although having no reason to deprecate its historicity, notes that "εἰς τὰ ὄρη *eis ta orē*, is again a phrase from the apocalyptic tradition and cannot be identified with a historical flight to Pella or anywhere else," and of the Eusebius tradition states "of course it has nothing to do with the φευγέτωσαν εἰς τὰ ὄρη *pheugetōsan eis ta orē* of Mark 13:14b," Hengel, *Studies*, 130 n.111.

Verse 14 had not defined οἱ ἐν τῇ Ἰουδαίᾳ *hoi en tē Ioudaia*.[137] The next two verses refer to particular people, variously located, who act as "focal instances," thus stressing that everyone will be affected by this impending judgment.[138] Likewise, the common apocalyptic theme of danger to pregnant women,[139] the note of woe (οὐαί *ouai*) and ἐν ἐκείναις ταῖς ἡμέραις *en ekeinais tais hēmerais* import an atmosphere of severe eschatological judgment (v.17).

In verse 18 the present imperative, which gives the disciples an instruction to carry out immediately, suggests a note of imminence (cf. 11:24). This impending time of judgment, from which escape is the best option by far, will be even worse if it strikes during winter. The extra difficulty afforded by winter can only be guessed at, although it may simply underline the judgment theme.[140] Whatever its exact nuances, the verse stresses the imminence and the severity of the coming event. The suggestion to pray also implies that it will come from God's hand and that he has the power to manipulate its timing.

The severity, imminence, and yet chronological uncertainty combine to add to the intrigue surrounding when this will occur. Like any puzzle, this raises expectations that the puzzle will eventually be solved.

The Last and Supreme Distress

Verses 19–20 resume the thought of vv.14–18 in order to explain it.[141] The hearer is invited to understand the reason (γάρ *gar*) for the urgent reaction

---

137. Lane, *Mark*, 471, wants to draw a distinction between the disciples and the people of Judea, but those in Judea are a subset of the ones who will see.

138. ἐπὶ τοῦ δώματος *epi tou dōmatos* (v.15), καὶ ὁ εἰς τὸν ἀγρόν *kai ho eis ton agron* (v.16). The reference to those inside and outside the city hearkens to Ezek 7:14-27. For focal instances see Tannehill, *Sword*, 67–77. Both situations stress the abandonment of normal life that is made necessary, cf. 1 Macc 2:28.

139. Cranfield, *Mark*, 403; Nineham, *Mark*, 355; Kee, "Function," 169.

140. Most cite the fullness of the normally dry wadis which would make flight a lot slower. There may be an Old Testament precedent in Zech 14:6. The Rabbis said that the exile occurred in the summer because of God's compassion, for he said "if they go out in the cold they will die"; Str-B, I.952. Winter is used as an apocalyptic motif in the Egyptian *Oracle of the Potter*, see O'Connell, "Potter's Oracle"; McCown, "Hebrew and Egyptian Apocalyptic Literature."

141. αἱ ἡμέραι ἐκεῖναι *hai hēmerai ekeinai*; cf. v.17. This is preferable to taking the γάρ *gar* closely with the imperative to prayer. "The opening words read like a homiletical comment on the preceding sayings," Taylor, *Mark*, 514, cf. Hengel, *Studies*, 131 n.114.

to the events of those future days, in terms of "a virtual citation of Dan 12:1," which links these events with a coming θλῖψις *thlipsis*.¹⁴² The quoted portion can be seen in Table 5.

The eschatological expectations of Daniel 12:1 involve "the last and supreme time of distress"¹⁴³ before the last day resurrection, which will surpass anything that has occurred since Israel was born as a nation. Thus it will be far greater than even the Babylonian exile which spelled the complete dismantling of God's people.

Jesus' additions to the verse separate the suffering even further into a class of its own. The addition of τοιαύτη ἀπ᾽ ἀρχῆς κτίσεως ἣν ἔκτισεν ὁ θεός *toiautē ap archēs ktiseōs hēn ektisen ho theos* underscores the severity of the judgment, through a time reference that stretches back to God's act of creation, that is, even beyond the birth of the nation in the exodus.¹⁴⁴ Jesus picks up the Danielic theme and increases the magnitude of the coming distress, saying that it will be greater than both the exodus and the exile.¹⁴⁵

The rule of end-stress and the fact that it is a most significant variation of the original quotation,¹⁴⁶ throws the emphasis upon ἕως τοῦ νῦν καὶ οὐ μὴ γένηται *heōs tou nyn kai ou mē genētai*. Daniel compares previous suffering to ἕως τῆς ἡμέρας ἐκείνης *heōs tēs hēmeras ekeinēs*, whereas Jesus makes his comparison with ἕως τοῦ νῦν *heōs tou nyn*, "until now".¹⁴⁷ This introduces a strong note of fulfillment. The promised day of suffering and

---

142. Taylor, *Mark*, 514; Lane, *Mark*, 471; Hengel, *Studies*, 131 n.114.

143. Hengel, *Studies*, 19.

144. Cf. the addition in Theodotion. The language is similar to Exod 9:24; 11:6; cf. Gen 41:19; Taylor, *Mark*, 514. The plagues of the exodus brought Egypt to its knees under the judgment of God, now a similar judgment is promised for the people of Israel. The End is frequently referred to as a second exodus; Beasley-Murray, *Mark 13*, 78.

145. Comparison with Josephus on the AD 70 fall of Jerusalem is therefore unnecessary. In any case it is unfruitful (Lane, *Mark*, 471) and unconvincing (Hengel, *Studies*, 16–18).

146. Tannehill, *Sword*, 11–58, for the significance of varying a common pattern.

147. In 10:30 equivalent to ἐν τῷ καιρῷ τούτῳ *en tō kairō toutō* and in contrast to ἐν τῷ αἰῶνι τῷ ἐρχομένῳ *en tō aiōni tō erchomenō*.

THE NARRATIVE INTEGRITY OF MARK 13:24-27

the events to which it is linked (i.e., 14–23), is vividly imminent (νῦν *nyn*, "now") at the time at which Jesus is speaking to his disciples.

Table 5: The Quotation of Daniel 12:1 in Mark 13:19

Daniel 12:1	Mark 13:19
καὶ κατὰ τὴν ὥραν ἐκείνην... *kai kata tēn hōran ekeinēn*...	
	ἔσονται γὰρ *esontai gar*
	For will be
ἐκείνη ἡ ἡμέρα	αἱ ἡμέραι ἐκεῖναι *hai ēmerai ekeinai*
that day	those days
Θλίψεως (Th: θλῖψις)	θλῖψις *thlipsis*
of suffering	a suffering
οἵα οὐκ ἐγενήθη (Th: γέγονεν) *hoia ouk egenēthē* (Th: *gegonen*)	οἵα οὐ γέγονεν τοιαύτη *hoia ou gegonen toiautē*
such as has not been	such as has not come about
ἀφ' οὗ ἐγενήθησαν *aph' hou egenēthēsan*	ἀπ' ἀρχῆς *ap' archēs*
from when came into being	from the beginning
(Th: ἀφ' οὗ γεγένηται ἔθνος ἐπὶ τῆς γῆς) (Th: *aph' hou gegenētai ethnos epi tēs gēs*)	κτίσεως ἣν ἔκτισεν ὁ θεὸς *ktiseōs hēn ektisen ho theos*
[the] nation upon the land	of the creation which God created
ἕως τῆς ἡμέρας ἐκείνης *heōs tēs hēmeras ekeinēs*	ἕως τοῦ νῦν *heōs tou nyn*
until that day	until now.
(Th: ἕως τοῦ καιροῦ ἐκείνου) (Th: *heōs tou kairou ekeinou*)	
until that time	
	καὶ οὐ μὴ γένηται. *kai ou mē genētai.*
	and will never again come about.

The significant variations all occur in the time reference:

ἀφ' οὗ ἐγενήθησαν *aph' hou egenēthēsan*	ἀπ' ἀρχῆς *ap' archēs*
from when came into being	from the beginning
ἔθνος ἐπὶ τῆς γῆς *ethnos epi tēs gēs*	κτίσεως ἣν ἔκτισεν ὁ θεὸς *ktiseōs hēn ektisen ho theos*
[the] nation upon the land	of the creation which God created
ἕως τῆς ἡμέρας ἐκείνης *heōs tēs hēmeras ekeinēs*	ἕως τοῦ νῦν *heōs tou nyn*
until that day	until now
	καὶ οὐ μὴ γένηται. *kai ou mē genētai.*
	and will never again come about.

The discourse is beginning to define its time references more carefully. The disciples had asked ὅταν μέλλῃ ταῦτα συντελεῖσθαι πάντα; *hotan mellē tauta synteleisthai panta?* (v.4). When Daniel had asked the same question he was told the things (including the abomination, 12:11) concern the End, but the time of revelation had not yet come (cf. Dan 12:6–8). The disciples, however, receive an answer in terms of "now," which adds to the already intense note of expectancy in the discourse.

The final "significant addition"[148] to the quote, καὶ οὐ μὴ γένηται *kai ou mē genētai*, "and will never come about again", increases the severity of the coming suffering to the utmost scale. The coming θλῖψις *thlipsis* will be the severest of all time. Whatever the referent, this language exalts the suffering to the highest plane possible, far too emphatically to be merely hyperbole.[149] It can only be describing the end time judgment expected by

---

148. Lane, *Mark*, 472.

149. Most take it as hyperbole conforming to the prophetic style when threatening an unprecedented catastrophe, cf. Mic 1:2–7; Isa 13:6–10; Jer 30:7; Joel 2:2; and, in Jewish literature, Baruch 2:2; 1 Macc 9:27; AssMos 8:1; plus Qumran examples; Lane, *Mark*, 471. Beasley-Murray, *Mark 13*, 78, in support of the thesis that this language has become almost proverbial, cites Josephus *BJ* 1.12 (Proem 4): "Accordingly it appears to me, that the misfortunes of all men, from the beginning of the world, if they be compared to these of the Jews, are not so considerable as they were"; 5.442 (5.10.5): "That neither did any other city ever suffer such miseries, nor did any age ever breed a generation more fruitful in wickedness that this was, from the beginning of the world"; 6.429 (6.9.4): "Accordingly the multitude of those that therein perished exceeded all the destructions that either men or God ever brought upon the world"; however these references do not

the Old Testament.[150] The general context of a world in turmoil and the last days of Israel (vv.5-13) will issue in the greatest distress of all time.

Verse 20 completes the explanation begun in verse 19 (καί *kai*), reinforcing the severity of the coming distress by reference to a divine decision to abbreviate those days of trouble.[151] Once again this imports eschatological overtones, since in Daniel 12 it is "the End"—resurrection and all—that ceases the terrible, unprecedented suffering and so a reference to its end is a reference to the resurrection day.[152]

Although the distress is still Judean,[153] its implications are universal, since πᾶσα σάρξ *pasa sarx*, unless limited by the context, is a general term for humanity.[154] If the Lord had not shortened this terrible time of suffering, no human being would have been saved. The meaning of ἐσώθη *esōthē* is now completely unambiguous (cf. v.13), since in Dan 12:1 salvation from the θλῖψις *thlipsis* is equivalent to the end-time resurrection (cf. Theodotion: σωθήσεται *sōthēsetai*). These incredible days of suffering will issue in the resurrection and the arrival of eternal salvation.

This hypothetical disaster has been thwarted (ἀλλά *alla*) by the Lord's decision to cut short, which is now explained further (διά *dia*). God shortened the days, for the sake of the elect, introduced as a balance to "all flesh."

---

have the emphatic denial of any future comparison (for which cf. Plato, *Republic* 6.492E). Beasley-Murray nevertheless states "by the use of traditional language Jesus describes an unprecedented time of suffering, to be followed in due time by the 'rest' of the kingdom."

150. As Nineham, *Mark*, 355, puts it: "It is clear that in v.20 and the last four words of v.19, the perspective has widened beyond any siege of Jerusalem or any other specific historical event even if understood as a divine judgment; what is here envisaged is the end of the world." At this point we can agree with what he denies but hold over a decision on what he affirms. For the End promised by the Old Testament may yet be modified by the New Testament.

151. According to Delling, "κολοβόω," the verb (only here, Matt 24:22 and 2 Sam 4:12 LXX) indicates that "[God] has made it shorter than it would normally have been in terms of the purpose and power of the oppressors." The aorist perhaps emphasizes that the divine decision has already been made, Nineham, *Mark*, 355.

152. Hengel, *Studies*, 28, therefore takes it as the parousia. Dan 12:7 uses the apocalyptic symbol for a time cut short before completion (three and a half), it is the "shattering of the power of the holy people" that is cut short by the accomplishment of "all these things."

153. Beasley-Murray, *Mark 13*, 80-81, notices that this therefore makes the verse contradictory to the usual explanation of vv.18-19 and unconvincingly attempts a rescue. This further reinforces that the verses aren't commanding an actual flight, but simply using the flight theme to reinforce the severity of the distress.

154. Nineham, *Mark*, 355, indicates the underlying Semitic idioms.

Although this term only appears in this chapter (vv.20,22,27), it is simply a new label for a group that has already been firmly established in principle, even if the boundaries are still blurred. This is a reference to the remnant, those "insiders" who long to do the will of God (3:31–35), those to whom the secret of the kingdom has been given (4:11) and who stand in marked contrast to unbelieving Israel who remain outside (4:11b–12).[155] Jesus has urged his disciples to come out of Israel to be a part of this group, the transition being effected through hearing his word.

This verse continues to underline the severity of the coming θλῖψις *thlipsis*. It will be so severe, that divine intervention will be necessary to ensure the survival even of the elect. Verse 13 promised salvation to those who lasted through to the end, but, in order for any to reach this destination, the Lord had to make his decision to cut the suffering short.

Temptation to Deny the Christ

Verses 21–22 complete the frame which began in vv.5–6. This encourages the reading of the intervening material in the light of the frame.[156]

Continuing the increasingly precise chronological links, καὶ τότε *kai tote* introduces "that which follows in time," as a consequence of something else.[157] The consequential event is another hypothetical situation in which an imperative will apply. Once again the hypothetical situation shouldn't be treated as "prediction"; instead it functions as a "focal instance" that, in fact, may work out in any number of ways.[158] The focus is therefore on the imperative, which will apply no matter what precise circumstances eventuate.

The hypothetical case is a second level narrative even with its own dialogue.[159] Within this narrative someone τις *tis*, who of course lacks specificity due to the future orientation of the narrative, will address the four disciples (ὑμῖν εἴπῃ *hymin eipē*). However, the reader has been educated about this vague τις *tis* from previous material. He appeared in verse 5b and was defined further as οἱ πολλοί *hoi polloi* who, through

---

155. This theme in Mark also has links to the OT remnant theme, Nineham, *Mark*, 355.

156. Most use the term "doublet," which has source-critical overtones. "Frame" labels it as a literary device, cf. chapter 4.

157. BAGD, 823–4. Mark always uses it in this sense (2:20; 3:27; 13:14,21,26,27).

158. Tannehill, *Sword*, 66–77.

159. Dewey, "Point of View."

their leadership of Israel, occupied the position properly belonging to the Messiah and lead many astray (v.6).

Verses 21-23 now specify that their method of leading astray is christological, for their potential statement seeks to point the direction to the Christ (Ἴδε ὦδε ὁ Χριστός, Ἴδε ἐκεῖ *Ide hōde ho Christos, Ide ekei*). The impression is that a number of options could be presented to the disciples, but it is not necessary to focus on either the identity of the ones pointed towards, or their understanding of ὁ Χριστός *ho Christos*. The significant thing is that they are pointed out *as an alternative* to Jesus and so they deny the identification which the disciples have already made of Jesus as the Christ. For the story has already revealed the identity of ὁ Χριστός *ho Christos*. The reader has known from 1:1 that Jesus is the Christ and has watched the disciples make the correct confession as well (8:29-30). The only ones who have not recognized Jesus as the Christ are his opponents, in accord with Isa 6:9,10 (cf. 4:12). They have disputed his claims (3:22-30; 11:27-12:37) and, in turn, he has disputed their christological understanding (11:27-33; 12:35-7). This verse warns that, even in the midst of the impending distress, the opponents will refuse to identify Jesus as the Christ, but will continue to look in another direction for their Messiah. Since Jesus feels that the disciples need to be warned about these distractions, then the suffering that lies ahead will be so severe that even their previous identification of Jesus as ὁ Χριστός *ho Christos* will be thrown into doubt. Whenever that happens and other alternatives seem much more attractive, they are to apply this imperative: μὴ πιστεύετε *mē pisteuete*, stop believing them.[160] For to go along with them would align the disciples with the γενεὰ ἄπιστος *genea apistos* (cf. 9:19), his opponents who failed to identify Jesus correctly, and theirs will be a terrible judgment (12:40).

Although the disciples have been slow to understand, see and believe, they have been shown that their faith ought to be directed to the gospel concerning Jesus as the Christ.[161] Their future performance may still be uncertain, yet the reader knows the standard by which to evaluate them. When the pressure comes, they will be faced with a choice to continue to

---

160. The present imperative used in this prohibition indicates that at the time the disciples will actually be believing these detractors and they should stop it. Their claims will be believable, so uncertain will the situation be with regard to Jesus.

161. Πιστεύειν *pisteuein* is always directed towards Jesus or the message about him (1:15; 5:36; 9:23-4,42; 11:23-4,31; 13:21; 15:32), as is πίστις *pistis* (2:5; 5:34; 10:52), except for 11:22. Cf. Marshall, *Faith*.

affirm Jesus as ὁ Χριστός *ho Christos*, or to deny their previous affirmation. The reader now awaits to see their choice in the face of the coming distress.

The γάρ *gar* clause (v.22), a scriptural allusion, explains the reason for the imperative.[162] Anyone pointing away from Jesus should not be believed because they are pointing to ψευδόχριστοι καὶ ψευδοπροφῆται *pseudochristoi kai pseudoprophētai*. As expected from the Old Testament,[163] these people may even perform σημεῖα καὶ τέρατα *sēmeia kai terata*, but their sole purpose is to lead astray. The exceptive, εἰ δυνατόν *ei dynaton*, speaks of this intent, but it also hints at the fact that it is an impossible task since the elect have the divine protection described in verse 20. Since this warning is derived from the general teaching of the Old Testament, merely in support of the imperative, the exact form of the future misleading is unknown. The main point is that these people will go to extraordinary lengths—perhaps even miracles!—to avoid identifying Jesus as the Christ. Only the subsequent story will reveal the specifics.[164]

A Warning for the Time of Distress

The discourse has now come full circle. In the first part of the frame, there is no equivalent to μὴ πιστεύετε *mē pisteuete* or to καὶ δώσουσιν σημεῖα καὶ τέρατα *kai dōsousin sēmeia kai terata*. These significant portions are reserved until the end. As Jesus sums up this first part of the discourse he reveals that the antidote to being led astray is continued belief in him as the Christ. He also reveals the special danger the future could hold for the disciples, for they could find people offering the signs they are seeking (cf. v.4), but these will take them away from the true Messiah.

Thus, rather than immediately answering the disciples' question (v.4), Jesus, firstly warns them against the attitude that it betrayed.[165] The

---

162. Dan 11:36–45, Deuteronomy 13; Kee, "Function," 169; Lane, *Mark*, 473. It is possible that Mark especially uses γάρ *gar* clauses to allude to the Old Testament, cf. Bird, "Some γάρ Clauses."

163. See Woodhouse, "Signs and Wonders."

164. It will also be no big deal if they do not do signs and wonders, for this merely outlines the extent to which the opponents can and may go, according to the Old Testament picture.

165. Cranfield, *Mark*, 405, states: "[The misleaders] will exploit to the full the natural craving of the disciples to escape from the painful paradoxes and tensions and indirectness of faith into the comfortable security of sight," although he fails to make the connection with their desire in v.4.

general context in which the disciples find themselves brings its own difficulties for those tied to Jesus' mission (vv.5–13). But, the pinnacle of these difficult times, the severest of all distresses, is now impending and it may well include alternative proposals to Jesus' messiahship, perhaps even backed up by signs and wonders. In such an environment their sign-seeking attitude would be a liability and would put them at risk of being led astray. They must not be led astray by the opponents of Jesus' mission, because the gospel of his messiahship must be preached to all the nations through their testimony. Therefore Jesus warns them not to believe any other christological alternative.

Verse 23 forms an inclusio with verse 5 and obviously rounds off the first part of the discourse. The imperative (βλέπετε *blepete*) summarizes the point Jesus has made, using the emphatic pronoun (ὑμεῖς *humeis*): *their activity should consist of looking out for themselves rather than signs*. The final phrase should not be translated as if Jesus has imparted the information they required, but, rather, that he has "warned them."[166]

What to Look For (vv.24–27)

These verses are the "climax of the synoptic apocalypse."[167] Although informed by a plethora of Old Testament quotes, allusions and influences,[168] the central quotation is that of Daniel 7:13 (v.26) and the other Old Testament material is added to this reference to the Son of Man.[169]

---

166. This is the sense in every usage of this word in the New Testament (2 Cor 13:2; Gal 5:21; 1 Thess 3:4; Matt 24:25). Cranfield, *Mark*, 405, also critiques those who feel the meaning is "I have given you an apocalyptic program for the future," but with different reasoning.

167. Kee, "Function," 176; Robinson, *Jesus and His Coming*, 56; Nineham, *Mark*, 356; Beasley-Murray, *Mark 13*, 6 (agreeing with Colani).

168. Cranfield, *Mark*, 405; Lane, *Mark*, 474; Hartmann, "Survey," 156–57; Nineham, *Mark*, 356; Robinson, *Jesus and His Coming*, 56; Beasley-Murray, *Mark 13*, 87.

169. For other quotations and allusions cf. Cranfield, *Mark*, 405–06; Nineham, *Mark*, 357; Kee, "Function," 169; Lane, *Mark*, 475.

The Quoted: Dan 7:13

Daniel 7, a "paradigm of apocalyptic thought"[170] which introduces the unit Daniel 7–12,[171] consists of the vision (vv.1–14) and its application (vv.15–28).[172] Rather than vv.15–28 "interpreting" the heavenly vision[173] and so the Son of Man "standing for" the saints in some way, these verses "apply" the heavenly vision to the earthly situation of the saints.[174] Daniel asks for the significance of what he sees in heaven for life on earth. Thus, "the function of the Son of Man is generally representative in that what he has done or will do will affect [the saints'] position."[175]

In the vision, the "one like a son of man" is given dominion in the heavenly court, but the earthly realization of this still awaits manifestation.[176] Although the heavenly decision has been made, its significance for the earthly saints is still awaited, for their share in his kingdom is still future.[177] In the meantime, the vision functions as an encouragement to them that

> with the approach of the Son of Man to the throne of the Ancient of Days, the judgment process is loosed. [. . .] the historical processes may sweep over and will scar the people of God but their reward is sure. The world system has already been condemned

---

170. Dumbrell, "Daniel 7," 17.

171. Dumbrell, "Daniel 7," 22–3, drawing on Collins, "Son of Man."

172. Dumbrell, "Daniel 7," 17. It is more usual to use the term "interpretation," which has the precedent of the English versions of Dan 7:16. However, since the word "interpretation" tends to conjure up the task of detecting a one-to-one correspondence between the two—e.g., the Son of Man (v.13) = the saints (v.22), an interpretation which operates on a simplistic view of prophecy as being "straightforward prediction and fulfillment" and misses the complexity of Biblical prophecy—it is preferable to talk of the vision and its application. Dumbrell uses the latter term in his essay (p.20).

173. That is its appropriate location, Dumbrell, "Daniel 7," 19; *Faith*, 262; *pace* Beasley-Murray, *Kingdom,* 26–35, "Jesus and Apocalyptic," who gives it an earthly locale. His argument assumes that the Son of Man is a divine figure, however in the context he appears to be human (contrast the beasts), which destroys the theophany theory.

174. The Son of Man is interpreted as standing for the saints either narrowly representatively or collectively; cf. Dumbrell, "Daniel 7," 19. An illuminating parallel in the Old Testament is 2 Kgs 6:15–17, in which the vision doesn't "stand for" anything on earth, but it certainly had significance for those of the earth to have the chariots of fire with them—it *applied* to them.

175. Dumbrell, "Daniel 7," 20.

176. Dumbrell, "Daniel 7," 21.

177. Dumbrell, "Daniel 7," 22.

and the decision of the heavenly high-court must be brought to bear on particular historical cases. [. . .] Faith is thus sustained by the recognition that beyond the empirical world which seems so uncompromising to the high hopes of the Saints there is the sovereignty of God which orders human concerns.[178]

The Quotation

Some maintain Dan 7:13 is not quoted in its original sense because, in the Markan context, the Son of Man is not brought to God's throne and there is no allusion to a revelation to God but instead he comes to gather together the scattered people of God.[179]

However, it is better to begin with the assumption that the quotation ought to be taken in its Old Testament sense. Unless the text gives good reason to understand the quotation of Daniel 7:13 differently,[180] the very function of a quotation suggests an equivalent reading, for a quotation invites hearers to inform themselves with the appropriate theology drawn from the context of that quotation. The quotation becomes a reliable commentator on the context into which it is inserted, not vice versa.[181] This means that there *is* a "revelation to God in the context" because the quotation imports the theology of Daniel 7. Whatever that does to the understanding of Mark 13 remains to be seen, but the use of this quotation automatically recalls for the hearer the heavenly scene of Daniel 7. Furthermore, it can be argued that the "revelation to God" is not the focal theology, even in Daniel, but is the means to the Son of Man's reception of the kingdom,[182] a theme which is integral to both Mark's story and the immediate context of Mark 13:24–27. Mark's addition of the "gathering of the elect" theme to the Dan 7:13 quotation is also perfectly permissible, since a speaker / author is free to conjoin quotations in order to achieve the desired effect.

---

178. Dumbrell, "Daniel 7," 23.

179. Lane, *Mark*, 476.

180. Lane's arguments are not strong enough to do this.

181. The Old Testament was considered a "Sacred Text" by the New Testament writers, cf. Detweiler, "What is a Sacred Text?." This makes the assumption that they quote it with an equivalent sense a legitimate starting point. Any position arguing for non-equivalence has the burden of proof.

182. The kingdom is at the climactic position in the vision (vv.13–14) and the application (vv.26–27), as well as the theme of the entire book of Daniel.

The Eschatological Feel (vv.24–25)

Ἀλλά *alla*, the hingepoint of the discourse, introduces a strong contrast with the preceding. Jesus has corrected the disciples' attitude and warned them, now he begins to negotiate the positive direction of the shift.

The verse begins with a demonstrative reference to the time (ἐν ἐκείναις ταῖς ἡμέραις *en ekeinais tais hēmerais*) cast in terms of a stereotypical Old Testament expression which imports an eschatological atmosphere.[183] In itself, the phrase has no precise temporally locative value, simply meaning "a time subsequent to the time of tribulation of imprecise chronology."[184] However, by the use of the demonstrative, these eschatological overtones are fixed to a particular time, namely that of vv.19–20. Jesus is referring to a time which is closely associated with the time of distress already tabled in vv.14–23.[185]

This is confirmed by the next phrase in which the temporal vagueness is defined more closely: μετὰ τὴν θλῖψιν ἐκείνην *meta tēn thlipsin ekeinēn*, "after that distress". The dual definition emphasizes the temporal references, which provide a chronological precision to the discourse.[186] The impression given is that whatever is coming will follow hard on the intense and unprecedented suffering of vv.19–20. Although that suffering remains undefined,[187] it is clearly the immediate harbinger for the event(s) of vv.24b–27.

Vv.24b–25 contain three parallels chronicling the decline of the sun, moon and stars, summed up in a fourth.[188] All phrases, influenced by the Old Testament, convey an eschatological atmosphere. This is more than just "an important turning point in history,"[189] it is Old Testament last day

---

183. Cf. Isa 13:10; 34:4; Jer 3:16,18; 31:29; 33:15–16; Ezek 32:7,8; Joel 2:10,31; 3:15; Zech 8:23; etc; Kee, "Function," 169; Cranfield, *Mark*, 405.

184. Lane, *Mark*, 475.

185. Lane, *Mark*, 475.

186. Noticed by Nineham, *Mark*, 356. Although he attempts an historical explanation of this emphatic time reference asking "Had some expected it prematurely?"; cf. vv.7–8; Luke 19:11b; 2 Thess 2.

187. Nevertheless, commentators attempt to define the undefined. E.g. Cranfield, *Mark*, 405, with Calvin, "a general recapitulation of all the evils of which Christ had previously spoken," the "whole course of [the Church's] tribulations."

188. Lane, *Mark*, 475.

189. Lane, *Mark*, 475.

imagery. After the time of suffering, the End looked forward to by the Old Testament will come![190]

But all this just sets up the context. The text has not yet focused on any explicit event. This comes in verse 26.

The Coming of the Son of Man (v.26)

Verse 26 begins with another time reference, καὶ τότε *kai tote*, "and then"—introducing the next event to be seen in the series.[191]

Rather than assuming that the indefinite plural subject of ὄψονται *opsontai* means all people,[192] it is best to leave it intriguingly vague at this stage: whoever is there at the time "will see". The object to be seen is conveyed by the quotation from Dan 7:13,[193] τὸν υἱὸν τοῦ ἀνθρώπου ton huion tou anthrōpou etc. The Son of Man is no stranger to Jesus' hearers nor to Mark's readers and this verse therefore resumes all the expectations clustered around this figure that have been generated by the preceding narrative.[194] However, 13:26 is the first full-blooded quotation and so it is a climax. If there was any doubt about Jesus' previous use of the term, it is now clarified as the Daniel 7 figure. This verse unites the theology of Daniel 7 and Mark's presentation so far. What Daniel's vision necessarily left vague; Mark's story has now made explicit.[195]

Although this verse has been used to talk of Christ's "parousia," it should rather be read in the same way as its original context, i.e., not of a

---

190. Beasley-Murray, *Mark 13*, 88, notices that v.24a is separate from the poetry of the rest of the verse. "Jesus prefixed this indication of time before his citation of the Scriptures, which are to be read as in inverted commas: 'After the tribulation of those days, the Scriptures will be fulfilled which speak in this manner [. . .] The note of time is not to be watered down (so Swete). The tribulation is ended by the (events of vv.24–27)."

191. To talk of it as "the final eschatological 'then'—the end itself as opposed to the signs of the end," is perhaps reading too much in to this temporal indicator (Cranfield, *Mark*, 406). His opposition between "signs of the end" and "the end" can be restated in more textually descriptive language by saying "vv.24–27" is opposed to "vv.5–23."

192. As does Cranfield, *Mark*, 406; Nineham, *Mark*, 357. Presumably this interpretation is colored by a particular view of the referent of this verse (viz the parousia).

193. Kee, "Function," 169, also suggests the influence of Isa 19:1, for the "on the clouds" addition.

194. Cf. 2:10,28; 8:31,38; 9:9,12,31; 10:33,45; 13:26; 14:21,21,41,62.

195. Interpreters of Daniel should not assume that Daniel contains enough information to answer all its questions. Dan 12:7 indicates that the book remains a puzzle. It is only the events of a later time (i.e., the events of the gospel) that enable understanding.

coming to earth, but a coming to God, which can be described as an exaltation/vindication. At this point the "Fall of Jerusalem" interpreters have the strongest exegetical position.[196] Unlike Daniel (cf. 12:8–9), "they" will see, in fulfillment of his vision, the Son of Man coming to the ancient of Days and receiving an everlasting kingdom from his hand. They will see him clothed with the tokens of divinity (ἐρχόμενον ἐν νεφέλαις μετὰ δυνάμεως πολλῆς καὶ δόξης erchomenon en nephelais meta dynameōs pollēs kai doxēs), the glory that once bathed the Temple.[197] After the time of unparalleled distress, then "they" will see this magnificent event.

The hearer knows by now that Jesus is the Son of Man. Since Jesus has spoken of the Son of Man's betrayal, death and resurrection, it is a natural question to ask how the Daniel 7 coming and reception of the kingdom is related to his predicted death and resurrection. When they see this coming of the Son of Man, what form will it take?

The Harvest (v.27)

The definite chronological sequence continues with καὶ τότε *kai tote*, "and then", again pointing to the next item in the series. After his coming, the

---

196. Some invoke this interpretation elsewhere but not here. For example, Robinson, *Jesus and His Coming*; "The Second Coming," (with Colani) interpret 14:62 of the ascension, but 13:26 as the secondary addition of the parousia teaching of the early church. Cranfield happily reads 9:1 of the exaltation, at least in part, but not 13:26. However, 13:26 can also be interpreted consistently in this way.

This reading has such a long history (Holsten, Appel, Wellhausen, Smend, Lagrange, Glasson, Duncan, Stonehouse, Lowther-Clarke, Dom G. Dix, A.H. Curtis) that Beasley-Murray, *Mark 13*, 90–91, complains that "this view is becoming almost a new orthodoxy in Britain." Beasley-Murray, who strongly asserts that both 13:26 and 14:62 refer to the parousia, puts forward four objections, all of which can be disputed. 1. He claims that Daniel 7 is set on earth. This ignores the tenor of the vision, which is a heavenly judgment scene, not without OT precedent (e.g., 1 Kings 22; Isaiah 6). 2. Daniel 7 is reminiscent of the chariot vision of Ezekiel, which brought God to the earth. In fact, the similarities are superficial and there is a world of difference between the two. 3. There is no hint that the saints are transferred to heaven, but they rule on earth. This is true, but ignores the division of the chapter into heavenly vision/earthly application, consistent with apocalyptic material. 4. In Dan 7:22 the Ancient of Days came to the earth. This is also true, and can be explained as for the last point. It also needs to be said that the Ancient of Days is not the one like the son of man. Beasley Murray later shows that he is keen to tie Daniel 7 into an earthly theophany, rather than a heavenly vision, but this too is disputable, see *Jesus and the Kingdom*, 3–35, see also "Jesus and Apocalyptic."

197. Power, glory, and clouds; cf. the Shekinah; Nineham, *Mark*, 357, 235; Lane, *Mark*, 475.

THE NARRATIVE INTEGRITY OF MARK 13:24-27

Son of Man will send out his angels. ἄγγελος *aggelos* can be a human or heavenly messenger. Although Mark has used the verb ἀποστελλεῖν *apostellein* predominantly of humans, including those designated apostles,[198] the identity of these angels is best left as an open question at this stage.[199]

Their function, however, is clear: καὶ ἐπισυνάξει τοὺς ἐκλεκτοὺς [αὐτοῦ] *kai episynaxei tous eklektous [autou]*. Having been sent out, they will gather in the elect from the whole wide earth.[200] This appears to be the means by which the elect are brought to end-time salvation (cf. vv.20,22).

The gathering of the people of God resonates with the recurring Old Testament themes of scattering/judgment and regathering/salvation, clustering around the end time.[201] The Old Testament looked forward to the time when the people of God would be reunited again. They may have been scattered through their sinfulness and consequent judgment, but yet once more God would gather them together—and more besides. This gathering of the elect which would encompass even the nations is linked in with the Zion motifs.[202] Given Mark's presentation so far, it also links in nicely with the mission to the nations in vv.9–11. But the distinctive thing here is that Jesus has linked these themes with the Son of Man. The combined effect of this linkage is that, whereas the Son of Man comes in the context of judgment, he nevertheless comes with a salvific purpose. The unity of the people of God and the centre of the eschatological world mission is in the Son of Man.[203]

---

198. Cf. 1:2; 3:14,31; 6:7,17,27; 8:26; 9:37; 11:1; 12:2,3,4,5,6; 12:13; 14:13 (cf. ἀπόστολος *apostolos*: 3:14; 6:30). The only non-humans are a sickle 4:29, a donkey 11:3, and some demons 5:10.

199. Barth, *CD* III/3.369–519. Nineham, *Mark*, 357, for angels as messianic agents see 1 Enoch 61. In Mark's narrative ἄγγελος *aggelos* is sometimes clarified by the addition ἐν τοῖς οὐρανοῖς *en tois ouranois* (12:25; 13:32), other times, although associated with a heavenly figure (i.e., Son of Man) they are not explicitly identified (1:13; 8:38; 13:27) and once clearly human (1:2).

200. Both phrases (ἐκ τῶν τεσσάρων ἀνέμων *ek tōn tessarōn anemōn*/ ἀπ᾽ ἄκρου γῆς ἕως ἄκρου οὐρανοῦ *ap' akrou gēs heōs akrou ouranou*) indicate the same thing; cf. LXX of Zech 2:6; Deut 30:4; and 13:7; Nineham, *Mark*, 357; Beasley-Murray, *Mark 13*, 92.

201. Lane, *Mark*, 476; Nineham, *Mark*, 357; Kee, "Function," 169.

202. This, for example, is the thrust of Isaiah's eschatology, achieved through the ministry of the Servant (e.g., Isa 2:2–4; 42:1–4; 49:6; 56–66). See Dumbrell, "Purpose"; "Role of the Servant."

203. The Old Testament expected this unity to be around the Temple, as did the Jews (Lane, *Mark*, 476). Thus Temple motifs are overlaid upon Son of Man theology.

This is not as blunt a linkage as it may at first seem.[204] In Daniel 7 the Son of Man receives the kingdom from the Ancient of Days. In the application, it is clear that the effect of this happening in heaven is to give the saints on earth a share in the kingdom too. The Son of Man receives the kingdom, then the saints share in it. This same pattern is operating in the discourse. The Son of Man comes—i.e., to the Ancient of Days to receive the kingdom—and then he begins the process of sharing that kingdom with the saints—he sends out his angels to gather in the elect. The addition of the verse 27 material to the quotation of verse 26 highlights the means by which the saints will share in the Son of Man's kingdom and thus receive their salvation. They will receive their share as a result of this end-time gathering process.

The Timing

The disciples' original question concerned chronology. Once Jesus warns them against their mistaken attitude, he offers a chronological sequence. These three verses have a definite internal temporal sequence, which is also sequential upon the preceding. The sequence in Jesus' answer can now be summarised. There will be a time of unprecedented suffering, and then the Son of Man will come to the Ancient of Days to receive the kingdom of God. He will then send out his angels to gather the elect.

Watch for It (vv.28–37)

So far, rather than give signs, Jesus has warned the disciples against a sign-seeking attitude[205] in view of the generalized context of difficulty in which they operate (vv.5–13), and, in view of the severest of all distresses which they will see (vv.14–23). He then told them that they ought to be looking instead for the coming of the Son of Man. Although the exact contours of this event are still awaited, he now begins to tell them to watch for it.[206]

---

204. Lane, *Mark*, 476, considers it unusual.

205. This is characteristic of Jesus; see Dodd, *Parables*, 83–84; Manson, *Teaching of Jesus*, 261–62. The perspective of this paragraph will therefore be found to be entirely congruent with the preceding, *pace* Nineham, *Mark*, 358.

206. Thus Cranfield, *Mark*, 407, and Lane, *Mark*, 478, are correct that this is the third part of Jesus' answer, although the interpretation given here differs considerably in detail. Manson, *Teaching of Jesus*, 261–62, noticed the link between this paragraph and v.4 by

THE NARRATIVE INTEGRITY OF MARK 13:24-27

Verses 28-37 are closely linked together but fall into three parts.[207]

Learn from the Figtree (vv.28-32)

The opening phrase focuses upon τὴν συκῆν *tēn sykēn*. It is difficult to imagine that the disciples in the story would not have understood the definite article[208] of the figtree closest to their experience, i.e., the one that Jesus cursed the day before (11:12-14) and discussed this very morning (11:20-26)! Certainly it seems impossible for the reader not to link the two, especially since they occur respectively at the beginning and end of the same three day cycle and the saying points to the same visible sign of the leaves[209] stressed twice in 11:13.[210] This cursed figtree is a parable which ought to be learned (μάθετε τὴν παραβολήν *mathete tēn parabolēn*).[211] "The

---

suggesting it was the original answer to the question.

207. They are linked by a series of "hook-words" (ταῦτα γινόμενα *tauta ginomena* v.29 — ταῦτα πάντα γένηται *tauta panta genētai* v.30; παρέλθῃ *parelthē* v.30 — παρελεύσονται *pareleusontai* v.31; ἀγρυπνεῖτε *agrypneite* v.33 — γρηγορῇ *grēgorē* v.34 — γρηγορεῖτε *grēgoreite* vv.35,37; ἐπὶ θύραις *epi thyrais* v.29 — τῷ θυρωρῷ *tō thyrōrō* 34); Nineham, *Mark*, 358. The three divisions are given by vv.28-29 μάθετε *mathete*; vv.30-32 ἀμὴν λέγω *amēn legō*; vv.33-37 βλέπετε *blepete*; Cranfield, *Mark*, 407.

208. It has been taken variously as referring to 1. a definite symbol. McNicol, "Lesson," 194, 204, points out that Dispensational Pre-Millenialists use the figtree as "a reference to the restoration of the Hebrew people in Israel in 1948 after the Holocaust"; or 2. "generic as in many parables," Taylor, *Mark*, 520; or 3. to contrast the particular lesson of the figtree with other trees; Lane, *Mark*, 479.

209. Not so much to the tenderizing of the branches (Lane, *Mark*, 479), which would not be visible.

210. It is somewhat surprising how many miss the connection! Although some make passing comment merely to contrast the two (e.g., Harrington, *Mark*, 208; Tolbert, *Sowing the Gospel*, 267; Kelber, *Kingdom*, 70), most completely ignore the question of the relationship between the two figtrees (e.g., Alexander, *Mark*; Anderson, *Mark*; Barclay, *Mark*; Bowman, *Mark*; Branscomb, *Mark*; Cole, *Mark*; Cranfield, *Mark*; Crotty, *Mark*; Ferguson, *Understanding the Gospel*; Hendriksen, *Mark*; Hurtado, *Mark*; Hunter, *Mark*; Jones, *Mark*; Johnson, *Mark*; Lane, *Mark*; Nineham, *Mark*; Schweizer, *Mark*; Stock, *Method*; Swete, *Mark*; van Iersel, *Reading Mark*; Williamson, *Mark*). However, Wellhausen, Schwarz and E. Meyer said that it was the same figtree (Beasley-Murray, *Mark 13*, 97; Taylor, *Mark*, 520). There is no need to adopt their entire view of the verse (which Beasley-Murray calls "Gospel exegesis at its most degraded level"!) to notice the connection. Additional supportive evidence may be drawn from the observation that allusions to Micah 7 appear in both contexts.

211. Note that they are to learn τὴν παραβολήν *tēn parabolēn* (RSV the lesson) not *from* the parable: i.e., the parable is the content, not merely the instrument of learning.

figtree, whose parable should be understood, must be a definite one, which all know, even that one which the Lord had cursed (see Mark 11:20–25)."[212] When that story was narrated it created a gap which has been gradually closing. As we have seen, day three is a reflection on day two and now Jesus completes the reflection he began this morning by summarising the plain lesson of the cursed figtree.

This means that it is misguided to introduce too much symbolism into this saying. Symbolism was operative in the initial event, and contributed to its thrust. However, since this is a reflection upon the lesson of that event, the symbolism has now yielded to the import of the cursed figtree considered as a package. It is no longer a system of symbols, it has become a parable. But what does that parable teach? The thrust of that parable was that, in the midst of barren Israel, all the hopes of Israel have arrived with Jesus, and therefore the kingdom of God is at hand. Jesus now draws the same lesson, underlining its significance for the four disciples at this moment in the story.

The particular manner in which the figtree acts as a parable focuses upon the leaves (ὅταν ἤδη ὁ κλάδος αὐτῆς ἁπαλὸς γένηται καὶ ἐκφύῃ τὰ φύλλα *hotan ēdē ho klados autēs hapalos genētai kai ekphyē ta phylla*). The leaves give the watcher knowledge (γινώσκετε *ginōskete* in the indicative) ὅτι ἐγγὺς τὸ θέρος ἐστίν *hoti eggys to theros estin*. Rather than reading τὸ θέρος *to theros* as "the harvest,"[213] it is best to take it simply as an intra-

---

212. J. Wellhausen, quoted in Beasley-Murray, *Mark 13*, 97f.

213. Telford, *Barren Temple*, 242. 1. although admitting τὸ θέρος *to theros* means summer, Telford notes that its Old Testament equivalent קַיִץ *qayiṣ* can mean (i) summer, but can also mean (ii) summer fruits / fig harvest. Through this second meaning it is given eschatological overtones, e.g., notice the pun with קֵץ *qēṣ* (end of life, final punishment) in Amos 8:1–3. See also Kistemaker, *Parables*, 108 n.1. 2. Telford also notes that from θέρος *theros* is derived θερισμός *therismos* [harvest]. 3. He concludes that "the harvest, as the wedding and wine, are well-established symbols of the end of the old age and beginning of the new time in much Jewish religious thought of our first century era."

However, these arguments are not convincing. The second one commits the etymological fallacy. The first one rightly surveys the range of usage in the Old Testament. As the season (Gen 8:22; Pss 32:4; 74:17; Prov 6:8*; 10:5*; 26:1*; 30:25*; Jer 8:20*; Amos 3:15; Zech 14:8) it may well be the season for harvest (specific links marked *); Scott, "Summer and Winter." The summer fruits (2 Sam 16:1,2; Isa 16:9; 28:4; Jer 40:10,12; 48:32; Amos 8:1,2; Mic 7:1) appear to be those that first ripen, some time before the harvest proper. However, the eschatological associations are not patent. God's judgment causes the removal of joy over the קַיִץ *qayiṣ* for Moab (Isa 16:9, quoted in Jer 48:32), or the snatching away of Ephraim as quickly as the קַיִץ *qayiṣ* (Isa 28:4), or the similar comparison with Israel's קַיִץ *qayiṣ* (Amos 8:1,2), or the removal of the harvest from Israel (Jer 8:20, cf. 13) and so is heading towards eschatology, but in none of the other references do we have parabolic reference to summer.²¹⁴ Thus the point is simple: the focus is not on the summer itself, but on the sign of its imminence.

The Imminent Kingdom (v.29)

Jesus then explicitly draws the application of the parable (οὕτως καὶ ὑμεῖς *houtōs kai hymeis*, v.29), which resumes the positive side of Jesus discourse (ὅταν ἴδητε ταῦτα γινόμενα *hotan idēte tauta ginomena*, cf. v.14).²¹⁵ Whenever the disciples see the awful horror bringing the worst-ever distress, followed by the coming of the Son of Man and the gathering of the elect occurring (γινόμενα *ginomena*, present participle), they are to know (γινώσκετε *ginōskete* as imperative) that these things too signal an imminence:²¹⁶ ἐγγύς ἐστιν ἐπὶ θύραις *eggys estin epi thyrais*.

The unexpressed subject of ἐγγύς ἐστιν *eggys estin* could be personal, i.e., the Son of Man.²¹⁷ However, since the most natural reading of ταῦτα *tauta* includes the coming of the Son of Man, it is best to take the impersonal subject, i.e., the kingdom of God.²¹⁸ The imminence is underlined by

---

an unmistakable eschatological context so it seems too much to read in "eschatological harvest" so directly. The text seems to require the more indirect approach taken below.

214. Taylor, *Mark*, 520, takes it as summer not harvest.

215. Too much should not be made of the use of ταῦτα *tauta* in the disciples' question (v.4); cf. Lane, *Mark*, 479. After correcting their misunderstanding, Jesus determines his own agenda for the rest of the discourse.

216. I have rejected the idea that ταῦτα *tauta* refers merely to the "preliminary signs" of vv.5–23, *pace* many, e.g., Beasley-Murray, *Mark 13*, 96–97. It is generally agreed that the most natural reading of ταῦτα *tauta* includes vv.24–27, although this is also generally rejected due to its failure to fit with interpreters' historical conclusions for the rest of the chapter. So Cranfield, *Mark*, 407, rejects because it would be tautological with his view that the subject of ἐστιν *estin* is the Son of Man's parousia; Lane, *Mark*, 478, strongly dismisses this natural reading due to being convinced that vv.24–27 are about the second coming and ταῦτα *tauta* about vv.5–23, i.e., the fall of Jerusalem. The natural connection forces Nineham, *Mark*, 359, to take v.29 as obviously secondary, believing ταῦτα *tauta* to refer to the activities of Jesus' ministry (with Dodd, *Parables*, 137 n.; Jeremias, *Parables*, 96; Dibelius, *Message*, 72–73).

217. So McNicol, "Lesson," 200 n.13; Cranfield, *Mark*, 407–408.

218. Nineham, *Mark*, 358, mentions this possibility comparing with Luke 21:31. It is, perhaps, more in line with the allusion to Zeph 1:7,14 (Kee, "Function," 169). Hunter, *Interpreting the Parables*, 42, despite believing that the early church interpreted it of the second coming, recognizes this as the original sense. "The era of the kingdom of God whose advent prophets and kings had yearned so long to see was beginning [. . . .] The summer of God's salvation was at hand, his harvest was under way."

the addition of ἐπὶ θύραις *epi thyrais*.[219] When the disciples see the coming of the Son of Man, they must know that the kingdom of God is imminent, "at the very gates!"[220]

This interpretation yields perfect sense, for it is exactly what Daniel 7:13–14 would lead us to expect. The very reason the Son of Man comes to that heavenly throne is to receive the kingdom from God, which he then shares with the saints. Once his coming is sighted, of course the kingdom is the next thing on the agenda.

This saying therefore links in with a most important theme in Mark, harkening back to the beginning of Jesus' ministry (1:14–15):[221]

> The brief logion of the fig tree preserved by Mark in ch 13:28 *echoes Jesus' proclamation that the kingdom has come near* and clarifies why the nearness of the kingdom imposes radical demands upon men: [quotes verse] i.e., the summer is the next thing that comes.[222]

This parable therefore focuses upon the significance of the coming of the Son of Man. Once that event is seen the kingdom of God is imminent. That is why the disciples are to watch for this coming, rather than for the various signs sought and offered by others. The coming of the Son of Man augurs the arrival of God's everlasting kingdom. Thus it is the kingdom of God that is the focus, the coming of the Son of Man is the "sign" of the kingdom's inauguration.[223]

This discourse has erected certain expectations in a certain sequence. The disciples already stand in a world in turmoil which provides a general context of difficulty and opposition (vv.5–13). Jesus leads them to expect

---

219. Kistemaker, *Parables*, 109, takes this as pointing "to the imminent arrival of the Lord who is coming as Judge and Redeemer; cf. Jas 5:8,9; Rev 3:20." There is no need to explain the verse's imminence away due to embarrassment over historical conclusions, such as: i) the Church read-in apocalyptic ideas (Dodd, Glasson, Taylor etc.); ii) Jesus was mistaken (Schweitzer, Werner, Manson, Barrett, etc.); iii) A theological understanding of the nearness of end should be assumed (Cranfield), with a telescoping of incarnation—crucifixion—resurrection—ascension—parousia, so the parousia is always imminent.

220. To use the translation of ἐπὶ θύραις *epi thyrais* from Nineham, *Mark*, 358.

221. Notice the similarity of vocabulary. Taylor, *Mark*, 520, suggests the possibility that the original form of this parable related to 1:14–15. Without entering into authenticity debates, this indicates that others have noticed the relationship with these verses.

222. Lane, *Mark*, 66 (my emphasis).

223. *Contra* Lane, *Mark*, 478–79, who treats them as the same. Although beyond the scope of this discussion, this understanding helps to explain Matthew 24:30. [2021: Bolt, *Matthew*, 222–23.]

that there will come a time of great distress associated with the awful horror, followed by the coming of the Son of Man who will send out his angels and all this brings the kingdom of God to the very gates. The disciples now know what to expect, as do the readers, who are closely entwined with them at this stage. Because the reader has been taken into the story, the closure of these expectations is awaited, in the first instance, from within the story that Mark is quickly bringing to a climax.

A Limit is Set but the Hour is Unknown (vv.30–32)

Verses 30–31 contain two short sayings in support of vv.28–29. The solemn introductory formula (ἀμὴν λέγω ὑμῖν *amēn legō hymin*) demands attention, causing the hearer to await the following authoritative and revelatory saying. Since so little specific detail has been given thus far in this puzzling discourse, this formula raises expectations that the solution will soon be forthcoming. Jesus is perhaps about to conclude.[224]

The authoritative saying hammers home the previous note of imminent fulfillment, by giving a definite time limit for the arrival of the things of which he has been speaking. The concern for timing has held the discussion together so far and as Jesus draws his discourse to a conclusion, the emphatic negative future leaves no doubt that he is setting an absolute limit for all these things.

Although the referent of ταῦτα πάντα *tauta panta* is debated, it is obviously linked directly to v.29 by the hook word ταῦτα *tauta*.[225] Since the most natural reading is inclusive of the coming of the Son of Man, Jesus is clearly setting the limit for the occurrence of all the things in his discourse.[226] This opinion is strengthened by the use of πάντα *panta* and the quotation of Dan 12:7 (LXX), in which all the things of Daniel's vision, including the coming of the Son of Man, are in view.

---

224. See also 3:28; 8:12; 9:1,41; 10:15,29; 11:23; 12:43; 14:9,18,25,30. It thus performs a parallel function to the "if anyone has ears to hear let him hear" formula of 4:23.

225. The various positions being: i) The woes up to/ including the fall of Jerusalem and the destruction of the Temple (Bengel; Lagrange; Taylor says originally yes, but not in present context; McNicol, "Lesson"; Lane, *Mark*, 478); ii) Christ's passion and resurrection (Cullmann, "Return," 152–54; Barth, *CD* III/2.500–02; Lightfoot, "Connexion," 54); iii) Signs of the end in vv.5–23 "characteristic of the last times," Cranfield, *Mark*, with Calvin.

226. "At first sight Jesus seems to say that all the things of vv.5–27 will come to pass in his contemporaries' lifetime," Cranfield, *Mark*, 409; cf. Taylor, *Mark*, 521.

The limit is set prior to the passing of ἡ γενεὰ αὕτη *hē genea hautē*. Here, too, despite the various interpretations,²²⁷ the most obvious reading is to understand it of Jesus' contemporaries.²²⁸

> The significance of the temporal sequence is debated but 'this generation' clearly refers to the contemporaries of Jesus (cf. 8:12,38; 9:19) and there is no consideration from the context to support any other proposal.²²⁹

The generation amongst whom Jesus and the four disciples presently live will by no means pass away until all these things have occurred (cf. 9:1).

The enormous claim contained in v.31 reinforces the certainty of Jesus' promise.²³⁰ The first half imports a rich Old Testament "background feel,"²³¹ which sets God, his salvation, righteousness, and word over against created things. Jesus sets his own words on the side of God and claims that they will never pass away.²³² This strengthens his words in v.30, there is no way that ταῦτα πάντα *tauta panta* will not occur before the passing of ἡ γενεὰ αὕτη *hē genea hautē*.²³³ This would engender confidence in the disciples

---

227. Suggestions include: i) mankind in general (Jerome); ii) The Jewish people of Jesus' day; iii) The Jewish people as a race (Jerome; Schneiwind; Schofield; Dispensational Pre-millenial interpreters; Beasley-Murray). However, γενεά *genea* is not used this way except perhaps Luke 21:32, McNicol, "Lesson," 205 n.23; iv) Christians (Chrysostom; Victor of Antioch; Theophylact; Moore, *Literary Criticism*, 131–33; Kistemaker, *Parables*, 110 n.7, citing 1 QpHab 2:7, 7:2 in which the last generation is not literal [with Ellis, *Luke*, 246–47]; Calvin, *Harmony*; Nineham, *Mark*, 360, takes it this way on analogy with 9:1 of the parousia and employing the notion of prophetic foreshortening); v) Qualitative sense: "this sort" i.e., unbelievers. There will be unbelievers until the end (Michaelis). McNicol, "Lesson," 202, feels that Mark may have more than one sense.

228. Cranfield, *Mark*, 409 and Taylor, *Mark*, 521, admit this.

229. Lane, *Mark*, 480, who then interprets the verse of the destruction of Jerusalem.

230. That this has been felt is reflected in the discussions over authenticity. Because the saying is a claim hardly paralleled outside the Gospel of John many take it as an early church invention; Nineham, *Mark*, 360.

231. For references see Kee, "Function," 169; Cranfield, *Mark*, 409.

232. The Jews asserted the inviolability of their law until the earth passed away; Cranfield, *Mark*, 409. Note too the contrast with vv.24–25. There the earth and heaven does pass away. Jesus asserts that his words will abide even beyond the coming of the Son of Man, into the kingdom of God.

233. Lane, *Mark*, 480; Cranfield, *Mark*, 410; Calvin, *Harmony*, 152.

THE NARRATIVE INTEGRITY OF MARK 13:24-27

and invite them to see things from "the perspective of divine providence,"[234] i.e., from "the things of God" (8:33), not "the things of man."[235]

The closure of Jesus' discourse is fast approaching. The disciples had begun by affirming Jewish opinions of the inviolability of Zion (vv.1–2) which Jesus had trashed, since their statement about the buildings and their question betrayed wrong foci. Jesus has now reset their vision with words that are absolutely certain. He has shown them that true inviolability lies with himself. The Old Testament looked forward to the time when "the law will go forth from Zion,"[236] now Jesus states that he is the source of such inviolate words. He is the centre of Israel's Zion hopes and before this generation passes away, those hopes will be fulfilled. "The promise of the kingdom (v.31) was surer than the continuance of the universe."[237]

Although it has generated much debate, the meaning of verse 32 is clear: the exact timing is unknown to all but the Father.[238]

The particle δέ *de* connects with the preceding, although not necessarily adversatively.[239] The prepositional phrase locates the nature of the connection: we are about to hear more detail about that day or that hour.

In view of the eschatological atmosphere imported by τῆς ἡμέρας ἐκείνης *tēs hēmeras ekeinēs*,[240] this verse is commonly interpreted of the parousia, as opposed to the fall of Jerusalem.[241] However, caution against

---

234. Calvin, *Harmony*, 152.

235. A reversal of what they had been doing, cf. vv.1,4.

236. Isa 2:1–5; Mic 4:1–5, etc. In view of this, the textual variant of v.2 which imports 14:58 and is paralleled by John 2:20–22 is interesting, showing the early understanding that Jesus is the new Mount Zion / Temple from which the law will proceed. Cf. Geddert, *Watchwords*, Ch. 5.

237. Beasley-Murray, *Mark 13*, 105.

238. Despite being one of Schmiedal's "foundation pillars for a truly scientific life of Jesus" its authenticity has been disputed; Cranfield, *Mark*, 410. The problem generated by ignorance being ascribed to the Son was recognized very early and is reflected in the textual variants. For a brief discussion of the verse in the Fathers, see Martin, *Mark: Evangelist and Theologian*, 124–26.

239. The particle is given "full strength" as an adversative due to the perceived discrepancy between Jesus' ignorance here and knowledge in v.30. Once δέ *de* is adversative the two verses are interpreted of distinct events, Cranfield, *Mark*, 410; Lane, *Mark*, 482. However, the "full strength" adversative could have been conveyed by ἀλλά *alla* and the explanation adopted here dismisses the perceived discrepancy.

240. Lane, *Mark*, 481; Kee, "Function," 169: v.32a is influenced by Dan 12:13 (cf. Dan 2:28, 45; 10:14; 11:20), and v.32b alludes to Zech 14:7 and Ps Sol 17:23[21 LXX].

241. Nineham, *Mark*, 360; Lane, *Mark*, 481; Cranfield, *Mark*, 410; even France switches to the parousia at this verse.

begging conclusions still needs to be exercised and therefore it is best to use the language of the text. In the context ἐκείνης *ekeinēs* must refer to the only "day" mentioned, i.e., the day of the coming of the Son of Man, an event to which the eschatological atmosphere is entirely appropriate.

However, another phrase (ἢ τῆς ὥρας *ē tēs hōras*) is added to this stock Old Testament term, which conveys a strong note of imminence. What lay in the distant future in Old Testament eschatology now has the immediacy of a timetable reckoned by hours.[242] This increases the sense of imminence gained from vv.28–31 even more.[243]

The information given concerning this hour is that οὐδεὶς οἶδεν *oudeis oiden*. After correcting their sign-seeking attitude, and telling them to watch for the coming of the Son of Man, Jesus finally answers the disciples' question (v.4) by saying "No-one knows"! The universality of ignorance regarding the day of this coming is then underlined, since οὐδείς *oudeis* not only includes the angels in heaven—perhaps those who will gather the elect (v.27) —, but also the Son.

The absolute ὁ υἱός *ho huios* is ambiguous. The consensus considers it a short version of the title "Son of God," an opinion bolstered by the interrelation of the Son with the Father here (cf. 1:11; 9:7; 12:6).[244] However, the immediate context suggests this is τὸν υἱὸν τοῦ ἀνθρώπου *ton huion tou anthrōpou* (v.26),[245] who has also been associated with the Father (cf. 8:38). Both these titles have played a significant and interrelated role in Mark's narrative and neither the disciples nor the reader are in any doubt that both titles properly belong to Jesus. It therefore appears that the usage here is a studied ambiguity which continues to blur the two together and so unite the expectations clustering around both.

Even the Son does not know his own hour of glory! Although he knows that it will occur, and that it will be soon, as Jesus delivers his discourse no-one knows the exact time.[246] The only exception (εἰ μή *ei mē*) is

---

242. Contrast Dan 12:5–13 in which there is a series of intervals before the distant end. Note that Dan 12:1 also uses ὥρα *hōra*.

243. Cranfield, *Mark*, 410, with Lohmeyer. This imminence is obviously felt by the commentators.

244. Calvin, *Harmony*, 153; Nineham, *Mark*, 361; Cranfield, *Mark*, 411. Kümmel notes that this association is the chief (historical) critical problem of the verse; cf. Martin, *Mark: Evangelist and Theologian*, 125, referring to Kümmel, *Promise and Fulfilment*, 40.

245. So Lane, *Mark*, 482.

246. There is therefore no real clash with verse 30. Jesus' ignorance is explained by the fact that Jesus is not being spoken of purely as the divine Son of God, but also as the

the Father. Jesus discerns that the end is near and is eager to establish the remnant of Israel in "these last days." However, he is not separate from that remnant, but he, as the Servant of the Lord, is *part of that remnant*, in fact, he *is* the remnant. Because the exact timing of the end is at this point unknown, everyone, including Jesus, needs to be vigilant, which is the theme of the following parable.[247]

The "ignorance therefore vigilance" connection, rightly discerned, seems to strain the proposed historical referents. Since "nor the Son" "indicates that even Jesus had to live by faith and to make obedience and watchfulness the hallmark of his ministry"[248] then how can this be referring to either AD 70 or the parousia? Jesus will not be present in the capacity of an onlooker for either. Rather, since his own ignorance includes him in the need for vigilance, he is obviously expecting *the end promised by the Old Testament* and he is expecting it *in his own time*.[249]

Watch for It! (vv.33–37)

The γάρ *gar* clause of v.33 resumes both the disciples' question (πότε *pote*, v.4) and Jesus' "answer," namely that no-one knows the hour. This ignorance theme continues to the end of the paragraph (v.35) and the imperatives give the responsibilities necessitated by such ignorance. βλέπετε *blepete* resumes the warning of the earlier discourse and ἀγρυπνεῖτε *agrupneite* adds the need for what is described by commentators as "vigilance."[250]

The point of comparison (ὡς *hōs*, v.34) in the simile[251] is gradually unfolded from the general to the specific, finally arriving at the command to

---

perfect man, i.e., he needs to watch and wait, he cannot force his own vindication, that is up to the Father.

247. Note connection with ignorance motif (vv.32,33,35), Lane, *Mark*, 483.

248. Lane, *Mark*, 482.

249. This, of course, then raises another problem for the historical critics, which has given rise to the theory of the "delay of the parousia."

250. Lane, *Mark*, 482; Cranfield, *Mark*, 411. The use of a second person imperative does not exclude Jesus from also being vigilant, as the scene in Gethsemane illustrates. Rather, he had already discerned that the End was near and that vigilance was necessary and was now urging his disciples to adopt the same watchful attitude. He is (part of) the remnant of Israel, and urges them also to be a part of that remnant. Geddert, *Watchwords*, Ch. 4, supports the point.

251. Only Mark has the simile in entirety. However, partial "parallels" can be found whose relationship with Mark is extremely complicated. See Cranfield, *Mark*, 412;

the doorkeeper. The finite verb (ἐνετείλατο *eneteilato*) after two participles (ἀφείς *apheis*, δούς *dous*) clearly isolates the command to the doorkeeper as the focal point,[252] which warns against making too much mileage of the other details.[253] The ἵνα *hina* clause gives the content of the command and provides the conclusion to the parabolic section. The watchman's delegated authority and duty is to watch.[254]

The switch to the plural form of the verbs in verse 35, coupled with the οὖν *oun* indicates that Jesus has now moved into the application of the parable. The four disciples are told to do the same job as the watchman. They are also given a reason for this necessity in the γάρ *gar* clause. Watching is necessary due to their ignorance of the timing, to which, of course, they have already confessed (πότε *pote*, v.4). Thus Jesus has arrived back where he began (v.33), after using the parable to illustrate and reinforce his point.

However, Jesus makes a slight change to the specification of their area of ignorance. The πότε ὁ καιρός ἐστιν *pote ho kairos estin* (v.33) is now replaced by πότε ὁ κύριος τῆς οἰκίας ἔρχεται *pote ho kyrios tēs oikias erchetai* (v.35). In verse 33 the actual event was not mentioned, being assumed from the preceding context to be the coming of the Son of Man, immediately preceded by the distress associated with the awful horror. What is conveyed by the change in verse 35?

Verse 35 applies the illustrative parable to his original command (v.33). As such it is a bridge between the story and the disciples' reality. Jesus has imported the disciples into the story and speaks as if they were the watchman. Thus, rather than being allegorised,[255] πότε ὁ κύριος τῆς οἰκίας ἔρχεται *pote ho kyrios tēs oikias erchetai* ought to be taken as metaphor and

---

Jeremias, *Parables*, 53–55; Kistemaker, *Parables*, 114; Nineham, *Mark*, 361; Wenham, *Rediscovery*, 67–76.

252. This is reflected in Jeremias' title "The Doorkeeper," *Parables*, 53–55. See also Cole, *Mark*, 206.

253. Some find ἀπόδημος *apodēmos* appropriate to the parousia (Cole, *Mark*, 207), although this word need not imply a long journey, but it may simply imply going outside the province; Kistemaker, *Parables*, 114. Likewise, in v.35, the coming of ὁ κύριος τῆς οἰκίας *ho kyrios tēs oikias* is not the main point. Nor is the analogy between the master and the Son of Man, *pace* Kistemaker, *Parables*, 115. Geddert, *Watchwords*, Ch. 4, despite observing the connection with the passion narrative, also assumes a connection with the parousia.

254. Kistemaker, *Parables*, 115, gives historical details illustrating that the watchman held ultimate responsibility for the security of those within. cf. Str-B II:47. The figure of the porter may in fact have been suggested by v.29, see Nineham, *Mark*, 361.

255. This is done by interpreters who read in the parousia.

need not be burdened with any deeper christological significance.[256] The event they are waiting for is not given by this application, it has already been told them. However ἔρχεται *erchetai* does hook in with vv.24–27, which reinforces the fact that this is the event which ought to be paramount in their mind.

Like the watchman was vigilant for his event, they too need to be vigilant for their event, lest they too be surprised. The four watches[257] survey the possibilities for the moment of surprise. The fact that they refer to the cycle of daily time adds an immediacy and specificity that would cause the hearer to watch each time one of these indicators occurred. Listing them makes the actual timing all the more uncertain in the hearer. It produces the anxiety which the command for watchfulness then preys upon.

Verse 36 gives the reason for anxiety, still in metaphorical mode with an eye on the parable. The opposite of watchfulness is sleep, which indicates a shirking of delegated responsibility. This simply reinforces Jesus' command to watch.

In verse 37 Jesus reiterates his command, adding a sphere of wider application.[258] There are at least three options to consider:[259]

1. The πᾶσιν *pasin* could be "everyone of you three who listen." This would then be an emphasis of the special role of the inner core in the task of watching. Their role would be analogous with special role of the θυρωρός *thyrōros* compared with τοῖς δούλοις αὐτοῦ *tois doulois autou* in the similitude.

2. However, πᾶσιν *pasin* is usually taken to be Jesus extending the imperative beyond the four question-askers of verse 3.[260] Although it is correct to recognize the readers' involvement in the text, commentators usually extend it to Mark's readers too quickly.[261] Further sensitivity to the actual means of reader involvement allows a better understanding

---

256. E.g. Taylor, *Mark*, 525, "The church is daily expecting the return of her Lord."

257. Corresponding with the Roman usage, Cranfield, *Mark*, 411; Kistemaker, *Parables*, 115 n.3, who refers to Str-B, I:688; cf. Acts 12:4; Matt 14:25; Mark 6:48.

258. Primarily to the similitude. Then the whole package (vv.33–37), coming as it does at the end, forms the conclusion to the entire discourse; cf. Cranfield, *Mark*, 412.

259. If the verse is still intra-similitude, this then expands the doorkeeper's special charge to the rest of the servants. All of them need to be vigilant as they attend to their duties.

260. Lane, *Mark*, 483–84.

261. Kistemaker, *Parables*, 114; Jeremias, *Parables*, 53; Nineham, *Mark*, 361.

of the intended function (i.e., application) of the text itself *viz a viz* the reader.

3. Within the story, in the first instance, the extension would be to the other disciples, of whom the three are the inner core. Thus, as we emerge from the discourse, the reader expects to find the other disciples "watching" as well as the four.[262]

Rather than decide the question, it is better to first look at the effect of this section upon the reader. Prior to entry into this paragraph, the reader is already awaiting the kingdom of God bursting through the doors. He knows that is preceded by the coming of the Son of Man. He is already on board before Jesus commands the disciples to be vigilant. The reader listens to the imperatives as well.

The twofold οὐκ οἴδατε *ouk oidate* links the commands to vigilance in the reader's mind with the ignorance motif that runs through the discourse.[263] The situation of ignorance sets up a puzzle which strongly demands a solution. The reader is therefore thoroughly engaged by the text and awaits the hour of fulfillment.

The listing of the daily possibilities (which act like focal instances) increases both the feeling of ignorance and the anxiety about "when?" This puzzle reinforces the quest for fulfillment just as much for the reader as for those in the story.

The vagaries of verse 37 complete the reader's involvement in the text. The application appears to be extended, but to whom remains unclear. The reader, now thoroughly engaged in the story, naturally includes himself and so Jesus now addresses him! The reader is called to watch alongside the disciples.

The many links observed between vv.33–37 and the rest of the discourse make sense when this unit is considered to be Jesus' climactic application. The whole chapter is held together by this theme of alertness (vv.5,9,23,29).[264] Having read the chapter, we await the resolution of its expectations.

---

262. Cranfield, *Mark*, 412, includes all the possibilities: "The command to watch is addressed not only to the four, but also to the rest of the twelve, to Mark's readers in the church of Rome, and to the whole Church throughout the Last Times."

263. Lane, *Mark*, 483, notes the connection of vv.32,33,35 with this ignorance motif.

264. Nineham, *Mark*, 362, considers this an artificial unity because "the type of alertness called for and the things for or against which it is demanded, differ from one section of the chapter to another."

Reading with Apocalyptic Expectation

The chapter erects the expectation of the arrival of the kingdom of God (vv.28-31) made imminent by the coming of the Son of Man (vv.24-27), after the time of immense suffering associated with the awful horror (vv.14-23), which issues out of the general context of a fallen world and the last days of Israel, in which Jesus' mission is opposed (vv.5-13). The four disciples are alerted to expect this cluster of events in their immediate future, certainly before their generation passes away.

However, the reader too has been entangled with the four disciples. The story has puzzled, intrigued and involved the reader. Since readers expect puzzles to be resolved by the end of the reading experience, the puzzles of this discourse are expected to be resolved before Mark's story is done. Rather than enforcing a sense of delay,[265] the "involvement" of the reader in the application of the apocalyptic discourse increases the expectation of imminent fulfillment. In the ensuing narrative the disciples can be expected to carry out their watching. While reading that narrative the reader watches their watching to see if they find the events to which they have been alerted. We now watch for the coming of the Son of Man, in the first instance within the remainder of Mark's narrative.[266]

---

265. As with the interpretation of, for example, Jeremias, *Parables*, 63.

266. This reading also explains the "whole church" extensions. They have been affected by the text in the right way, but have too quickly jumped to an answer outside of the text, rather than awaiting the answer the text provides.

Although Jeremias, *Parables*, 55, considers the parable has been molded by the early church into a "parousia parable," he nevertheless recognizes the effect of the parable in its original setting was to "arouse a deluded people and their leaders to a realization of the awful gravity of the moment" (p. 63).

6

Mark 13 in Retrospect (Mark 14–16)

Mark 13 as Part of the Rising Action

BY THIS STAGE IT is obvious that Mark 13 does not contain enough information to interpret it in isolation. As part of Mark's story, chapter 13 has tapped into the previous narrative and made its contribution to the development of that story. It has raised various anticipations for the reader which, presumably, ought to find corresponding retrospections in the subsequent narrative. Although it will not be possible here to discuss Mark's passion narrative (Mark 14–16) in detail, the intention is to simply outline the contours of its story in order to discern whether it delivers the expectations raised by chapter 13. In this way these chapters exercise a textual control over the interpretation of Mark 13 in retrospect.

Not only is it unusual to interpret Mark 13 as a significant continuation of the narrative of Mark 1–12, but it is also unusual to link it to the passion narrative in any significant way.[1] However, if Mark 13 is granted proper integrity within the narrative, then, since it is positioned amidst the rising action, its function as the immediate precursor to the passion narrative needs to be explored.

---

1. This is despite the fact that chs.1–13 are given the passing nod of being the "extended introduction" to Mark's "Passion narrative," see Nineham, *Mark*, 366 n. Lightfoot, "Connexion," 50: "the divorce between chapter 13 [. . .] and chapters 14–15 [. . .] seems at first sight absolute". Such is this divorce for Trocmé, *Formation*, 224, that he suggests that "original" Mark ceased at the end of chapter 13 and 14–16 were later additions.

Mark 13 and the Passion Narrative

The discourse had insisted on the disciples being ready for the Son of Man's coming, since "no-one knows the hour." The final parable had associated a series of hypothetical time indicators with this event (evening, midnight, cock-crow, and dawn, v.35) which then effectively shape the hearer's expectations. This coming is now a daily possibility, and, as each one of the four daily watches arrives, the disciples ought to be ready for the Son of Man's awaited hour.

Lightfoot asked, in a question which has hardly received the attention it deserves, whether these time notes were "a tacit reference to the events of that supreme night before the passion?"[2] A partial answer can be given immediately, in that once the time notes are mentioned they travel with the reader into the narrative concerning the events of that supreme night. After being erected as hypothetical temporal landmarks for the major event expected by chapter 13, they cannot help but also guide the reading experience. On turning to the passion narrative, the reader has been educated to watch for *this* event *at these times*. As the watches successively appear, the expectation of the Son of Man's coming will increase. As they pass by disappointed, the expectation is increased even more at the next landmark. Since any of these landmarks could be the significant one, each is watched for with great eagerness.[3]

The story has moved relentlessly towards Jesus' death. As the passion narrative unfolds it becomes clear that each of its units centers around this predicted passion, either by way of preparation or reflection.[4]

---

2. Lightfoot, "Connexion," 53. Geddert, *Watchwords*, Ch. 4, follows and extends Lightfoot.

3. This is especially true given the importance of time to a narrative, see above, chapter 2. It is no great problem that midnight is not mentioned explicitly in the passion narrative (cf. 14:41; Lane, *Mark*, 24), nor that evening appears twice and other time references are also given. Once these particular landmarks are overlaid with an expectation, as each time reference appears it will cause the reader to watch more closely for fulfilment.

4. [2021: I later examined Mark's narrative portrayal of Jesus' death in "Feeling the Cross" and *Cross from a Distance*.]

MARK 13 IN RETROSPECT (MARK 14–16)

Preparation for Jesus' Death (14:1–11)

An Horrific Betrayal (14:1-11)

14:1–11 is a sandwich which prepares for Jesus' death. It begins by resuming the opponent's plot to kill him (vv.1–2), which had previously come to a stand-still (12:28–34). Their public tactics (12:13–34) had failed before a crowd they feared (12:12,37), now they seek a "sly way" (ἐν δόλῳ *en dolō*) to arrest and kill Jesus.

The middle portion of the sandwich (vv.3–6) climaxes when Jesus explains the woman's anointing as preparation for his burial. The story's most reliable character reveals that his death is inevitable and so the reader knows that the opponents will find the sly way they are after.

The closing frame of the sandwich (vv.10–11) reveals that the opportunity they were after arrives when Judas offers to betray Jesus to them. With this offer, Judas' commissioned role begins to be played out (3:19) and the opponent's commissioned role (3:6; 12:12; 14:1) is revived. The imminent closure of these earlier expectations gives the sense that the narrative is rising towards its end.

The focus of this passage is not on Jesus' betrayal as such, since this is by now a well-established fact (8:31; 9:31; 10:33), but on the horrendous manner in which it occurred. This brief, unembellished narrative in which "one of the twelve" quite definitely leaves Jesus' company and is firmly aligned with his opponents, succeeds at both increasing the distance between Judas and the reader, who remains aligned with Jesus, and erecting an atmosphere of pathos and tragedy at his heinous act of betrayal.[5]

In 14:1–11 Jesus is prepared to die, and the reader learns the horrendous fact that his death will come through one of his closest companions joining forces with his opponents.

---

5. This effect is the result of a number of factors: The contrast between the "beautiful" act of preparation for Jesus' death, and this deceitful one; the naming of Judas as "one of the twelve" underlines his betrayal of the one who called him to "be with him" (3:14); since there has been distance between the reader and the opponents from the beginning, their delight at this act turns the reader off it; the crass commercialism in the offer of money recalls previous scenes in which the opponents were portrayed negatively (12:13–17; 12:38–44; 14:4–5) and reverses the tenor of the previous scene in which it was more important to have Jesus than a well-stocked wallet (10:17–31); and Judas' deliberate, premeditated posture of betrayal (v.11b) removes any last shred of sympathy the reader may feel towards Judas.

Explanation of Jesus' Death (14:12–25)

The next unit (14:12–25) explains his forthcoming death in terms of the Passover sacrifice (note vv.12,12,14,16).[6] The deliberate preparations (vv.12–16) recall Jesus' previous careful preparations made for his entry to Jerusalem. Then he was hailed as Israel's king,[7] now he comes to be sacrificed. Jesus arrives "when evening came" (v.17, ὀψίας γενομένης *opsias genomenēs*), that is, at the first of the timing milestones (13:35) being watched for. Through the time notice, the previous expectations are brought into the last supper and this Passover feast becomes a potential candidate for the Son of Man's coming.

It is therefore no surprise that the Son of Man theme is explicitly reinforced by the narrative. Jesus reveals to his disciples what the reader already knows: the Son of Man will be betrayed by one of the twelve. Although this betrayal will be a fulfilment of the Scriptures, the horrendous nature of the betrayer's action is underlined (v.21).

Jesus then explains the Passover meal in terms of his own forthcoming death understood in terms of Isaiah 53 (v.24; cf. 10:45). He will die as the Suffering Servant, the Passover sacrifice, whose "blood of the covenant" will have salvific implications for many.

The section ends with Jesus once again emphatically declaring the imminence of the kingdom of God (v.25; cf. 13:30). This would be his last drink before he drinks again in the kingdom.

Although the last supper has not delivered "the hour," it has reinforced the expectations generated by the apocalyptic discourse, through continuing the well-established links between the death of Jesus, the Son of Man, and the imminent kingdom. These narrative expectations are kept to the forefront at the end of the scene, for Jesus once again stands on the Mount of Olives (v.26; cf. 13:3–37).

---

6. The significance of this unit for Mark's story is often missed through the preoccupation with reading this section as "the institution of the Lord's Supper," rather than as Jesus' Last Supper.

7. Lightfoot, "Passion Narrative," 138.

Warning about Jesus' Death (14:26-31)

Much in this short dialogue recalls the themes of chapter 13, thus keeping its expectations alive.[8] For, once again standing on the Mount of Olives and using apocalyptic language (Zech 13:7), Jesus warns the disciples of coming disaster primarily directed at the shepherd, who will be struck down, but also having disastrous consequences for the sheep. In the pattern that is by now familiar, Jesus then adds a word about his resurrection, which he promises will be followed by a time of restoration for the disciples in Galilee (v.28). This raises another expectation for the narrative to fulfil.

The severity of this projected disaster is reinforced when Peter denies Jesus' prediction of a complete apostasy (v.27)—at least in his case (v.29). Commentators have often condemned Peter for his petulance, but the narrative does not encourage any condemnation of such an outburst from this sympathetic character.[9] These are rather the earnest protestations of loyalty, cast in terms of his previous hard-learned lesson (8:31-34)[10] and continuing strongly even after Jesus emphatically states that Peter, too, will fall (vv.30-31). Jesus' prediction of Peter's apostasy does not encourage condemnation, but horror—the coming distress will be so bad that even this loyal chief disciple will fall.

His fall is imminent indeed, given with a most explicit threefold time reference (v.30). It will be "today" (σήμερον *sēmeron*), "this night" (ταύτῃ τῇ νυκτί *tautē tē nykti*), indeed, before the cock crows twice (πρὶν ἢ δὶς ἀλέκτορα φωνῆσαι *prin ē dis alektora phōnēsai*). Since Peter's denial is pinpointed with reference to the cockcrow, the terrible distress associated with the striking of the shepherd is also pinpointed to this time. Since this is also one of the temporal indicators associated with the coming of the Son

---

8. There are many links with Chapter 13: the Son of Man; the emphatic "truly I say to you", ἀμὴν λέγω ὑμῖν *amēn legō hymin*, v.25; ἕως τῆς ἡμέρας ἐκείνης *heōs tēs hēmeras ekeinēs*, v.25; the imminent Kingdom, v.25; the Mount of Olives, v.26.

9. Read against the narrative norms, the denial is obviously wrong, for true discipleship is denial of self rather than of Jesus (8:34—9:1). However, Peter is nevertheless sympathetically portrayed. He has been with Jesus from the beginning (1:16-20), he is one of the inner circle of disciples, he was the first to identify Jesus correctly as the Christ. Even the fact that he is told beforehand, ameliorates his failure. For the notion of sympathetic characters, see Boomershine, "Mark 16:8"; "Peter's Denial"; Vorster, "Characterization".

10. Ἐὰν δέῃ με συναποθανεῖν σοι, οὐ μή σε ἀπαρνήσομαι *Ean deē me synapothanein soi, ou mē se aparnēsomai* (14:31), "Even if I must suffer with you, I will never deny you", is reminiscent of 8:31 (δεῖ ... παθεῖν *dei ... pathein*); cf. also 8:34-36; 10:28-31.

of Man (13:35), these events are brought into relationship in the reader's expectation.

This warning is so plainly reminiscent of the previous warning Jesus issued at this same location, that it is impossible not to link the two together and adopt the natural assumption that he is talking of the same event. In Mark 13 the terrible distress was followed by the coming of the Son of Man. Here, where he speaks more plainly than in Mark 13, he is obviously talking of his own death,[11] and, in line with the previous passion predictions, the death of the Son of Man is followed by his resurrection. Since the middle term is the Son of Man, the question is raised whether these two patterns are describing the one thing.

Mark 13	Mark 14:26-31	Combined effect?
Coming distress (?of the Son of Man)	Coming death of the Son of Man	Coming distress = death
Coming of the Son of Man	resurrection (?of the Son of Man)	resurrection = coming of Son of Man
Gathering of elect	Go ahead to Galilee	Galilee = gathering?

The two discourses on the Mount of Olives frame the narrative that prepares for Jesus' death (14:1-25). It is consistent with Mark's use of sandwich and framing techniques to read the two discourses in the light of the intervening material. Although both use apocalyptic language, the sequence "Lengthy Olivet discourse—preparations for death—Shortened Olivet discourse," suggests that this unit begins to explain in plainer language what Mark 13 had expressed in symbol. This return to the Mount of Olives after the preparation and explanation of the death of the Son of Man (14:1-40) reinforces the warning given to the disciples in Mark 13 and strongly suggests that the coming distress, previously described even more strongly in apocalyptic mode, is Jesus' death.

This hint is further clarified by the following narrative.

---

11. There is no doubt that this means he will be killed, cf. Zechariah 6-8. This is reinforced by the previous passion predictions (cf. 8:31; 9:31; 10:33) and 14:1-40 (v.28).

Mark 13 in Retrospect (Mark 14–16)

The Advent of the Hour (14:32–42)

Gethsemane

In this pericope Jesus withdraws to pray, taking three of our four disciples with him (cf. 13:3). The theme of the paragraph is his command for them to watch (vv.34,37,38) and their failure to do so (vv.37,40,41). The time of testing is upon them (v.38) but they sleep, leaving Jesus to endure his great distress alone (v.33).

The horror of the coming distress is evident in Jesus' words (v.34), and set up by the narrator's introduction (v.33, καὶ ἤρξατο ἐκθαμβεῖσθαι καὶ ἀδημονεῖν *kai ērxato ekthambeisthai kai adēmonein*). This horrifying hour, which Jesus prayed might pass (v.35), is then clearly revealed to be the moment when Jesus will drink the cup of God's wrath as the obedient Servant of the Lord (v.36; cf. 10:38,45; 14:24).[12]

This paragraph echoes the apocalyptic discourse and reinforces its narrative thrust. There the four disciples were told to pray (13:18) about the timing of the great abomination that would cause unprecedented suffering and they were told to watch for that suffering, for it would herald the coming of the Son of Man and the gathering of the elect. "The hour" was unknown (13:32) therefore they were to watch, lest they be found asleep (13:36) when that climactic event took place.

This section explicitly echoes the apocalyptic discourse, which justifies the claim that it is a deliberate "redundancy" that is meant to guide the reading of the Gospel. On leaving chapter 13 the reader was entangled in the story, watching for the resolution of the expectations generated by the discourse. This paragraph makes contact with the reader's expectations, and begins their resolution. What was imminent now begins to arrive.

Jesus' final words commence the closure of the narrative's sustained expectations (vv.41–42). They explicitly echo the plain language of the previous passion predictions (8:31; 9:31; 10:33–34), and hook in with the other expectations of Jesus' inevitable death.[13] They also echo the apocalyptic language of chapter 13 and so hook in with the expectations erected there.[14] However, what is significant about Jesus' words is that they echo

---

12. The horrifying nature of Jesus' impending death is brought out well by Grassi, "Abba, Father."

13. These are both explicit (e.g., 3:6; 3:19; 12:1–12; 14:1–2,10–11) and implicit (e.g., 2:20; 1:14; 6:14–29).

14. Καθεύδετε *katheudete*, cf. 13:36; ἡ ὥρα *hē hōra*, cf. 13:32; ὁ υἱὸς τοῦ ἀνθρώπου

previous expectations in order to begin their closure. From the mouth of Jesus himself, the reader learns that his long-expected death has arrived, for, using the language erected by chapter 13, he *declares that the time for watching is over since the "hour" has come* (v.41).[15]

The hour that was previously unknown (13:32) has now been made manifest by the arrival of the betrayer. Here this hour is plainly the hour of Jesus' impending crucifixion. Now that this has been clarified by the subsequent story, the *"horrifying sacrilege" is retrospectively interpreted as the apocalyptic prefigurement of the horrific betrayal of the Son of Man into the hands of sinners (v.41) so that he might be destroyed.*[16]

This partial closure of the expectations erected by Jesus' last major discourse strongly increases the expectancy of complete closure. That it is the betrayal of "the Son of Man" reminds the reader that this time of severe distress is merely the precursor to the "coming" of the Son of Man.

The Desertion of Jesus (14:43–52)

The closure of narrative expectations continues with the arrival of the betrayer in full consort with the opponents (v.43), which increases the horror of the narrative when a symbol of affection is corrupted into a sign of betrayal (vv.44,45).[17] The arrest occurs (v.46) and, after one rather pathetic show of violence (v.47) and Jesus' resignation to the necessary fulfilment of the Scriptures (vv.48–49; cf. 9:11–13), everyone deserts him (v.50).

This flight of the disciples is the climax of the arrest scene. Jesus' mention of the fulfilment of Scripture recalls the last such formula (v.49, cf. v.27) before the fulfilment of that particular quotation is reported (v.50). Despite their protestations of loyalty (14:26–31), the pathetic disciples now desert the Son of Man in his hour of need, closing the expectations generated by

---

ho huios tou anthrōpou, cf. 13:26; and perhaps even the use of ἤγγικεν *eggiken*, cf. 13:29. "The links between the Doorkeeper parable (13:33–37) and the Gethsemane account (14:32–42) are so remarkable that the burden of proof is surely on anyone who wants to consider them coincidental," Geddert, *Watchwords*, 91.

15. Lightfoot, "Connexion", 52–53.

16. Note the added link to chapter 13, and confirmation of this position from the variant reading for v.41 ἀπέχει τὸ τέλος· ἦλθεν *apechei to telos; ēlthen*; cf. 13:7,13, which reflects the way Luke tells the story cf. Luke 22:37.

17. The narrator ensures that the reader feels this horror, by firstly imparting some privileged information (v.44) about this despicable arrangement and then narrating it in operation, with κατεφίλησεν *katephilēsen* in the emphatic final position (v.45).

Jesus' quotation of Zech 13:7. The disciples did not heed Jesus' warning, failed to watch, and now the sheep have been scattered, just as the striking of the shepherd begins.[18]

When read against previous textual norms (8:31—9:1; 9:42—50; 10:38—40; 13:5—37; 14:30—31,32—38) this flight is obviously a failure of discipleship. However, the text does not encourage an outright condemnation of the disciples. Besides the fact that they are portrayed sympathetically throughout the story of their decline,[19] there is another textual norm that puts their flight in a more positive light. In 13:14—23 the disciples were told to flee urgently whenever they recognized the arrival of the awful horror, with all its attendant distress. Here, as "the hour" arrives, the disciples quickly flee, indicating that *they have recognized the arrival of the terrible distress foreshadowed in the apocalyptic discourse*. Although they recognize the moment, they fail to endure as the remnant should have done.

The account of the one brave man left following in Jesus' way,[20] who only fled after actually being seized by the garment, not only underlines Jesus' desolation,[21] but also reinforces the intense distress of this hour. This graphic allusion to Amos 2:16 informs the reader that the impending judgment is so severe that even the valiant of heart flee away naked.[22] The

18. Lightfoot, "Connexion", 52, notes that despite being informed beforehand, all of them were led astray (cf. 13:22—23).

19. The reader is told of: i. their desire to prepare for what will be Jesus' last meal (v.12), which aligns them with the woman of the previous scene, a most sympathetic character (14:3—6); ii. their grief at the betrayal, by use of an inside view, a grief shared by the reader (v.19, ἤρξαντο λυπεῖσθαι *ērxanto lypeisthai*); iii. their protestations of loyalty (vv.19,29,31b); iv. an explanation for their sleep in the garden and their lack of excuse, both of which, in the reader's mind, ameliorate their failure (v.40); v. the rude attempt at protection (v.47). For devices that encourage sympathy in the reader, see Booth, *Rhetoric of Fiction*, 5, 6, 12, 44, 64, 129—33, 158, 194, 271, 378; Boomershine, "Peter's Denial"; "Mark 16:8." The fact that Jesus' work is described as being in their favour (14:23—25, cf. 10:45) and the promise of reunion (14:28), also encourages sympathy. When combined with their failure, this reminds the reader that "all things [i.e., entry to the kingdom] are possible with God" (10:27).

20. Recall the significance of this theme for Mark's Gospel, see for example, Best, *Following Jesus, passim*.

21. Lane, *Mark*, 527—28. For Mark taking pains in chs. 14—15 to show the increasing dereliction of Jesus, see Lightfoot, "Connexion", 55. [2021: see also Bolt, "Feeling the Cross".]

22. *Pace* the suggestions of Cranfield, *Mark*, 438, and Taylor, *Mark*, 561, that the identification of this allusion is "desperate in the extreme." Note that γύμνος *gymnos* is used twice, which indicates that it is the significant point and so cements the allusion to Amos.

Servant will endure the distress of "that day" absolutely alone, the one for the many (cf. 10:45).

The Son of Man Will Come (14:53-72)

The narrative continues with a sandwich (14:53-72) that both reinforces the narrative expectations and guarantees their fulfilment.

As expected, Jesus is handed over to his opponents (v.53; cf. 8:31; 9:31; 10:33-34). After the previous scene, it is a pleasant surprise that Peter is still following him, albeit at a distance (v.54).[23] The fact that he still remains loyal indicates that Jesus' prediction (vv.27-31) is not yet completely fulfilled and Peter's denial before cockcrow is still outstanding. This also means that the great distress is also still awaited.

Before hearing any more of Peter the scene shifts to the Sanhedrin inside. The reader has no doubt about the outcome of this trial scene (cf. 3:6,19; 8:31; 9:31; 10:33-4; 12:1-12; 13:9; 14:1-2,10,41,42-43). Judas, the betrayer, has done his work and now the real enemies of Jesus will reject him and hand him over to the Gentiles to be abused and killed. In case there remains any doubt, the narrator clarifies their deadly motives (14:55). The only concrete charge made at the trial is the enigmatic saying about the Temple (14:58). The reader recalls Jesus' brief dismissal of the disciple's focus on the Temple (13:1-2), but nothing comparable to this puzzling claim.[24] Nevertheless, this solitary reported charge flounders due to a lack of evidence (vv.55b-59), which leads to the High Priest himself beginning his examination.[25] After an unsuccessful attempt to draw Jesus into the false testimony (vv.60-61a), he puts a direct question (v.61b) concerning Jesus' messianic claim.[26] His question recalls the last discussion concerning the Christ, in which Jesus had propounded a riddle at his opponents' expense (12:35-37). Since there was no answer given, that incident created

---

23. Recall that this is discipleship language for Mark, which therefore continues the sympathetic portrayal of this chief apostle. Lightfoot, "Passion Narrative," 150-51, comments on the pleasant surprise of Peter's loyalty at this point.

24. This puzzle prepares the way for 15:38, see below.

25. Εἰς μέσον *eis meson* may help to focus upon this great one taking the floor.

26. Marcus, "Are You the Messiah-Son-of-God?," 139, has shown that this is a question concerning the nature of Jesus' messianic claim, not whether Jesus is the Davidic Messiah (which apparently would not have been blasphemous), but whether Jesus is claiming a messiahship "understood in terms of participation in God's cosmic lordship."

a gap which still remains open. By recalling this gap, the High Priest's question raises the expectation that it may now be closed.

Jesus' answer is the climax of the trial scene and contains its significant point.[27] He gives an affirmative answer, breaking his previous secrecy by publicly disclosing his identity as Israel's Messiah, God's Son, for the first time.[28] He then goes public with the two quotations he had previously used privately (Ps 110:1; Dan 7:13). The first quotation closes the gap created by his previous riddle (12:35-37), for he now gives the answer:[29] The Messiah is greater than David for he is the Son of the Blessed one[30] and the Son of Man. This second quotation taps into the outstanding expectation from 13:26, which, rather than being closed, is given further momentum since the coming is still a projected event. Nevertheless it is imminent, for the Sanhedrin is told that they will see the Son of Man exalted, vindicated and given the kingdom of God.[31] His enemies may seem to be in control, but they will see this moment which will also be the hour of their own defeat, in fulfilment of Ps 110:1 (cf. 12:36).

This claim then becomes the reason for his death (14:63-65).[32] As expected, Jesus is killed as the Son of Man, which continues the expectation that, as the Son of Man, he will also arise (8:31; 9:9,31; 10:33-34). In this way the trial scene reinforces the previous narrative expectations, before

---

27. It comes at the conclusion of the trial and then becomes the cause of his death (vv.63-64). It is also the christological highpoint of the story so far. For the connection of Jesus' before the Sanhedrin with 13:9, see Lightfoot, "Connexion", 52.

28. He previously revealed himself as "I am" to the disciples (6:50), but now it is to his enemies. By thus breaking the "Messianic Secret" theme (Perrin, "The High Priest's Question."), the narrative continues to move towards closure. Since 9:9 had projected this openness would occur beyond Jesus' death and resurrection, Jesus' openness here makes those events loom large in the reader's expectation.

29. Noted also by Beasley-Murray, *Jesus and the Kingdom*, 298 (with Neugebauer).

30. The filial son theme is therefore prominent; cf. 12:1-12,35-7; and perhaps 13:32. It will also be present at 14:36; see Grassi, "Abba, Father."

31. This verse is read consistently with Dan 7:13 and Mark 13:26 of the exaltation/vindication. Cf. Lightfoot, "Connexion", 54. The mention of "with the clouds," being part of the quotation from Dan 7:13, signifies his enthronement rather than hinting at further judgment to come. Its' retrospective and prospective nature is noticed by Perrin, "The High Priest's Question," *passim*, and Jackson, "Death," 25-26. Following Vielhauer, "Erwägungen zur Christologie," they both consider it as prospective of the crucifixion, but I will argue below that it ultimately looks to the resurrection.

32. In a touch of Markan irony as they declare his words to be blasphemy, the opponents complete their blasphemy against the Holy Spirit against which Jesus warned them in their very earliest encounter (3:28-9). Bolt, "Spirit", 48-49.

ending with the ironic mockery of Jesus—ironic because the ones who demand a prophecy in the very act fulfil one Jesus has already given (10:34).[33] This irony is carried over into the next scene.

Switching to the courtyard reveals that another prophecy is being fulfilled, as Peter denies Jesus (14:66–72). His triple failure to fulfil his own prediction (14:29) is presented in a way that shocks the reader and is plainly a failure of discipleship.[34] However, even this horrendous denial is somewhat ameliorated by the end of the scene,[35] where Peter remembers Jesus' word, before breaking down to weep.[36] This inside view and expression of intense emotion encourages sympathy in the reader and underlines the great distress of the moment. While the soldiers demand a prophesy inside, one is being fulfilled in the courtyard outside. For Jesus' prediction has come true: even the loyal chief disciple has fallen in this hour of testing (14:30). Only Jesus has endured as the righteous remnant.[37]

As predicted, the denial takes place before cockcrow (v.72). The appearance of this temporal landmark, also means that another indicator has passed by without the coming of the Son of Man. However, since the last sheep has now fallen away and the hour of distress is pressing in upon the shepherd, the coming of the Son of Man must be imminent indeed.

The inside of this sandwich had reinforced the expectation of the Son of Man's coming. The outside shows one of Jesus' predictions fulfilled, underlines the incredible distress of this moment, and flags one of the potential temporal moments for the Son of Man's arrival. The combined

---

33. Mark's Passion narrative is full of irony. See Booth, *Rhetoric of Irony*, 28–29, 91–92.

34. The accusations are blunt (vv.67,69,70, contrast those of John 18:15–18,25–27) and the denials are equally emphatic (vv.68,70), culminating in curses and a denial of any relationship with Jesus at all (v.71)! ἀρνέομαι *arneomai* is used in 8:34 where, basically because of Peter (cf. 8:33), the crowd is told that true discipleship is to deny oneself rather than Jesus. Here Peter makes exactly the opposite choice. He still has his mind on the things of men, not God!

35. Peter is the last remaining disciple; the denial is gradual and twice suggested by the questioner.

36. Although the meaning of ἐπιβαλών *epiballōn* here is difficult to grasp, it quite clearly supports the main verb in some way.

37. Lightfoot, "Connexion", 52–53. "The faithful people of God has gradually narrowed and finally identified with the person of Jesus alone. Jesus will now die in order to redeem his disciples," Geddert, *Watchwords*, 102; "according to Mark the faithful remnant of Israel was finally reduced through the passion to Jesus alone. He alone carried the destiny of the nation," 133, cf. 93 nn.16,17. [2021: Bolt, "Feeling the Cross".]

effect of the sandwich is not only to reassert these expectations, but also to guarantee that this prediction will likewise be fulfilled, thus increasing the reader's momentum towards the resolution of the story.

The Great Distress (15:1–39)

Once his opponents have decided his fate, Jesus is tried before Pilate (15:1–5), subject to a mock enthronement (vv.16–19)[38] and then crucified and mocked again (vv.21–32), before he dramatically breathes his last (vv.33–39).

Throughout the account it is clear that Jesus, innocent of any other charge (v.14), is killed as King of the Jews, Israel's Christ (vv.2,9,12,17,18,19,26,31–32). It is equally clear that this is orchestrated by Israel's leadership (vv.1,3–4,10,11,31–32), who, in their mockery, show perfect understanding of Jesus' mission and identity (vv.31–32) even though their demand for a final sign shows that they remain hard-hearted and unbelieving (cf. 8:11–13; 13:4,21–22).[39]

Their blindness is further contrasted by the climax of the Gospel.[40] Rather than mock Jesus, the Gentile centurion, whether in full faith or in partial recognition, discerns that this man was the Son of God (v.39). When he dies as the one who came to serve and give his life as a ransom for many (10:45), Israel's Messiah is recognized by a non-Israelite, while Israel remains "seeing and never perceiving" right up to the end (cf. 4:11–12).

The opponents' action is horrifying. Even Pilate seems surprised that the Jews would release a murderer to kill their King (vv.9–14). Their actions are patently unjust and dislikeable throughout.[41] The tragic tone of the nar-

---

38. The scene is ironically cast as a mock enthronement: he is led into the palace, a king's proper abode; the whole battalion is called; purple cloak, crown, salutes, and homage.

39. Jesus warned against the sign-seeking attitude and it is now clear where it leads. The disciples have abandoned the Messiah to his death, just as surely as the opponents have done.

40. The climax of a narrative is "that part of a story [. . .] at which a crisis is reached and resolution is achieved," Cuddon, "Climax," 125; cf. "Crisis," 166). Despite the arguments of Johnson, "Is Mark 15:39 the Key?," 15:39 is generally regarded as Mark's climax.

41. They insist on accusing him of many things (v.3), even though the trial had found no evidence, and they passed sentence on one item only. They choose a murderer over an innocent man. Their motive is patently obvious even to the Roman Governor, let alone the reader who knows so much more (v.10). In their mockery they are no better than the Roman soldiers, perhaps even worse since they understand Jesus' mission better. Their

rative is reinforced by its matter-of-fact style, in which Jesus has the passive role of a victim (cf. Isa 53:7) and overall there is an increase in the distance between the hero and the reader. Jesus has been divorced from his disciples, and now from the reader too, adding to the horror of the moment.[42]

The tragic irony of the narrative,[43] in which the religious leaders kill their long-awaited King, and the reader's attendant sense of horror combine with the previous narrative expectations to suggest that *in the story of the crucifixion the promised awful horror has arrived. As Israel's hard-hearted leadership succeeds in abusing, mocking and destroying Israel's Messiah, the greatest sacrilege of all time has been committed.* The owner of the vineyard has played his last card and his own son has been destroyed (12:1–12; cf. 15:39). However, in the same event in which Israel passes judgment on God's Messiah, God passes judgment on Israel (15:38).[44]

The time references focus the narrative around the climactic moment when Jesus dies.[45] Time is reckoned in hours (vv.25,33,34), which slows the story down and adds to its pathos. The story reaches its full depths of pathos at the hour of Jesus' death (vv.33–38), for when the king finally dies, he dies utterly forsaken: forsaken by his disciples, forsaken by the Jerusalem leadership, forsaken by God (v.34). He dies as the remnant of Israel who redeems Israel, the elect of God who redeems the elect. At this moment he endures the worst distress ever known to humanity, utterly God-forsaken, drinking the cup of God's wrath on behalf of the Israel who rejected their king. Here is "the destructive sacrilege", ὁ βδέλυγμα τῆς ἐρημώσεως

---

post-crucifixion mockery has a gloating and insulting tone that grates on the reader who is firmly on Jesus' side (vv.31–32).

42. For Mark's portrayal of Jesus' increasing dereliction in chs. 14–15, see Lightfoot, "Connexion", 55. [2021: Bolt, "Feeling the Cross".]

43. The crucifixion account is filled with irony, for in all the mockery, the reader recognizes that these people speak words of sober truth.

44. The usual explanation is that Jesus' death does away with the necessity of the Temple. Cf. Lightfoot, "Connexion", 55–56. Bailey, "Fall of Jerusalem," however, goes even further to say that Jesus *is* the Temple, who is both destroyed (crucifixion) and rebuilt (resurrection). If this reading is connected with the Temple associations of the abomination of desolation in Daniel, then it is yet another piece of evidence for the thesis argued here. This connection is of course made explicit in John 2:13–22, and it is interesting to note some early scribes made the same connection in 13:2 (D W it).

45. The problem with the chiastic structure proposed by Bailey, "Fall of Jerusalem," 103, is that the central emphatic position is not given to this event. Rather than being chiastic, the rhetorical structure, actually consists of three, linear scenes (crucified, vv.21–24; mocked, vv.25–32; dead, vv.33–39), with the "rule of three" throwing emphasis upon the last. The threefold desire for de-crucifixion (vv.30,32,36) reinforces this structure.

ἑστηκότα ὅπου οὐ δεῖ *ho bdelygma tēs erēmōseōs hestēkota hopou ou dei* (13:14): the Christ arrives, and Jerusalem kills him.[46]

The crucifixion account continues the closure of narrative expectations. It is what the opponents had planned from the outset. However, behind the opponents' plot there is a greater divine necessity and so his death is exactly what Jesus had promised (8:31; 9:9,31; 10:33; 14:28). The last event to occur before the coming kingdom of God / resurrection day has now happened (cf. 9:11–13).

The allusion to the trial charge adds to the sense of closure (15:29–30; cf. 14:58, and 15:38), but, since it also reminds the reader that it wasn't the charge that stuck, its' more important contribution is to raise the Son of Man expectation generated by the claim for which Jesus was crucified (14:62). The Son of Man allusions are reinforced by the darkness which enveloped the entire death scene (v.33, cf. 13:24–25), for his arrival could be expected as the next event in the series after this apocalyptic symbol of judgment is sighted.[47]

Despite these closures, the crucifixion should not be seen as the complete closure of the 13:26/14:62 expectation.[48] Although the crucifixion may be called Jesus' enthronement, in the sense that here he is declared to be King, it is an ironic enthronement, in the eye of the reader alone. The expectations generated by 12:35–37 (Ps 110:1), 13:26 (Dan 7:13) and 14:62 (both) were that the enemies would see the Son of Man coming, in victory over his enemies.[49] At the crucifixion Jesus may be ironically recognized as King, but his enemies are gloating in their victory and the righteous Messiah still cries out for his hour of victory (v.34, quoting Psalm 22:1). The crucifixion account still looks forward to the complete closure of the narrative expectations surrounding the Son of Man.

---

46. Of course Jesus dies according to the divine δεῖ *dei*, however, this expression underlines the awful horror of Israel's crime: they should have embraced their Messiah, not murdered him; cf. 12:1–12; 14:21; or Acts 2:23.

47. Geddert, *Watchwords*, 106 n.57, recognizes that "the 'apocalyptic' signs accompanying the first fulfilment of 'the day and the hour' happen when Jesus is already on the cross." I would argue that this is not just the "first fulfilment," but the correct reading of the textual retrospection to Mark 13.

48. *Pace* Perrin, "The High Priest's Question"; Jackson, "Death"; Vielhauer, "Erwägungen zur Christologie"; Radcliffe, "'The Coming of the Son of Man," 184.

49. I argue below that it comes in the resurrection, which therefore brings Mark's usage of Psalm 110 into line with elsewhere in the New Testament, where it refers to Jesus' session as an expression of his resurrection/ascension victory.

The account contains several features that continue previous expectations. In the mockery, the emphasis is on Jesus coming down from the cross (vv.29-30,31-32,35-36).[50] The proof of messiahship that these mocking Israelites wished to see was a powerful reversal of crucifixion.[51] The three day time-note of the mockery, based on the charge made at the trial (vv.29-30, cf. 14:58),[52] uses the same time-frame given for the resurrection predictions (8:31; 9:31; 10:33-34). In this way the text constructs another irony, for the reader realizes that what the mockers demand (de-crucifixion), Jesus has already promised to fulfil.

The careful, deliberate time references recall the itemization of 13:35, and once again raise expectations for the coming of the Son of Man. Likewise, the repeated mention of Jesus as King, re-erects the expectation of the coming kingdom in power, and his refusal to drink the wine (v.23) reminds us that the kingdom of God had not yet arrived (14:25). Another offer of drink to Jesus at the moment of his death (15:36), sustains this expectation and the lack of any report of Jesus drinking it leaves the expectation open. If he did not drink, then the kingdom of God has not yet come, even though the necessary conditions for its arrival have been fulfilled (cf. 9:11-13).

Even the climactic confession by the centurion is only a partial closure. His recognition certainly ends the Son of God expectations.[53] However, the preference in Mark's Christology has been towards the Son of Man and the enigmatic 13:32 has blurred these two together. Now that Jesus has been recognized by someone in the enemy camp as Son of God, the expectation is that he is yet to be recognized as the Son of Man.

The passion predictions have been partially fulfilled, the Son of Man has been crucified. The expectations of chapter 13 have also been partially fulfilled, for the time of great distress has occurred, veiled in a cloak of apocalyptic darkness (13:24; 15:33). The Son of Man is still awaited. The narrative now has two outstanding expectations. The passion predictions promised the resurrection of the Son of Man[54] and the apocalyptic dis-

---

50. Bailey, "Fall of Jerusalem," misses this feature in his "literary analysis" of 15:20-39. The threefold repetition makes it a most significant feature.

51. The irony is that these were probably taunts of defeat rather than genuine expectations of fulfilment.

52. This closes the gap erected by 14:58, since it is now apparent that this charge at the trial prepared for the mockery scene at the cross.

53. 1:1,11; 3:11; 5:7; 9:7; 12:6; 13:32. Cf. Lightfoot, "Connexion", 56-57.

54. 8:31; 9:9,31; 10:33-34. Once again it is Jesus' identity as the Son of Man that provides the middle term in the expectations.

course promised the coming of the Son of Man, his kingdom and the gathering of the elect. By this stage these expectations have been clearly fused together in the reader's mind and the narrative now strains ahead for the resolution of these expectations in the dénouement of the story.

The Coming Kingdom?

The Dénouement: The Followers of a Dead King

Mark's dénouement[55] is delivered in a final sandwich (15:40—16:8),[56] the significance of which lies in the interrelationship of its components.

The Watching Women (15:40–41)

It opens with a group of women who are named and positively characterized as those who previously followed and cared for Jesus in Galilee. For the time being merely their state is described and their action is left in abeyance (v.40).[57] The emotional portrayal of their former relationship with Jesus, the implicit reminder of the whole sweep of his ministry (Galilee to the cross) and their distant impotence all underline the tragedy of the scene.[58]

The Watching Man (15:42–47)

The next paragraph has a more significant role than simply underlining the fact that Jesus was dead.[59] This middle portion of the sandwich introduces another new character, Joseph of Arimathea (vv.42–47). He is described as a prominent member of the council (εὐσχήμων βουλευτής *euschēmōn*

---

55. A dénouement is "the event or events following the major climax of a plot, or the unravelling of a plot's complications at the end"; Cuddon, "Dénouement," 181.

56. The view taken here is that Mark intentionally ended at verse 8. See the discussions by Petersen, "End," 151–66; Boomershine, "Mark 16:8."

57. Ἦσαν δὲ καὶ γυναῖκες ἀπὸ μακρόθεν θεωροῦσαι *Ēsan de kai gynaikes apo makrothen theōrousai*. The introduction of new characters raises the expectation that they will act.

58. Notice that the same language is used of Peter in 14:54.

59. This emphasis is conveyed by Joseph's request for the body (v.43), Pilate's inquiry (vv.44–45), and the double reference to the shroud and the tomb (v.46). The sealing of the door of the tomb with the stone adds a note of finality. The burial is discussed by Brown, "Burial," although he fails to discuss its function in the narrative.

bouleutēs) which creates some distance between him and the reader, since this council condemned Jesus. However, his actions are entirely positive. The description of him burying Jesus in lieu of his disciples (cf. 6:29) involves five verbs, underlining the great effort taken.[60]

However, the Joseph story does not simply provide a burial scene, but it has a greater importance for the dénouement of Mark. Its significance is revealed by Joseph's description as one "who was himself waiting eagerly for the kingdom of God" (v.43), which acts as a redundancy that keeps the reader on track. The kingdom of God has been increasingly imminent since the beginning of the story and it is still part of the reader's outstanding expectations.[61] Joseph reminds readers that they too are still eagerly awaiting the coming of the Son of Man and his kingdom. In this way the reference to Joseph keeps the story straining forward to resolution.

The mention of two of the women from the previous scene (v.47; cf. vv.40–41) reinforces the expectation that they have a role to perform.

The watched-for Event (16:1–8)

Their role is played out in 16:1–8 when, at the first opportunity, they bought spices (v.1) . . . discussed . . . and saw (vv.4,5) the empty tomb before fleeing, silent and afraid (v.8).

There are two significant time references attached to the women's action. The first dates this event to the third day after the crucifixion (v.1; cf. 15:42), that is, the expected day of resurrection (cf. Hosea 6:2). The second, twice-given to ensure the point is not missed, dates this event *by reference to the final time landmark that was mooted as the time of the Son of Man's coming* (13:35).[62] Thus, once again, the expectations drawn from the

---

60. He boldly entered, [. . .] he asked [. . .] after buying linen and removing the body from the cross he wrapped it, [. . .] then buried it, [. . .] then rolled a stone across the entrance.

61. This expectation of imminence has been increased and excited along the way (1:15; 9:1; 13:29; 14:25) and reached enormous proportions in chapter 15 where the King arrives—but with no obvious kingdom. The kingdom of God is related to the Son of Man's coming (Dan 7:13–14) and the story has also engaged the reader to watch for this coming (13:24–27). The reader has seen the hour of distress in the crucifixion, but where is his coming in which he receives and then parcels out his kingdom?

62. λίαν πρωΐ [. . .] ἀνατείλαντος τοῦ ἡλίου *lian prōi* [. . .] *anateilantos tou hēliou* v.2. Although the words used are different to 13:35, it is plainly the same time. Evening has passed by, cockcrow likewise passed by, and now we arrive at dawn. The third time-reference (on the first day of the week) may also be significant as a pointer to the

passion predictions and those from the apocalyptic discourse—i.e., those concerning the resurrection and those concerning the Son of Man's coming—coalesce, and now the expectation becomes intense.

Despite being portrayed with masterly understatement the scene is clearly the closure of all previous expectations. The disengaged stone, coupled with the young man's words, reveal that the resurrection has occurred as expected. Since the hope of resurrection has become closely entangled with the hope of the Son of Man's coming, *then this too can be taken as having occurred.*[63] The interaction between the parts of this final sandwich unit also suggests that this is so. Joseph puts the stone against the tomb, still awaiting the kingdom of God. The stone is then removed—by God's activity—and so presumably the kingdom of God has arrived in power!

The ending of the story also confirms this reading. According to Daniel 7, once the Son of Man comes and receives his kingdom he shares it out with the saints. In Mark, in terms of the next item in the chain of events expected from the apocalyptic discourse, the Son of Man sends out his angels to gather in the elect (13:27). In this final scene an angel has been sent out with a message for the disciples which he passes on through the women (16:7). The message is reminiscent of 14:28 and promises the closure of the expectation generated in the second Olivet discourse. Presumably, now that it is the appropriate time for the messianic secret to be declared in an open way (9:9), this projected reunion would involve Jesus finishing the work he had begun in the disciples and sending them out as fishers of men (1:16–20), with a top priority gospel that must go to all the nations (cf. 13:10; 14:9). The strange ending, in which the women ignore this command (v.8), challenges readers about their own involvement in this mission.[64]

---

eighth day of the kingdom of God. This would certainly support the reading offered here. However, Mark's story has not really set us up for interpreting this reference in this way.

63. In actual fact, Mark simply continues the link between the resurrection, the kingdom of God and the coming of the Son of Man found in the book of Daniel.

64. Following Boomershine and Bartholomew, "Narrative Technique," the inside view ("they were afraid") aligns the reader with the women sympathetically while still recognising their silence as wrong. Thus Mark closes with the reader understanding the temptation to be silent about the resurrection and yet being implicitly challenged to repent of such silence and speak out. The readers of Mark heard at the beginning that they were about to hear the beginning of the gospel of Jesus Christ (1:1). They knew that gospel, for someone had proclaimed it to them. Now at the end of the Gospel, the bridge is made. The beginning of gospelling is here in the story of the women at the tomb and the proleptic trip back to where it all began (16:7).

It is therefore clear that the last remaining expectations of the story are closed off. With the young man's word of command to the women, the gathering of the elect in the end-time harvest is begun, closing the expectation of 13:27 and therefore implying that the preceding expectations are also over: the Son of Man has come, the kingdom of God has come with power!

Mark 13: The Apocalyptic Precursor to the Passion Narrative

This examination has notice that significant portions of chapters 14–16 are clearly retrospective to anticipations in chapter 13. Rather than being isolated from its narrative context, in a profound way Mark 13 forms an apocalyptic precursor to the passion.

7

Conclusion

Mark 13:24–27. In Search of a Referent

THE INTERPRETIVE PROBLEMS OF Mark 13 revolve around the interpretation of its central key verses. All three readings of the chapter agree that these verses generate expectations to be fulfilled beyond the chapter and they each therefore seek after the referent to Mark 13:24–27. The two prevailing views opt for an historical referent *external to the events narrated by Mark*. This assumes that there is no closure of the expectations of Mark 13 within the subsequent story, i.e., what vv.13:24–27 anticipate finds no retrospection in Mark 14–16. Consequently, the referent must be looked for beyond the pages of the Gospel in subsequent history (the fall of Jerusalem) or at the end of history (the parousia).

However, the third reading—hinted at elsewhere, but more fully developed here—seeks an *intratextual referent* for these verses. Lightfoot recognized that Mark 13's narrative position made it "the climax of all that part of the Gospel which precedes the passion narrative itself." He therefore expressed surprise that there was "no reference in it to (Jesus') own approaching, almost immediate death."[1] He also recognized that chapter 13 "is undoubtedly designed by the evangelist as the immediate introduction to the Passion narrative"[2] and yet found difficulty in relating Mark 13 and

---

1. Lightfoot, "Content," 124, cf. 94.
2. Lightfoot, "Connexion," 50. Note also the observation of Derrett, *Making*, 218, that "Chapter 13 prepares the hearer for the passion narrative."

the passion narrative (which he considered to be independent). However, the argument presented in the present work has demonstrated that Mark 13 can in fact be legitimately read within the immediate literary context of the Gospel, both against the backdrop of the preceding story, and as preparation for the following passion narrative, and, despite Lightfoot's comments, that it includes a symbolic—or, better, an *apocalyptic*—reference to both the death and resurrection of Jesus Christ. In short, Mark 13:24–27 can be read within their narrative integrity.

Mark 13:24–27. Narrative Integrity

Regarding the narrative integrity of Mark 13:24–27 the argument in this book has demonstrated that:

1. the form of Mark 13 encourages its reading against the narrative in which it is embedded.

2. Mark 13 can be read against the preceding story, which deals with the arrival of the Servant-Messiah in the midst of hard-hearted Israel. He immediately clashes with Israel's corrupt leadership and seeks to establish a remnant of Israel, before the universal kingdom of God harvest begins. After the conflict escalates and his end is fast approaching, as a counterpart to his earlier parables discourse, Jesus delivers the apocalyptic discourse. It has the same function, to establish a remnant, but it has a greater urgency since the end is now imminent, only delayed by his necessary suffering which lurks on the immediate horizon. The disciples are warned and urged that from now on they must face the turmoil of the last days and, for the sake of the gospel, they must endure to the end (vv.5–13). The need to watch themselves is extremely urgent, for they will see the greatest distress of all time (vv.14–23) which will then be immediately followed by the coming of the Son of Man and the subsequent gathering of the elect (vv.24–27).

3. the narrative of Mark 14–16 contains enough retrospections to the anticipations of Mark 13 to conclude that the horrific spectacle of Israel's leadership crucifying Israel's Messiah is the anticipated "abomination of desolation," and the resurrection on the third day signals the coming of the Son of Man to the Ancient of Days to receive the kingdom of God in power.

4. the expectations generated by Mark 13 that do not find closure within the narrative are not the abomination of desolation, nor the coming of the Son of Man, but only the gathering of the elect. There is only a promise of closure of this expectation (16:7; 14:28), which presumably also links up with the unclosed expectation of Jesus making the disciples fishers of men (1:16-20). This prospect hints that the disciples were restored and constituted as Israel's remnant, and that the gathering of the elect began with them. The closure of other themes ensures that the reader has no doubt about the prospect of the closure of this one, however, it still remains true that at this point Mark's story has an open-endedness.[3]

The gathering of the elect has its terminus when the saints share completely in the kingdom of God already given to the Son of Man (Dan 7:15-27). By implication, Mark's Gospel expects the time when the saints enter into their eternal life in the age to come (10:30). In the meantime, the difficulties of the last days will continue (10:29-30; 13:5-13), but the open-endedness of the story encourages Mark's readers to continue in the mission launched by the Son of Man, for he is now gathering in the elect from the four corners of the earth. The end has begun with Jesus' death and resurrection, but before the saints enter into their rest, the end-time harvest must be completed.[4]

Mark 13:24-27. A Referent Discovered

The method adopted in this book set aside questions of history in the interests of reading Mark on its own terms. Having explored Mark 13:24-27 in their narrative integrity, it is appropriate to return to the quest for a referent

---

3. This means that the theme of mission is crucial, not merely *part of* discipleship (so Geddert), but *the reason for* discipleship. To be a disciple is to be joined to Jesus' mission, to lose your life for him and his gospel's sake (8:31—9:1).

4. In this way Mark 13 retains its relevance for modern disciples. At the time of the discourse Jesus spoke of the end *as expected by the Old Testament, especially Dan 7:13-14.* This end arrived when he died and rose again and yet human history has continued. This interval of borrowed time means that, although the *specific expectations* of Mark 13 (i.e., vv.14-26) have occurred, *the general context of the last days* have continued, and so the warnings given to the disciples concerning those last days retain their relevance (vv.5-13). The difference is that our vigilance is no longer for the Son of Man's coming, but for the time when he shares his kingdom with his saints. From elsewhere in the New Testament we know that this will occur when Jesus returns, for then the saints enter into the resurrection of the kingdom of God (1 Cor 15:23-28). In the meantime the mission (v.27) continues.

to these key verses. Having done the work of a reader, the question is now simply answered. For, since Mark's story itself invites the reader to recognize the fulfillment of Mark 13:24–27 in the resurrection of Jesus, and the subsequent launch of the mission to the nations, there is no need to search for fulfillment in events beyond the those reported in the pages of the Gospel story. Granted their narrative integrity, Mark 13:24–27 are not referring to the fall of Jerusalem, nor to a still distant parousia, but to the climax of Jesus' ministry, namely, his vindication/ exaltation begun with the resurrection.

The parousia is certainly an *implication* of the coming of the Son of Man. Although the Son of Man has received the kingdom of God in power, the saints are yet to fully share in his kingdom. That is, the vision of Dan 7:1–14 has been fulfilled, but its application for the saints remains outstanding (Dan 7:15–27). Evidence from elsewhere in the New Testament confirms that Jesus will return to share his kingdom with his people.

The fall of Jerusalem in AD 70 may also be an *implication* of the coming of the Son of Man, with a legitimate place in salvation-history as a sign of the end having come upon Israel. However, on my understanding this would be a complete argument from silence as there is no interpretation of this event in these terms within the New Testament.

When the story is listened to on its own terms, the historical referent to these verses does not need to be implied, but it is made explicit: it is the resurrection of Jesus, considered as his hour of victory as the Son of Man. This means that there is no necessity to search for another historical referent. Rather than the chapter being about an implication of the exaltation, it is *about* the exaltation. Rather than being about the consummation, it is about *the historical event that guarantees the consummation*. The historical event symbolically discussed in Mark 13:24–27 is not the fall of Jerusalem in AD 70, nor is it the parousia, but it is the resurrection of Jesus from the dead, three days after the "appalling sacrilege" in which the Jewish leadership crucified the one rightly called "King of the Jews." Indeed, to reuse the words of Barth:

> *The discourse of Mk. 13 is a repetition of the three prophecies of the passion and resurrection of Jesus elevated to a cosmic scale.* Jesus is primarily foretelling *His own impending death* when He speaks of these imminent events, *and His resurrection.*[5]

---

5. Barth, *CD* III.2, 501 (my emphasis). As noted in Chapter 1, despite saying these words, Barth still spoke of the chapter in terms of the fall of Jerusalem and the parousia.

APPENDIX I

The Parallels

Support from the Parallels

ALTHOUGH A FULL DISCUSSION of the parallels is beyond the focus of this work, I will offer some brief comments for three reasons. Firstly, within traditional Gospels criticism, discussion of the parallels is conventional. Even if what is offered here is cursory, it points the general direction that would be taken in a fuller discussion of all four Gospels. Secondly, even from the point of view of my chosen method an argument could be mounted that Matthew and Luke provide insight into how Mark 13 was read in the early days of its literary history (that is, assuming Markan priority). Thirdly, the parallels—and indeed the rest of the New Testament—appear to support the perspective on Mark argued here, in that *they can be read along similar lines.*[1]

The Synoptic Parallels and Acts

Matthew

Robinson[2] lists only five distinctive features of Matthew's account:

---

1. The function of this Appendix is therefore not so much to argue for each point, but merely to suggest that such a reading can be done. As I have stated above, the parallels do not demonstrate the case, they merely play a supportive role.

2. Robinson, *Redating*, 21–25.

APPENDIX 1: THE PARALLELS

1. The question (24:3) is broadened to ask what is the signal of the coming and the end of the age. Robinson's interest is with verses potentially referring to the fall of Jerusalem and he therefore does not discuss Matthew's distinctive addition of παρουσία *parousia* (vv.3,27,37,39). For some, the appearance of this word is enough to clinch the interpretive deal since it is taken as a 'technical term' for the second coming of Christ. However, this "technical" status can be questioned. The word παρουσία *parousia* connotes "presence" or "arrival," the context determining its precise meaning, and it is clearly used in both ways in the New Testament.[3] The use of this "presence" language in the apocalyptic discourse fits nicely into Matthew's distinctive "Emmanuel" theme.[4] Jesus states that the sign of his presence (v.3) is the coming of the Son of Man (v.30).[5] This means that the meaning of this coming will determine the meaning of παρουσία *parousia*, not vice versa. In the same way as we have seen for Mark, Matthew's story then reveals that the fulfillment of this expectation is in the resurrection. This is additionally clarified by the use of Dan 7:13–14 language as an established fact after Jesus has risen (28:18). Once the Son of Man has come, Jesus assures his disciples of his continued presence (28:20).[6]

2. The persecution prophecies are relocated to 10:17–21 and replaced by a section regarding divisions and defections in the church. "Whatever the motives for this, the effect is to see the prediction fulfilled earlier rather than later, and evidently they are not intended by Matthew to have any reference to the sufferings of the Jewish war."[7] This relocation into the pre-resurrection mission to Israel,[8] observed by Robinson, also confirms the interpretation of Mark 13:9–13 offered above.

---

3. Oepke, "παρουσία, πάρειμι."
4. Cf. Burnett, "Prolegomenon"; Combrink, "Structure."
5. The genitive is epexegetic.
6. Burnett, "Prolegomenon," 100, recognizes that the question of 24:3 creates a gap, but fails to recognise that this also applies to the word παρουσία *parousia*. [2021: Since the original thesis, see Bolt, *Matthew*, 217–29, on Matthew 24–25.]
7. Robinson, *Redating*, 22.
8. Note 10:23, interpreted consistently with Dan 7:13–14. The view that this chapter refers to the Gentile mission context rests on the slim evidence of v.18 and is overturned by the overwhelmingly Israelite context (vv.5,6,17,21–23,34 land, i.e. of Israel, 34–36; cf. Mic 7:6). It refers rather to the pre-resurrection mission to Israel, which later finds its counterpart in the post-resurrection mission to the nations, Matt 28:16–20. [2021: See Bolt, *Matthew*, 100–06, on Matthew 10:16–23.]

3. In 24:15 the abomination of desolation is specifically attributed to Daniel, and ὅπου οὐ δεῖ *hopou ou dei* is replaced by ἐν τόπῳ ἁγίῳ *en topō hagiō*, which has its background in Daniel 8:13 (cf. 1 Macc 2:7). This simply strengthens the link with Daniel and accords with Matthew's desire to show the fulfillment of OT prophecy. He also makes the grammatical change to the neuter ἑστός *hestos*, confirming that Mark's masculine does not signify a person.

4. In 24:20 the additions "when you have to make your escape," "or Sabbath" (which may be an allusion to 1 Macc 2:29–41, in which the Jews were slaughtered without resistence due to their Sabbath scruples) simply draw out what is meant by Mark.

5. Other material unparalleled in Mark fails to add any further specificity in the direction of the fall of Jerusalem (24:26–28; 24:37—25:46), but focuses on "the consummation" (like 24:30–31), despite being in Judea. At this point I repeat my observation that this must be understood within the story as the consummation expected by the Old Testament, which is still future to those in the story. As the story proceeds, it becomes obvious that the consummation begins with Jesus' death and resurrection (cf. 26:58 "to see the end").[9]

Robinson also notes that Matthew adds to the imminence found in Mark. The distress is to be followed *immediately* (εὐθέως, *eutheōs* v.29) by the coming of the Son of Man.[10] Once again, the best solution is that offered by the story, that Jesus' death and resurrection fulfill these expectations.

Luke

If some feel Matthew's παρουσία *parousia* tips interpretation towards Jesus' second coming, some insist that Luke tips the balance in the opposite direction, towards the fall of Jerusalem, since his details "correspond exactly to descriptions [. . .] of the action of Titus against Jerusalem".[11] It is possible

---

9. [2021: See Bolt, *Matthew*, 242–44, on 26:57–75.]

10. Robinson, *Redating*, 23–24. He also observes that 24:34 preserves Mark's note of imminence unaltered, as does 16:28 (cf. Mark 9:1), and that Matt 10:23 is added to the persecution sayings transported from the apocalyptic discourse. He also throws substantial doubt upon the idea that Matt 22:6–7 (pp.19–21) and 23:35 (pp.25–26) refer to the fall of Jerusalem.

11. Kümmel, *Introduction*, 150; Robinson, *Redating*, 26.

APPENDIX 1: THE PARALLELS

that Luke has drawn out the implications of Mark's apocalyptic discourse for subsequent Jewish history. However, Dodd has convincingly shown that

> not only are the two Lucan oracles (i.e. 21:20–24; 19:41–44.) composed entirely from the language of the Old Testament, but the conception of the coming disaster which the author has in mind is a generalized picture of the fall of Jerusalem as imaginatively presented by the prophets. So far as any historical event has colored the picture, *it is not Titus's capture of Jerusalem in* AD *70, but Nebuchadrezzar's capture in 586* BC. There is no single trait of the forecast which cannot be documented directly out of the Old Testament.[12]

Dodd wishes to argue that this is consistent with a genuine prediction of the fall of Jerusalem. However, once it is admitted that the language is "a generalized picture [...] as imaginatively presented by the prophets" its fulfillment is open to question, for it need not be to a political catastrophe for the city at all. Rather than being a prediction that *the events of 586* BC *will be repeated*, it may well be that the theological language of Jerusalem's destruction in 586 BC is *applied symbolically to another event with similar theological import*. The event to which Jesus was actually referring needs to be determined by the retrospections within Luke's story.[13]

Collison has also shown that Luke's story awaits the imminent fulfillment of eschatological expectations.[14] When this story is examined it is plain to see that the expected judgment occurs at the cross, and that Luke's previous references to the judgment on Jerusalem were employed to symbolically point to that event. Just like Job described the judgment of

---

12. Dodd, "Fall of Jerusalem," 79, my italics. He is followed by Robinson, *Redating*, 27 n.54, who adds the independent comment from Torrey: "Every particle of Luke's prediction not provided by Mark was furnished by familiar and oft quoted Old Testament passages." Reicke independently agrees, "Synoptic Prophecies." In view of the weight given to Luke 21:20 in the argument for fulfilment in AD 70, I must also add that this verse too is thoroughly Old Testament. Στρατοπέδος *stratopedos* need not connote *Roman* armies, for it is patent of a more generalised meaning as well and is used of the 586 BC catastrophe in the LXX (Jer 41[34]:1), as is κυκλόω *kykloō* (Jer 52:7 A).

13. The same can be said for Robinson's argument. In showing that the parallels do not match the events of AD 70, his concern is to destroy the prophecy *ex eventu* theory, and so to redate the New Testament. However, his arguments can also be used to underline the interpretation offered above. [2021: See now, in part, Bolt, "Preparing Israel."]

14. Collison, "Eschatology." This is, of course, opposed to those in Conzelmann's tradition who stress that Luke expects a delay. Their distinction between "suddenness" not "imminence" actually amounts to the same thing when understood in the context of the pre-resurrection period in which Jesus exercised his ministry.

God upon him using military symbolism (Job 19:12), and Jeremiah symbolically became "a fortified city" (Jer 1:18–19; 15:20) and later symbolically took on the persona of the besieged city (Lam 3:1–8), so too at the crucifixion, Jesus was "surrounded by armies" (Luke 21:20; cf. 23:35–39), and was "shut up in a besieged city" (Ps 31:21, a Psalm that only Luke records Jesus as quoting from the cross: Luke 23:46, cf. Ps 31:5). The later narrative of Luke reveals that his death was both the day of vengeance on Israel (21:21–24; cf. 23:26–31,48–49) and the day of redemption for Israel (21:28; cf. 24:21,45–49). Luke's narrative also reveals that the Son of Man's kingdom comes in Jerusalem.[15] Luke's peculiar reference to Jesus' "exodus" (9:31) and his "lifting up" (9:51) in the ascension (24:50), confirms that he understood Dan 7:13–14 as fulfilled in these events. In other words, Luke strengthens Mark's apocalypse through using the symbolism drawn from 586 BC to talk of Jesus' death, and maintains the interpretation of the exaltation by means of Dan 7:13–14.[16]

Acts

Luke's second volume provides a unique opportunity to check such an interpretation of his first volume, since it narrates the story which took place after Jesus' death, resurrection and ascension, and yet before the second coming. It is therefore significant that in Acts 7:56 Stephen sees the Son of Man *having already come to the right hand of God* (Luke 22:69; cf. Mark 14:62); that a similar conception of political opposition to that used in the Gospel (Luke 21:20) is used of Jesus' crucifixion (Acts 4:23–30; cf. Psalm 2);[17] and that, on the rare occasions in which the second coming is mentioned, it is never spoken of in terms of the Son of Man coming, but *in*

---

15. He delays reference to the imminence of the Kingdom until the time Jesus heads for Jerusalem (9:27; 10:9,11) after which he stresses the urgent need for faith (18:8), entry (18:16,17,24–27), for recognition of the real king (19:11–27; cf. vv.28–44). His record of the words to the dying thief reinforce that the Kingdom of the Son of Man comes in association with the last events of Jesus' life (23:42–43). [2021: Bolt, "Preparing Israel."]

16. This means that Luke "spiritualizes" all of the main Old Testament events to apply them to Jesus redemptive work: the exodus (Luke 9:31), the fall of Jerusalem (as in text), the return from exile / redemption of Jerusalem (Luke 2:25,38; 21:28; 24:47).

17. Even though the repetition of such a prophecy would have ideally suited the polemic with Judaism of both the apostles within the story and Luke's purpose for the story. It is significant that they choose instead to talk of Jesus' death and resurrection in this context (e.g. 2:36; 3:13–15; 5:30–31; 13:27–31).

different terms altogether (e.g. 3:21; 17:31), or as an extension of what has already occurred (1:11).[18]

Other New Testament Material

John

Further confirmation can be found in the Gospel of John, where the "lifting up" of the Son of Man occurs at "the hour" of Jesus' glorification, namely the death/ resurrection/ ascension.[19] However, when John explicitly mentions the second coming it is not in Son of Man terms (14:3;[20] 21:22–23). It is also significant that there is no mention of the destruction of the physical temple as in AD 70 (whether as a fact or a prophecy)[21] and yet John provides explicit warrant for a symbolic interpretation of Jesus' words regarding the destruction of the temple in terms of his own death and resurrection (2:18–22).[22]

The Epistles

2 Thessalonians 2 is a passage that is often specifically linked to the apocalyptic discourse, although it is debatable whether it is a legitimate parallel.[23]

---

18. The several mentions of the Kingdom as future (14:22; ?19:8; 28:31) certainly emphasize that the consummation is yet to come, but do not deny the fact that the Son of Man has already received the Kingdom in the resurrection/ascension. He has received his Kingdom (cf. Dan 7:1–14), but is yet to share it out with the saints (cf. Dan 7:15–28). It is also significant that this future event is spoken of in terms of this sharing with the saints (e.g. entering kingdom, 14:22; 28:31; salvation, e.g. 16:31; judgement, 17:31; 24:25; inheritance with the saints, 20:32; 26:18; and especially the general resurrection, 23:6; 24:15,21; 26:6-8; 28:20; which began with Jesus' resurrection; cf. 4:2; 25:19; 26:23).

19. Indeed, part of the inspiration for Lightfoot's exploration was the suggestion that this element of the Gospel of John may have derived from Mark's earlier presentation, see "Connexion", 51. [2021: See now Bolt, "What Fruit?"]

20. Note also that here ἔρχομαι *erchomai* is qualified by πάλιν *palin*. This sense then carries over into John 21:22–23.

21. This would have suited the Jewish polemic of both John's Jesus, and John's purpose.

22. The textual variation at Mark 13:2 which interpolates Mark 14:58, appears to parallel this symbolic interpretation offered by John and therefore provides evidence of an early stream of tradition that understood Mark's "temple destruction" saying in a symbolic way, namely of Jesus' death.

23. Wenham, *Rediscovery*, 176–77, suggests that Paul is drawing on a pre-synoptic

Without even attempting any explanation of this difficult passage, I suggest that it should not be used to *interpret* the apocalyptic discourse in Mark, but both passages need to be understood in their own right and then related in whatever way is fitting.

The epistles bear eloquent testimony by their silence, that the fall of Jerusalem was a non-issue, even though such a prediction could have provided a useful weapon in their armoury. They also reveal that the second coming is never spoken of in terms of "the coming of the Son of Man," but always in other ways, usually focusing upon the saints' share. On the other hand, the prevailing talk of Jesus as Lord, confirms the Gospels' picture that the Son of Man comes, receives his kingdom, and begins to reign, seated at the right hand of God (cf. Mark 14:62). In other words, the Son of Man category is no longer used, for his work is completed and he is now reigning in terms of Ps 110:1 "until all his enemies are placed under his feet."

Revelation

In regard to the book of Revelation, I simply note that the interpretation of the Gospels offered here also fits well with this book. Jesus as ascended Son of Man is in view from the beginning.[24] Once the position of Jesus is established, then all else in the book is implication. It is also clear that Revelation works out the twofold pattern of Daniel 7, in that it clearly shows that Jesus is the Son of Man, who has received the Kingdom, but the saints are yet to share in that Kingdom. Although the Son of Man is already victorious, the cry of the book is towards the day when that victory is ultimately shared with the saints (cf. 6:10; 22:20).

---

eschatological discourse. However, this is not necessary. If, as I have argued above, Jesus delivers his discourse as an address to his disciples, using "last days" categories drawn from the Old Testament, it would not be unusual for Paul to use similar language and warnings to address his hearers once it has become plain that the last days began with Jesus' death and resurrection, and that they abide still until his return.

24. 1:7 should be taken as a quotation in support of the fact that Dan 7:13 is fulfilled already in Jesus, as the book goes on to show (e.g. 1:13; 5:1–14).

APPENDIX 2

A Brief Note on T. J. Geddert, *Watchwords*

COMING TO MY ATTENTION on the eve of the submission of my original thesis, T.J. Geddert, *Watchwords. Mark 13 in Markan Eschatology* shares the same aim, namely, to understand Mark 13 in the context of Mark's Gospel, and independently arrives at many of the same conclusions.

The Points of Agreement

As well as many points of agreement in detail, Geddert also argues for the following significant points:

1. that the disciples' request in Mark 13:4 must be read against Mark's previous negative presentation of sign-seeking, that Jesus corrects this attitude in the following discourse, and that 13:1–4 therefore does *not* set the agenda of the chapter;

2. that Mark 13 needs to be set in the context of the leadership clash between Jesus and the Jewish leadership, and that chapters 11–12 are not explicitly concerned with the temple, but about this clash of leadership. We differ in that Geddert hypothesizes that this implies an attack upon the Temple as well, whereas I prefer to remain with what the text encourages explicitly;

3. that the passion narrative is constructed deliberately on the basis of Mark 13:33–37, and that Jesus' death is "the Day of eschatological fulfillment *par excellence*" (p.199), the "first fulfillment of that Day and

the Hour" (pp.106, n.57, 107–108), "on one level at least" (p.104, n.51). Where we differ is that Geddert qualifies this, like Lightfoot, with the adjective *first* and with the words "on one level at least," whereas I have argued that this is the *only fulfillment that the text actually encourages*;

4. that Jesus is recruiting the disciples to be part of the faithful remnant of Israel, although the subsequent events reveal that Jesus ends up being the only representative of that group, and that Jesus himself, being included as one who is ignorant of the End at this stage, also shares the need to be watchful (13:32–37) for he acts not as the Master, but as one of the servants.

The Differences

Assumptions

Although agreeing on many points about the context in which Mark 13 is to be read, the fundamental difference with Geddert is over Mark 13 itself. Perhaps due to the constraints of the interpretive community in which he reads,[1] my contention is that Geddert does not read Mark 13 consistently with his understanding of the context. His reading of Mark 13 simply assumes previous interpretations on fundamental matters, which ought to be thrown wide open by his observations on the Markan context. It is disappointing that he assumes without argument that Mark 13:5–23 addresses the post-resurrection context; that he still reads the destruction of the temple as a major issue in Mark 13:14–23, despite obliterating it from the context and admitting that the reasons for finding it in Mark 13 are meager indeed (pp.205–07); and that he assumes 13:24–27 to be about the parousia without offering any arguments at all, (and not even interacting with the position of France, et al).

Mark's "Temple Theology"?

In the discussion of Mark 13, Geddert ignores the implications of his own argument on chapters 11–12. There, he argued that the leadership struggle was the issue, and, when allowing the destruction of the temple as merely

---

[1]. This is not meant as a criticism, merely a possible explanation. For the restraints of the interpretive community, see Fish, *Is There a Text?*

APPENDIX 2: A BRIEF NOTE ON T. J. GEDDERT, *WATCHWORDS*

an implication of this struggle he used a series of hypothetical-type words. However, in the subsequent discussion of Mark 13, the destruction of the temple somehow gained the exalted status of "Mark's temple destruction theology" and is burdened with tremendous significance, on a par with that of the resurrection! Reading between the lines, the only real textual support that Geddert can find for any temple destruction is 13:2, and if this is read, as I have done, as a passing remark by Jesus that the much-revered temple is part of the creation that is passing away, rather than a specific "prediction of AD 70," this verse is little support for such exalted theologizing of that later event in Jewish history.

Mark's Ambiguity

Geddert's major point is that much of Mark 13 is intentionally ambiguous. Although I go along with this to some degree, I would analyze this observation differently:

1. Jesus' call to discernment is usually directed to a better christological understanding, and not into the significance of other events (such as the temple destruction), and so this observation can support my reading;

2. If the suggestion is true that Mark 13 is deliberately ambiguous in order to prevent people asking the "when" questions, then Mark/Jesus has chosen exactly the wrong method. Ambiguity does not stop people asking questions, but, on the contrary, it *forces* them to ask questions. Once a writer has introduced puzzles, it is a sound assumption that their story will also provide answers for those puzzles. In addition, in Mark the *when* question is not wrong, but the *signs* question is wrong. In fact, the when question was asked in 9:9-13 and Jesus answered plainly "the kingdom comes after the Son of Man suffers." In Mark 13, it is asked and answered in apocalyptic guise with exactly the same answer.

3. Geddert's evidence of ambiguity is most often derived from a lack of scholarly consensus over interpretation. There is no doubt that this is a helpful procedure (cf. the masterly use of it by S.E. Fish, *Surprised by Sin*), but I have argued that the text of Mark 13 is understood quite readily, but it's plain meaning is then dismissed *because that meaning*

doesn't fit with the common scholarly assumptions about the historical referent(s) of the chapter;

4. Apparently this is also the case for Geddert. Despite persistently feeling the connection of Mark 13 with the passion narrative, and even despite being prepared to say that it is *fulfilled* in the events of the passion narrative, albeit in a qualified sense ("first," "on one level"), the constraints of a particular interpretive community, desperately trying to find theological significance in AD 70, apparently hold sway. However, the arguments in this work suggest that that particular interpretive community ought to glory in the theological significance of the events of some 40 years earlier—as should the interpretive community centred finding the parousia in Mark 13.

The Dynamics of Reading

Although Geddert's contribution to the understanding of Mark's narrative is excellent, it fails to pay adequate attention to the dynamics of reading operative in the story. This is evident, for example, when he is too quickly side-tracked by his assumptions that apply Mark 13 to the post-resurrection context without firstly analysing it as part of the story. Although Mark 13 does end up saying something about the post-resurrection context, I have suggested that this occurs by a much more profound means than simply addressing it outright with no regard for the original context of utterance. It is also evident in the desire to apply the passion narrative to discipleship in the post-resurrection period, sometimes almost at the expense of its primary story, namely the passion itself. Although Jesus' passion may well be a paradigm for later servants, it is first and foremost to be read as the story of The Servant.

Bibliography

Albertz, Martin. *Die synoptischen Streitgespräche: ein Beitrag zur Formengeschichte des Urchristentums*. Berlin, Trowitzsch, 1921.
Alexander, Joseph A. *A Commentary on the Gospel of Mark*. Geneva and Edinburgh: Banner of Truth, 1858, reprint 1960.
Allen, Willoughby C. *The Gospel according to St Mark with Introduction and Notes*. London: Rivington, 1915.
Anderson, George W. *A Critical Introduction to the Old Testament*. Studies in Theology. London: Duckworth, 1959.
Anderson, Hugh. *The Gospel of Mark*. New Century Bible. London: Oliphants, 1976.
Anderson, Janice Capel. "Double and Triple Stories, The Implied Reader, and Redundancy in Matthew", *Semeia* 31 (1985) 71–89.
Bailey, Kenneth E. "The Fall of Jerusalem and Mark's Account of the Cross", *ExpT* 102.4 (1991) 102–105.
Barclay, William. *The Gospel of Mark*. Daily Study Bible. Edinburgh: St Andrew, 1954, ²1956.
Barrois, Georges A. "Zion", *IDB*, IV.959–60.
Barth, Karl. *Church Dogmatics* III.2. Translated by Harold Knight et al. Edinburgh: T&T Clark, 1960 [German: 1948].
———. *Church Dogmatics* IV.4. Translated by Geoffrey W. Bromiley. Edinburgh: T&T Clark, 1969 [German: 1967].
Bartlet, J.V. *St Mark*. Century Bible. Edinburgh: Jack, 1925.
Barton, John. *Reading the Old Testament: Method in Biblical Study*. London: Darton, Longman & Todd, 1984.
Bassler, Jouette M. "The Parable of the Loaves", *JR* 66.2 (1986) 157–72.
Beasley-Murray, George R. *A Commentary on Mark 13*. London: Macmillan, 1957.
———. "Jesus and Apocalyptic: With Special Reference to Mark 14,62", *L'Apocalypse Johanique et l'Apocalyptique dans le Nouveau Testament*, edited by Jan Lambrecht, 415–29. Gembloux: Duculot, 1980.

———. *Jesus and the Future. An Examination of the Criticism of the Eschatological Discourse, Mark 13, with Special Reference to the Little Apocalypse Theory*. London: Macmillan, 1954.

———. *Jesus and the Kingdom of God*. Grand Rapids and Exeter: Eerdmans and Paternoster, 1986.

Best, Ernest. *Following Jesus: Discipleship in the Gospel of Mark*. JSNTSup 4. Sheffield: JSOT, 1981.

———. "Jesus as the one who cares", *Mark. The Gospel as Story*, 55–65. Edinburgh: T&T Clark, 1983.

———. "The Role of the Disciples in Mark", *Disciples and Discipleship: Studies in the Gospel according to Mark*, 98–130. Edinburgh: T&T Clark, 1986.

Bird, C.H. "Some γάρ Clauses in St. Mark's Gospel", *JTS* ns 4 (1953) 171–87.

Bleich, David. *Readers and Feelings: an Introduction to Subjective Criticism*. Urbana: National Council of Teachers of English, 1975.

———. *Subjective Criticism*. Baltimore: Johns Hopkins University Press, 1978.

Blomberg, Craig L. "Synoptic Studies: Some Recent Developments and Debates", *Themelios* 12.2 (1987) 38–45.

Blunt, Arthur W.F. *The Gospel according to Saint Mark*. Oxford: Clarendon, 1929, ²1940.

———. *The Gospel and the Critic*. London: Oxford University Press, 1936.

Bolt, Peter G. *The Cross from a Distance. Atonement in Mark's Gospel* (NSBT 18). Leicester: IVP, 2004.

———. "The Faith of Jesus Christ: Synoptics & Acts", *The Faith of Jesus Christ: Exegetical, Biblical, and Theological Studies*, edited by Michael F. Bird and Preston M. Sprinkle, 209–222. Peabody & Carlisle: Hendrickson & Paternoster, 2009.

———. "Feeling the Cross: Mark's Message of Atonement", *RefThR* 60.1 (2001) 1–17.

———. *Jesus' Defeat of Death. Persuading Mark's Early Readers*. Society of New Testament Studies Monograph Series 125. Cambridge: Cambridge University Press, 2003.

———. "Mark 13: An Apocalyptic Precursor to the Passion Narrative", *RefThR* 54.1 (1995) 10–32.

———. *Matthew. A Great Light Dawns*. Reading the Bible Today Series. Sydney South: Aquila, 2014.

———. "Preparing Israel for the Arrival of the Son of Man. Jesus' Kingship Parable (Luke 19:11–28) in its Historical and Literary Context", *Journal of Gospels and Acts Research* 1 (2017) 23–41.

———. "The Spirit in the Synoptic Gospels: the Equipment of the Servant", *Spirit of the Living God, Part 1*, edited by Barry G. Webb, 45–75. Explorations 5. Homebush West, Lancer, 1991.

———. "What Fruit does the Vine Bear? Some Pastoral Implications of St John 15:1–8", *RefThR* 51.1 (1992) 11–19.

———. "What is the gospel for Today's Church?", *Exploring the Missionary Church*, edited by B.G. Webb, 27–61. Explorations 7. Homebush West: Lancer, 1993.

———. "What Were the Sadducees Reading? An Enquiry into the Literary Background to Mark 12:18–23", *TynBul* 45.2 (1994) 369–94.

———. "'With a View to the Forgiveness of Sins': Jesus and Forgiveness in Mark's Gospel", *RefThR* 57.2 (1998), 53–69.

Boomershine, Thomas E., and Gilbert L. Bartholomew. "The Narrative Technique of Mark 16:8", *JBL* 100.2 (1981) 213–223.

Boomershine, Thomas E. "Biblical Megatrends: Towards a paradigm for the Interpretation of the Bible in Electronic Media", *SBL 1987 Seminar Papers*, edited by Kent H. Richards, 144–55. Atlanta: Scholars, 1987.
———. "Mark 16:8 and the Apostolic Commission", *JBL* 100.2 (1981) 225–39.
———. "Peter's Denial as Polemic or Confession: The implications of Media Criticism for Biblical Hermeneutics", *Semeia* 39 (1987) 47–68.
———. *Story Journey: An Introduction to the Gospel as Storytelling*. Nashville: Abingdon, 1988.
Booth, Wayne C. *The Company We Keep. An Ethics of Fiction*. Berkeley: University of California Press, 1988.
———. *The Rhetoric of Fiction*. Chicago: University of Chicago Press, 1961, ²1983.
———. *A Rhetoric of Irony*. Chicago & London: University of Chicago Press, 1974.
Bowker, John W. "Mystery and Parable: Mark iv.1–20", *JTS* 25 (1974) 300–317.
Bowman, John. *The Gospel of Mark. The New Christian Jewish Passover Haggadah*. Leiden: E. J. Brill, 1965.
Brandon, Samuel G.F. "The Date of the Markan Gospel", *NTS* 7 (1960–61) 126–41.
———. *The Fall of Jerusalem and the Christian Church: a Study of the Effects of the Jewish Overthrow of AD 70 on Christianity*. London: SPCK, 1951, ²1957.
Branscomb, B. Harvie. *The Gospel of Mark*. London: Hodder & Stoughton, 1937.
Brower, Kent E. "'Let the Reader Understand': Temple and Eschatology in Mark", *The Reader Must Understand. Eschatology in Bible and Theology*, edited by Kent E. Brower and Mark W. Elliott, 119–143. Leicester: IVP, 1998.
Brown, Raymond E. "The Burial of Jesus (Mark 15:42–47)", *CBQ* 50.2 (1988) 233–245.
Bruce, F.F. *New Testament History*. New York: Doubleday, 1969, ²1980.
Bultmann, Rudolf. *The History of the Synoptic Tradition*. Translated by J. Marsh. Oxford: Blackwell, 1963.
———. "The Study of the Synoptic Gospels", *Form Criticism*. Translated by Frederick C. Grant. New York: Harper, 1934.
Burkill, T.A. "Strain on the Secret: An Examination of Mark 11:1—13:37", *ZNTW* 51.1–2 (1960) 31–46.
Burnett, Frederick W. "Prolegomenon to reading Matthew's Eschatological Discourse: Redundancy and the education of the reader in Matthew", *Semeia* 31 (1985) 91–109.
Buse, I. "The Markan Account of the Baptism of Jesus and Isaiah LXIII", *JTS* 7 (1956) 74–75.
Butterworth, R. "The Composition of Mark 1–12," *HeyJ* 13 (1972) 5–26.
Caird, George B. *The Language and Imagery of the Bible*. London and Philadelphia: Duckworth and Westminster, 1980.
Calvin, John. *Commentary on a Harmony of the Evangelists*. 3 volumes. Translated by William H. Pringle. Grand Rapids: Baker, 1845 [original: 1555], reprint 1979.
Carson, Donald A. *Exegetical Fallacies*. Grand Rapids: Baker, 1984.
———. "Recent developments in the Doctrine of Scripture", *Hermeneutics, Authority and Canon*, edited by Donald A. Carson and John D. Woodbridge, 1–48. Leicester: IVP, 1986.
———. "Matthew", *The Expositors Bible Commentary*, edited by F.E. Gaebelein, 8.3–602. Grand Rapids: Zondervan, 1984.
Chatman, Seymour. *Story and Discourse: Narrative Structure in Fiction and Film*. Ithaca: Cornell University Press, 1978.
Cohen, Ralph. "History and Genre", *New Literary History* 17.2 (1986) 203–18.

Cole, R. Alan. *The Gospel according to St Mark*. Tyndale New Testament Commentary. Grand Rapids: Eerdmans, 1961, reprint 1980.
Collins, John J. "The Jewish Apocalypses", *Semeia* 14 (1979) 21–59.
———. "Towards a Morphology of a Genre", *Semeia* 14 (1979) 1–19.
———. "The Son of Man and the Saints of the Most High in the Book of Daniel", *JBL* 93 (1974) 50–66.
Collison, J.G.F. "Eschatology in the Gospel of Luke", *New Synoptic Studies*, edited by William R. Farmer, 363–71. Macon: Mercer University Press, 1983.
Combrink, H.J.B. "The Structure of the Gospel of Matthew as Narrative", *TynB* 34 (1983) 61–88.
Cranfield, C.E.B. *The Gospel according to St Mark*. Cambridge: Cambridge University Press, 1959, reprint 1979.
Crotty, Robert B. *Good News in Mark*. Glasgow: Fontana, 1975.
Cuddon, J.A., ed. *A Dictionary of Literary Terms*. Harmondsworth: Penguin, 1977, reprint 1986.
Cullmann, Oscar. *The Christology of the New Testament*. Translated by Shirley C. Guthrie and Charles A.M. Hall. London: SCM, 1959 [German: 1957].
———. "The Return of Christ", *The Early Church*, edited by Angus J. B. Higgins, 152–54. London: SCM, 1956.
Daube, David. "Four Types of Question", *JTS ns* 2 (1951) 45–48.
Delling, Gerhard. "κολοβόω", *TDNT*, 3.823–24.
Derrett, J. Duncan M. *The Making of Mark. The Scriptural Bases of the Earliest Gospel*. 2 volumes. Shipston-on-Stour: Drinkwater, 1985.
Detweiler, Robert. "What is a Sacred Text ?", *Semeia* 31 (1985) 213–30.
Dewey, Joanna. *Markan Public Debate*. SBLDS 48. Chico: Scholars Press, 1980.
———. "Point of View and the Disciples in Mark", *SBL 1982 Seminar* Papers, edited by Kent H. Richards, 97–106. Chico: Scholars, 1982.
Dibelius, Martin. *From Tradition to Gospel*. Translated by B.L. Woolff. London: Nicholson & Watson, 1934 [German: 1919].
———. *The Message of Jesus*. London: Nicholson & Watson, 1939.
Dodd, Charles H. *The Apostolic Preaching and its Developments*. London: Hodder & Stoughton, 1936.
———. "The Fall of Jerusalem and the 'Abomination of Desolation'", *More New Testament Studies*, 69–83. Manchester: Manchester University Press, 1968.
———. *The Parables of the Kingdom*. London: Collins, 1935, ²1961.
Donahue, John R. *The Gospel in Parable: Metaphor, Narrative, and Theology in the Synoptic Gospels*. Philadelphia: Fortress, 1988.
———. "A Neglected Factor in the Theology of Mark", *JBL* 101.4 (1982) 563–94.
Dumbrell, William J. *Covenant and Creation. An Old Testament Covenantal Theology*. Exeter: Paternoster, 1984.
———. "Daniel 7 and the Function of Old Testament Apocalyptic", *RefThR* 34.1 (1975) 16–23.
———. *The End of the Beginning: Revelation 21–22 and the Old Testament*. Homebush West: Lancer, 1985.
———. *The Faith of Israel: Its Expression in the Books of the Old Testament*. Leicester: Apollos [IVP], 1989.
———. "The Purpose of the Book of Isaiah", *TynBul* 36 (1985) 111–28.
———. "The Role of the Servant in Isaiah 40–55", *RefThR* 48.3 (1989) 105–13.

———. "Some Observations on the Political Origins of Israel's Eschatology", *RefThR* 36.2 (1977) 33–41.

Dyer, Keith D. "'But Concerning *that* Day' (Mark 13:32). 'Prophetic' and 'Apocalyptic' Eschatology in Mark 13", *SBL Seminar Papers 1999*, 104–122. Atlanta: Scholars, 1999.

———. *The Prophecy on the Mount. Mark 13 and the Gathering of the New Community*, Bern: Peter Lang, 1998.

Earle, Ralph. *The Gospel of Mark*. London: Oliphants, 1962.

Edwards, James R. "Markan Sandwiches: The Significance of Interpolations in Markan Narratives", *NovT* 21.3 (1989) 193–216.

Ellis, E. Earle. *The Gospel of Luke*. New Century Bible. London: Oliphants, 1974.

———. "How the New Testament uses the Old", *New Testament Interpretation: Essays on Principles and Methods*, edited by I. Howard Marshall, 119–219. Exeter: Paternoster, 1979.

Evans, Craig A. "Jesus' Action in the Temple: Cleansing or Portent of Destruction", *CBQ* 51.2 (1989) 237–70.

Fenton, John C. *Preaching the Cross. The Passion and Resurrection according to St Mark*. London: SPCK, 1958.

Ferguson, Sinclair B. *Understanding the Gospel*. Eastbourne: Kingsway, 1989.

Fish, Stanley E. *Is there a Text in this Class? The Authority of Interpretive Communities*. Cambridge: Harvard University Press, 1980.

———. *Self-consuming Artifacts: The Experience of Seventeenth-Century Literature*. Berkeley: University of California Press, 1972.

———. *Surprised by Sin: the Reader in Paradise Lost*. Berkeley: University of California Press, 1967, ²1971.

Fleddermann, Harry T. "The Discipleship Discourse (Mark 9:33–50)", *CBQ* 43.1 (1981) 57–75.

———. "A Warning about the Scribes (Mark 12:37b–40)", *CBQ* 44.1 (1982) 52–67.

Fowler, Robert M. *Let the Reader Understand: Reader Response Criticism and the Gospel of Mark*. Philadelphia: Fortress, 1991.

———. *Loaves and Fishes: The Function of the Feeding Stories in the Gospel of Mark*. Chico: Scholars, 1981.

———. "Reading Matthew Reading Mark: Observing the First Steps toward Meaning-as-Reference in the Synoptic Gospels", *SBL 1986 Seminar* Papers, edited by Kent H. Richards, 1–16. Atlanta: Scholars, 1986.

———. "The Rhetoric of Direction and Indirection in the Gospel of Mark", *Semeia* 48 (1989) 115–34.

———. "Using Literary Criticism on the Gospels", *ChrCent* (26 May, 1982) 626–29.

———. "Who is 'the Reader' in Reader Response Criticism?", *Semeia* 31 (1985) 5–23.

———. "Who is 'the Reader' of Mark's Gospel ?", *SBL 1983 Seminar* Papers, edited by Kent H. Richards, 31–53. Chico: Scholars, 1983.

France, Richard T. *Divine Government: God's Kingship in the Gospel of Mark*. London & Homebush West: SPCK & Lancer, 1990.

———. *Jesus and the Old Testament. His Application of Old Testament Passages to Himself and His Mission*. Grand Rapids: Baker reprint, 1982 [1971].

Gaston, Lloyd. *No Stone on Another: Studies in the Significance of the Fall of Jerusalem in the Synoptic Gospels*. NovTSup 23. Leiden: Brill, 1970.

Geddert, Timothy J. *Watchwords. Mark 13 in Markan Eschatology*. JSNTSup 26. Sheffield: JSOT, 1989.

Genette, Gerard. *Narrative Discourse: An Essay in Method*. Translated by Jane E. Lewin. Ithaca: Cornell University Press, 1980.
Goldsworthy, Graeme L. *Gospel and Kingdom: A Christian Interpretation of the Old Testament*. Exeter: Paternoster, 1981, reprint, 1984.
———. *Preaching the Whole Bible as Christian Scripture: The Application of Biblical Theology to Expository Preaching*. Grand Rapids: Eerdmans, 2000.
Goodwin, Harvey. *A Commentary on the Gospel of S. Mark*. Cambridge: Deighton, Bell & Co, 1860.
Gould, Ezra P. *The Gospel according to St Mark*. International Critical Commentary. Edinburgh: T & T Clark, 1897.
Grassi, Joseph A. "Abba, Father (Mark 14:36): Another Approach", *JAAR* 50.3 (1982) 449–58.
Gros Louis, Kenneth R.R. "The Gospel of Mark", *Literary Interpretations of Biblical Narratives*, edited by Kenneth R.R. Gros Louis et al., 296–329. Nashville: Abingdon, 1974.
Guelich, Robert A. *Mark 1—8:26*. Word Biblical Commentary 34A. Waco: Word, 1989.
Gutting, Gary, ed. *Paradigms and Revolutions: Applications and Appraisals of Thomas Kuhn's Philosophy of Science*. London: University of Notre Dame Press, 1980.
Hanson, Paul D. *The Dawn of Apocalyptic*. Philadelphia: Fortress, 1975.
———. "Apocalypse, Genre", *IDBSup*, 27–28. Nashville: Abingdon, 1976.
———. "Apocalypticism", *IDBSup*, 28–34. Nashville: Abingdon, 1976.
———. "Old Testament Apocalyptic Reexamined", *Int* 25.4 (1971) 454–479.
Hargreaves, John. *A Guide to St Mark's Gospel*. London: SPCK, 1969.
Harrington, Wilfrid J. *Mark*. Wilmington: Glazier, 1979.
Hartman, Lars. "Survey of the Problem of Apocalyptic Genre", *Apocalypticism in the Mediterranean World and the Near East: Proceedings of the International Colloquium on Apocalypticism. Uppsala, August 12–17, 1979*, edited by David Hellholm, 330–43. Tubingen: Mohr, 1983.
Head, Peter M. "A Text-Critical Study of Mark 1.1 'The Beginning of the Gospel of Jesus Christ'", *NTS* 37.4 (1991) 621–29.
Hendriksen, William. *The Gospel of Mark*. Edinburgh: Banner of Truth, 1975.
Hengel, Martin. *Studies in the Gospel of Mark*. London: SCM, 1985.
Holland, Norman N. *5 Readers Reading*. New Haven: Yale University Press, 1975.
———. "UNITY IDENTITY TEXT SELF", *Publications of the Modern Language Association* 90 (1975) 813–22.
Hollenbach, Bruce. "Lest they should turn and be forgiven: Irony", *Bible Translator* 34.3 (1983) 312–21.
Hood, Jason B. "Evangelicals and the Imitation of the Cross: Peter Bolt on Mark 13 as a Test Case", *Evangelical Quarterly* 81.2 (2009) 116–25.
Hooker, Morna D. *Jesus the Servant*. London: SPCK, 1959.
———. "Trial and Tribulation in Mark XIII", *BJRL* 65.1 (1982) 78–99.
Hunter, Archibald M. *The Gospel according to St Mark*. London: SCM, 1948.
———. *Interpreting the Parables*. London: SCM, 1960, ²1964.
Hurtado, Larry W. *Mark*. Good News Commentary. San Francisco, Harper & Row, 1983.
Iser, Wolfgang. "Interaction between text and reader", *The Reader in the Text. Essays on Audience and Interpretation*, edited by Susan R. Suleiman and Inge Crosman, 106–19. Princeton: Princeton University Press, 1980.

———. "The Reading Process: A phenomenological Approach", *New Literary History* 3 (1972) 272-99.
Jackson, Howard M. "The Death of Jesus in Mark and the Miracle from the Cross", *NTS* 33.1 (1987) 16-37.
Jauss, Hans R. *Towards an Aesthetics of Reception*. Translated by Timothy Bahti. Minneapolis: University of Minnesota Press, 1982.
Jeremias, Joiachim. *The Parables of Jesus*. Translated by Samuel H. Hooke. London: SCM, ³1972 [German: 1962].
Johnson, Earl S. "Is Mark 15:39 the Key to Mark's Christology?", *JSNT* 31 (1987) 3-22.
Johnson, Sherman E. *The Gospel according to St Mark*. London: Black, 1960.
Jones, Alexander. *The Gospel according to St Mark*. London: Chapman, 1963.
Kaiser, Walter C. *Toward an Exegetical Theology: Biblical Exegesis for Preaching and Teaching*. Grand Rapids: Baker, 1981.
Kee, Howard C. "The Function of Scriptural Quotations and Allusions in Mark 11-16", *Jesus und Paulus. Festschrift für Werner Georg Kümmel zum 70 Geburtstag*, edited by E. Earle Ellis and Erich Grässer, 165-88. Göttingen: Vandenhoeck & Ruprecht, 1975.
Kelber, Werner H. *The Kingdom in Mark: a New Place, a New Time*. Philadelphia: Fortress, 1974.
Kilpatrick, George D. "BLEPETE PHILIPPIANS 3_2", *In Memoriam Paul Kahle*, edited by Matthew Black and Georg Fohrer, 145-48. Berlin: Töpelmann, 1968.
———. "The Gentile Mission in Mark and Mk 13:9-11", *Studies in the Gospels. Essays in Memory of R.H. Lightfoot*, edited by Dennis E. Nineham, 145-58. Oxford: B. Blackwell, 1955.
Kingsbury, Jack D. *Conflict in Mark: Jesus, Authorities, Disciples*. Minneapolis: Fortress, 1989.
Kistemaker, Simon J. *The Parables of Jesus*. Grand Rapids: Baker, 1980.
Kuhn, Thomas S. *The Structure of Scientific Revolutions*. Chicago: University of Chicago Press: 1962, 1970.
Kümmel, W.G. *Introduction to the New Testament*. Translated by Howard C. Kee. London: SCM, 1975 [German: 1973].
Lambrecht, Jan. *Die Redaktion der Markus-Apokalypse: Literarische Analyse und Strukturuntersuchung*. Analecta Biblica 28. Rome: Pontifical Biblical Institute, 1967.
Lane, William L. *The Gospel of Mark*. New International Commentary on the New Testament. Grand Rapids: Eerdmans, 1974.
Licht, Jacob. *Storytelling in the Bible*. Jerusalem: Magnes, 1978.
Lightfoot, Robert H. "The Connexion of Chapter Thirteen with the Passion Narrative", *The Gospel Message of St Mark*, 48-59. Oxford: Clarendon, 1950.
———. "The Content of the Gospel according to St. Mark", *History and Interpretation in the Gospels*, 97-125. London: Hodder & Stoughton, 1935.
———. "The Passion Narrative in St Mark", *History and Interpretation in the Gospels*, 126-51. London: Hodder & Stoughton, 1935.
Long, Thomas G. "Shaping Sermons by Plotting the Text's Claim Upon Us", *Preaching Biblically: Creating Sermons in the Shape of Scripture*, edited by Don M. Wardlaw, 84-100. Philadelphia: Westminster, 1983.
Lundin, Roger, Anthony C. Thistleton, and Clarence Walhout. *The Responsibility of Hermeneutics*. Grand Rapids and Exeter: Eerdmans and Paternoster, 1985.
McCown, Chester C. "Hebrew and Egyptian Apocalyptic Literature", *HTR* 18 (1925) 357-411.

BIBLIOGRAPHY

McNicol, Allan J. "The Lesson of the Fig Tree in Mark 13:28-32: A Comparison Between Two Exegetical Methodologies", *Rest Q* 27.4 (1984) 193-207.
Mailloux, Steven. *Interpretive Conventions: The Reader in the Study of American Fiction*. Ithaca: Cornell University Press, 1982.
Malbon, Elizabeth Struthers. "Galilee and Jerusalem: History and Literature in Marcan Interpretation", *CBQ* 44.2 (1982) 242-55.
———. "The Jesus of Mark and the Sea of Galilee", *JBL* 103.3 (1984) 363-77.
Manson, Thomas W. *The Teaching of Jesus. Studies in its Form and Content*. Cambridge: Cambridge University Press, 1943, 1945.
Marcus, Joel. "Are You the Messiah-Son-Of-God?", *NovT* 31.2 (1989) 125-41.
Marshall, Christopher D. *Faith as a Theme in Mark's Narrative*. Society of New Testament Studies Monograph Series 64. Cambridge: Cambridge University Press, 1989.
Marshall, I. Howard, ed. *New Testament Interpretation: Essays on Principles and Methods*. Exeter: Paternoster, 1979.
Martin, Ralph P. *Mark: Evangelist and Theologian*. Exeter: Paternoster, 1972.
Meagher, John C. *Clumsy Construction in Mark's Gospel. A Critique of Form- and Redaktionsgeschichte*. Toronto Studies in Theology 3. New York: Mellen, 1979.
———. "Die Form- und Redaktionsungeschickliche Methoden: The Principle of Clumsiness and the Gospel of Mark", *JAAR* 43.3 (1975) 459-72.
Moiser, Jeremy. "'She was twelve years old' (Mk 5:42). A note on Jewish-Gentile Controversy in Mark's Gospel", *IBS* 3.4 (1981) 179-86.
Moo, Douglas J. "The Problem of Sensus Plenior", *Hermeneutics, Authority and Canon*, edited by Donald A. Carson & John D. Woodbridge, 175-212. Leicester: IVP, 1986.
Moule, Charles F.D. *An Idiom Book of the New Testament*. Cambridge: Cambridge University Press, 1953, 21959.
Morris, Leon L. *Apocalyptic*. Grand Rapids: Eerdmans, 1972, reprint 1984.
Moore, Stephen D. *Literary Criticism and the Gospels: The Theoretical Challenge*. New Haven and London: Yale University Press, 1989.
Murray, Gregory. "The Questioning of Jesus", *DownRev* 102.349 (1984) 271-75.
Nardoni, Enrique. "A Redactional Interpretation of Mark 9:1", *CBQ* 43.3 (1981) 365-84.
Nineham, Dennis E. *Saint Mark*. Harmondsworth: Penguin, 1963, reprint 1981.
O'Connell, B. "The Potter's Oracle", *AncSociety* 13/3 (1983) 151-60.
Oepke, Albrecht. "παρουσία, πάρειμι", *TDNT* 5.858-71.
Osburn, Carroll D. "The Historical Present in Mark as a Text-Critical Criterion", *Biblica* 64.4 (1983) 486-500.
Patte, Daniel. *What is Structural Exegesis?*. Philadelphia: Fortress, 1976.
Perrin, Norman. "The High Priest's Question and Jesus' Answer (Mark 14:61-62)", *The Passion in Mark*, edited by Werner H. Kelber, 80-95. Philadelphia: Fortress, 1976.
Pesch, Rudolf. *Naherwartungen: Tradition und Redaktion in Markus 13*. Dusseldorf: Patmos, 1968.
Petersen, Norman R. *Literary Criticism for New Testament Critics*. Philadelphia: Fortress, 1975.
———. "The Reader in the Gospel", *Neot* 18 (1984) 38-51.
———. "When is the End not the End?: Literary Reflections on the Ending of Mark's Narrative", *Int* 34.2 (1980) 151-66.
Porter, Stanley E. "Why Hasn't Reader-Response Criticism Caught on in New Testament Studies ?", *JLit & Theol* 4.3 (1990) 278-92.
Prince, Gerald. "Introduction to the Study of the Narratee", *Poetique* 14 (1973) 177-96.

Radcliffe, Timothy. "'The Coming of the Son of Man'. Mark's Gospel and the subversion of 'the apocalyptic imagination'", *Language, Meaning and God: Essays in honour of Herbert McCabe O.P.*, edited by B. Davies, 176–89. London: Chapman, 1987.

Räisänen, Heikki. "The 'Messianic Secret' in Mark's Gospel", *The Messianic Secret*, edited by Christopher M. Tuckett, 132–40. Issues in Religion and Theology 1. Philadelphia & London: Fortress & SPCK, 1983.

———. *The 'Messianic Secret' in Mark's Gospel*. Studies in the New Testament and its World. Translated by Christopher M. Tuckett. Edinburgh: T&T Clark, 1976, ET 1990.

Reicke, Bo. "Synoptic Prophecies on the Destruction of Jerusalem", *Studies in the New Testament and Early Christian Literature*, edited by David E. Aune, 121–34. Leiden: Brill, 1972.

Resseguie, James L. "Reader-Response Criticism and the Synoptic Gospels", *JAAR* LII.2 (1984) 307–24.

Rimmon-Kenan, Shlomith. *Narrative Fiction: Contemporary Poetics*. New Accents. London & New York: Methuen, 1983.

Rist, Martin. "Apocalypticism", *IDB*, I.157–61.

Roberts, Jimmy J. M. "Zion Tradition", *IDBSup*, 985–86.

Robertson, D. "Literature, the Bible as", *IDBSup*, 547–551.

Robinson, John A. T. *Jesus and His Coming. The Emergence of a Doctrine*. London: SCM, 1957.

———. *Redating the New Testament*. London: SCM, 1976.

———. "The Second Coming—Mark xiv.62", *ExpT* 67.11 (1956) 336–40.

Robbins, Vernon K. "A Rhetorical Typology for Classifying and Analyzing Pronouncement Stories", *SBL Seminar 1984 Papers*, edited by Kent H. Richards, 93–122. Chico: Scholars, 1984.

Rowley, Harold H. *The Relevance of Apocalyptic. A Study of Jewish and Christian Apocalypses from Daniel to Revelation*. London: Lutterworth, 1963.

Sandmel, Samuel. "Parallelomania", *JBL* 81 (1962) 2–13.

Savran, George W. *Telling and Retelling—Quotation in Biblical Narrative*. Bloomington: Indiana University Press, 1988.

Schneidau, Herbert N. "Let the Reader Understand", *Semeia* 39 (1987) 135–45.

Schneider, Carl. "κάθημαι κτλ", *TDNT*, III.440–44.

Schrenk, Gottlob. "ἱερος κτλ", *TDNT*, III.221–83.

Schweizer, Eduard. *The Good News according to Mark*. Translated by D.H. Madrig. London: SPCK, 1971.

Scott, R.B.Y. "Summer and Winter", *IDB*, IV.463.

Silva, Moisés. "The New Testament Use of The Old Testament: Text Form and Authority", *Scripture and Truth*, edited by Donald A. Carson & John D. Woodbridge, 147–72. Leicester: IVP, 1983.

Slawinski, J. "Reading & Reader in the Literary Historical Process", *New Literary History* 19.3 (1988) 521–39.

Smith, Marion. "The Composition of Mark 11–16", *HeyJ* 22.4 (1981) 363–77.

Smith, Stephen H. "The Literary Structure of Mark 11:1—12:40", *NovT* 31.2 (1989) 104–23.

———. "The Role of Jesus' Opponents in the Markan Drama", *NTS* 35 (1989) 161–82.

Stein, Robert H. *Difficult Sayings in the Gospels: Jesus' Use of Overstatement and Hyperbole*. Grand Rapids: Baker, 1985.

BIBLIOGRAPHY

Stock, Augustine. *The Method and Message of Mark*. Wilmington: Glazier, 1989.
Strathmann, Hermann. "μάρτυς κτλ", *TDNT* IV.474–514.
Suleiman, Susan R., and Inge Crosman, eds. *The Reader in the Text. Essays on Audience and Interpretation*. Princeton: Princeton University Press, 1980.
Suleiman, Susan R. "Introduction: Varieties of Audience-Oriented Criticism", *The Reader in the Text. Essays on Audience and Interpretation*, edited by Susan R. Suleiman and Inge Crosman, 3–45. Princeton: Princeton University Press, 1980.
Suleiman, S.R. "Redundancy and the 'Readable' Text", *Poetics Today* 1 (1980) 119–142.
Suppe, Frederick, ed. *The Structure of Scientific Theories*. Urbana: University of Illinois Press, ²1970.
Swete, Henry B. *The Gospel according to St Mark*. London: Macmillan, 1898, ³1913.
Tannehill, Robert C. "Attitudinal shift in Synoptic Pronouncement Stories", *Orientation by Disorientation: Studies in Literary Criticism and Biblical Literary Criticism in Honor of William A. Beardslee*, edited by Richard A. Spencer, 183–97. Pittsburgh: Pickwick, 1980.
———. "The Gospel of Mark as Narrative Christology", *Semeia* 16 (1975) 57–95.
———. "Introduction: The Pronouncement Story and its Types", *Semeia* 20 (1981) 1–13.
———. *The Sword of His Mouth*. Philadelphia and Missoula: Fortress and Scholars, 1975.
———. "Synoptic Pronouncement Stories: Form and Function", *SBL 1980 Seminar Papers*, edited by Paul J. Achtemeier, 51–55. Chico: Scholars, 1980.
———. "Tension in Synoptic Sayings and Stories", *Int* 34.2 (1980) 138–50.
———. "Varieties of Synoptic Pronouncement Stories", *Semeia* 20 (1981) 101–19
Taylor, Vincent. *The Formation of the Gospel Tradition*. London: Macmillan, 1935.
———. *The Gospel according to St Mark*. Grand Rapids: Baker, ²1966, reprint 1981.
Telford, William R. *The Barren Temple and the Withered Tree: a Redaction Critical Analysis of the Cursing of the Figtree Pericope in Mark's Gospel and its Relation to the Cleansing of the Temple Tradition*. JSNTSup 1. Sheffield: JSOT, 1980.
Tolbert, Mary Ann. *Sowing the Gospel: Mark's World in Literary-Historical Perspective*. Minneapolis: Fortress, 1989.
Tompkins, Jane P., ed. *Reader-Response Criticism: From Formalism to Post-Structuralism*. Baltimore and London: Johns Hopkins University Press, 1980.
Torrance, James B. "Olivet Discourse", *New Bible Dictionary*, 908–09. Leicester: IVP, 1962.
Trocmé, Étienne. *The Formation of the Gospel according to Mark*. Translated by P. Gaughan. London: SPCK, 1975 [French: 1963].
Van Iersel, Bas M.F. "He will Baptize you with Holy Spirit (Mark 1,8). The time perspective of βαπτίσει", *Text and Testimony: Essays in Honour of A.F.J. Klijn*, 132–41. Edited by Tjitze Baarda et al. Kampen: Kok, 1988.
———. "The Reader of Mark As Operator of a System of Connotations", *Semeia* 48 (1989) 83–114.
———. *Reading Mark*. Translated by W.H. Bisscheroux. Edinburgh: T&T Clark, ET 1989 [Dutch: 1986].
Vielhauer, Philipp. "Erwägungen zur Christologie des Markusevangeliums", *Aufsätze zum Neuen Testament*, 199–214. Munich: Kaiser Verlag, 1965.
Vieth, David M. "Entrapment in Restoration and Early Eighteenth Century English Literature", *Papers on Language and Literature* 18.3 (1982) 227–33.
von Rad, Gerhard. "The City on the Hill", *Problem of the Hexateuch and other Essays*, 232–44. Translated by E.W. Truman Dicken. Edinburgh: Oliver & Boyd, 1966 [German: 1958].

Vorster, Willem S. "Characterization of Peter in the Gospel of Mark", *Neot* 21 (1987) 57–76.

———. "Literary reflections on Mark 13:5–37: A Narrated Speech of Jesus", *Neot* 21 (1987) 203–24.

Walhout, Clarence. "Texts and Actions", in Roger Lundin, Anthony C. Thistelton, and Clarence Walhout, *The Responsibility of Hermeneutics*, 31–78. Grand Rapids and Exeter: Eerdmans and Paternoster, 1985.

Wenham, D. "Recent study of Mark 13 (Part 1)", *TSF Bulletin* 71 (1975) 6–15.

———. "Recent study of Mark 13 (Part 2)", *TSF Bulletin* 72 (1975) 1–9.

———. "Additional Notes": Additional notes to "Recent Study—parts 1 & 2" kindly supplied to me by the author.

———. *The Rediscovery of Jesus' Eschatological Discourse*. Gospel Perspectives 4. Sheffield: JSOT, 1984.

Wheelwright, Philip E. *Metaphor and Reality*. Bloomington: Indiana University Press, 1962.

Williamson, Lamar. *Mark*. Atlanta: John Knox, 1983.

Wimsatt, William K. "The Intentional Fallacy (1946)", reprinted in *The Verbal Icon. Studies in the Meaning of Poetry*, edited by William K. Wimsatt & Monroe C. Beardsley, 3–19. Lexington: University Press of Kentucky, 1954.

Wittig, Susan. "Formulaic Style and the Problem of Redundancy", *Centrum* 1 (1973) 123–36.

———. *Stylistic and Narrative Structures in the Middle English Romances*. Austin: University of Texas, 1978.

Woodbridge, John D. "Some Misconceptions of the Impact of the 'Enlightenment' on the Doctrine of Scripture", *Hermeneutics, Authority and Canon*, edited by Donald A. Carson and John D. Woodbridge, 237–70. Leicester: IVP, 1986.

Woodhouse, John W. "Signs and Wonders in the Bible", *Signs and Wonders and Evangelicals: A response to the Teaching of John Wimber*, edited by Robert C. Doyle, 17–35. Homebush West: Lancer, 1987.

Wright, Addison G. "The Widow's Mites: Praise or Lament?—A Matter of Context", *CBQ* 44.2 (1982) 256–65.

Wright, N.T. *History and Eschatology: Jesus and the Promise of Natural Theology*. London: SPCK, 2019.

Modern Author Index

Albertz, M., 53n11, 54n12
Alexander, J.A., 4n18, 114n210
Allen, W.C., 4n17
Anderson, G.W., 65nn65 & 66
Anderson, H., 4n18
Anderson, J.C., 20n21, 75n32

Bailey, K.E., 140nn44 & 45, 142n50
Barclay, W., 4n17, 114n210
Barrois, G.A., 72n14
Barth, K., 10, 11n42, 43n71, 112n119, 118n225, 150, 150n5
Bartholomew, G.L., 145n64
Bartlet, J.V., 4n17
Barton, J., 14n62, 18n17
Bassler, J.M., 34n29
Beardsley, M.C., 17n17
Beasley-Murray, G.R., 1n2, 2n10, 4n17, 9n40, 71n13, 72n14, 73n24, 74n27, 77nn40 & 43, 80nn53 54 & 57, 82n65, 83nn69 & 70, 86n81, 87n88, 90nn98 & 102, 91nn104 & 106, 93n114, 94n121, 97n134, 99n144, 101n149, 102n153, 106nn167 & 168, 107n173, 110n190, 111n196, 112n200, 114n210, 115n212, 116n216, 119n227, 120n237, 137n29
Best, E., 42nn61 & 66, 70n5, 71n9, 135n20
Bird, C.H., 105n162
Bleich, D., 16n3, 17n5
Blomberg, C.L., 16nn1 & 2, 17n8, 18nn12 & 13, 21n26
Blunt, A.W.F., 4n17, 53n11
Bolt, P.G., xi– xiv, xii nn1&2, xiii nn3–6, 14n62, 24n37, 25n42, 27n52, 29nn6 & 8, 43n70, 47n86, 48n90, 87n91, 117n223, 135n21, 137n32, 138n37, 140n42, 152nn6 & 8, 153n9, 154n13, 155n15, 156n19
Boomershine, T.E., xii, 21n28, 29n9, 43n69, 44n73, 44n77, 131n9, 135n19, 143n56, 145n64
Booth, W.C., xii, 17n6, 25n42, 26n51, 30n10, 57nn28–31, 69n1, 95n126, 135n19, 138n33
Bowker, J.W., 34n26
Bowman, J., 4n17, 114n210
Brandon, S.G.F., 1n4, 9n39, 97n136
Branscomb, B.H., 4n17, 114n210
Brower, K.E., xiin2
Brown, R.E., 143n59
Bruce, F.F., 92n102

MODERN AUTHOR INDEX

Bultmann, R., 53n11, 54nn12 13 16 & 17, 71n13
Burkill, T.A., 39n44
Burnett, F.W., 20n21, 70n2, 75n31, 80n56, 152nn4 & 6
Buse, I., 29n8
Butterworth, R., 28n2

Caird, G.B., 61nn44 & 47
Calvin, J., 86n82, 109n187, 118n225, 119nn227 & 233, 120n234, 121n244
Carson, D.A., 1n1, 4n18, 7n32, 8n37, 14n62, 15n65, 77n40
Chatman, S., xii, 18n14, 24n37, 32n19
Cohen, R., 64nn 60 & 61
Cole, R.A., 4n17, 114n210, 123nn252 & 253
Collins, J.J., 65nn64 & 65, 107n171
Collison, J.G.F., 154
Combrink, H.J.B., 152n4
Cranfield, C.E.B., 4n17, 12n50, 40n55, 42n61, 44nn72 & 74, 45nn75 & 77, 62n52, 71n11, 73nn19 & 22, 76nn37 & 38, 77n41, 78n46, 80n57, 81n61, 82nn64 & 65, 83nn68 & 72, 84n73, 86nn82 & 85, 87nn88 & 89, 89n96, 90nn98 & 99, 91n103, 92n109, 93nn114 & 116, 94n121, 97n134, 98n139, 105n165, 106nn166 & 168-69, 109nn183 & 187, 110nn191 & 192, 111n196, 113n206, 114nn207 & 210, 116nn216-217 & 219, 118nn225-226, 119nn228 & 231-33, 120nn238-239 & 241, 121nn243 & 244, 122nn250 & 251, 124nn257 & 258, 125n262, 135n22
Crotty, R.B., 4n17, 114n210
Cuddon, J.A., 17n7, 19n17, 20nn22 & 23, 21n26, 39n45, 45n78, 56nn26 & 27, 58n33, 93n117, 94n120, 139n40, 143n55
Cullmann, O., 11n46, 29n7, 118n225

Daube, D., 48n90

Delling, G., 102n151
Derrett, J.D.M., 62n51, 147n2
Detweiler, R., 108n101
Dewey, J., xii, 1n1, 14n62, 15n64, 18n13, 20n20, 25nn43 & 44, 26nn46 & 47, 53n9, 54n12, 57nn29 & 31, 58n33, 71nn9 & 13, 80n54, 89n94, 94n122, 95n125, 103n159
Dibelius, M., 53n11, 54n16, 70n2, 116n216
Dodd, C.H., 27n52, 113n205, 116n216, 117n219, 154, 154n12
Donahue, J.R., 32nn18 20 &22, 34n26, 82n67, 87n89
Dumbrell, W.J., 27n53, 66n68, 67nn73 & 76, 68nn78-80, 71n12, 72nn14 17 & 17, 107nn170-177, 108n178, 112n201
Dyer, K.D., xiin2

Earle, R., 4n17
Edwards, J.R., 31n17, 58n33
Ellis, E.E., 62n56, 119n227
Evans, C.A., 46n83

Fenton, J.C., 12n49
Ferguson, S.B., 114n210
Fish, S.E., 16n3, 17nn5 &6, 21n28, 70n7, 96n131, 159n1, 160
Fleddermann, H.T., 42n62, 49n94
Fowler, R.M., xii, 4n19, 14n62, 17n6, 18nn13-15, 19n16, 20n24, 21nn25 & 28, 22nn29 & 31, 23n36, 24nn37-39 & 40, 25n41, 26n45 49 & 50, 30n11, 31n14, 33n22 & 23, 34nn27 & 28, 35nn30 & 31, 37n40, 43n67, 48n89, 52n4, 70n7, 77n43
France, R.T., 2, 2nn9 & 11, 3nn12 & 14, 4n16, 5, 5nn21-25, 6, 6nn26 & 27, 7nn28 & 31-32, 8, 8nn33-36, 9, 9n38, 10, 11n47, 40n52, 59n39, 62nn54 & 56, 63, 78n44, 120n241, 159

Gaston, L., 9n39

MODERN AUTHOR INDEX

Geddert, T.J., xiii, xiiin7, xx, 4n19, 10n41, 11n45, 12n50, 18n13, 38n43, 46n84, 49n94, 56n23, 73n19, 75n29, 77n42, 78n44, 79n50, 120n236, 122n250, 123n253, 128n2, 133n14, 138n37, 141n47, 149n3, App2
Genette, G., 17n5, 25n43, 26n46, 94n122
Goldsworthy, G.L., xiin2, 66n67
Goodwin, H., 4n17
Gould, E.P., 5n22
Grassi, J.A., 133n12, 137n30
Gros Louis, K.R.R., 30n13
Guelich, R.A., 37n37
Gutting, G., 14n59

Hanson, P.D., 66n68
Hargreaves, J., 12n49
Harrington, W., 114n210
Hartman, L., 65n63, 66, 66nn69 & 70, 79n47, 106n168
Head, P.M., 29n5
Hendriksen, W., 114n210
Hengel, M., 1n4, 9, 9n40, 73nn21 & 23, 82nn63 & 64, 85n76, 86n83, 87nn88 & 89, 90n97, 93n116, 94nn118-119 & 121, 95n129, 97n136, 98n141, 99nn142-143 & 145, 102n152
Holland, N.N., 16n3, 17n5
Hollenbach, B., 33nn22 & 23
Hood, J.B., xiin2
Hooker, M.D., 1nn1 & 4, 14, 14n58, 29n7
Hunter, A.M., 114n210, 116n218
Hurtado, L.W., 114n210

Iser, W., xii, 16n3, 17n5, 21n28, 22, 22nn31-33, 23n34, 87n87

Jackson, H.M., 13, 13n56, 137n31, 141n48
Jauss, R.R., 64nn59 & 61
Jeremias, J., 32n22, 116n216, 122n251, 123n252, 124n261, 126nn265 & 266
Johnson, E.S., 114n210
Johnson, S.E., 20n22, 139n40

Jones, A., 114n210

Kaiser, W.C., 27n54
Kee, H.C., 62n52, 76n39, 79n47, 82n64, 83n72, 87n86, 89n96, 90n100, 91n104, 98n139, 105n162, 106nn167 & 169, 109n183, 110n193, 112n201, 116n218, 119n231, 120n240
Kelber, W.H., 10n41, 114n210
Kilpatrick, G.D., 59n40, 79n50, 84n74, 86nn82 & 85, 87n88
Kingsbury, J.D., 34n28
Kistemaker, S.J., 115n213, 117n219, 119n227, 122n251, 123nn253 & 254, 124n257 & 261
Kuhn, T.S., 14n59, 15n65
Kümmel, W.G., 121n244, 153n11

Lambrecht, J., 2n8
Lane, W.L., 4n17, 12nn49 & 50, 31n14, 40nn54 & 55, 41nn57 & 59, 42nn61 & 66, 43n68, 47n86, 62n52, 71n13, 74n28, 75n29, 76n37, 76n38, 77n40, 78n44, 79n47, 80n57, 83nn68-69 & 72, 92n102, 93nn114 & 116, 94n121, 95nn127-129, 97nn133-134 & 136, 98n137, 99n142 & 145, 101nn148 & 149, 105n162, 106nn168 & 169, 108nn179 & 180, 109nn184-185 & 188-89, 111n197, 112nn201 & 203, 113nn204 & 206, 114nn208-210, 116nn215 & 216, 117nn222 & 223, 118n225, 119nn229 & 233, 120nn239-241, 121n245, 122nn247-248 & 250, 124n260, 125n263, 128n3, 135n21
Licht, J., 19n19, 20n20, 52n2, 57n29
Lightfoot, R.H., xii, xiii, 11, 11nn43 & 45, 12, 12n50, 74n28, 118n225, 127n1, 128, 128n2, 130n7, 134n15, 135nn18 & 21, 136n23, 137nn27 & 31, 138n37, 140nn42 & 44, 142n53, 147, 147nn1 & 2, 148, 156n19, 159

MODERN AUTHOR INDEX

Long, T.G., 23n35

McCown, C.C., 98n140
McNicol, A.J., 114n208, 116n217, 118n225, 119n227
Mailloux, S., 16n3, 26n50
Malbon, E.S., 21n27, 22n30, 52n4
Manson, T.W., 79n49, 113nn205 & 206
Marcus, J., 136n26
Marshall, C.D., 104n161
Marshall, I.H., 14n61
Martin, R.P., 120n238, 121n244
Meagher, J.C., 27n55
Moiser, J., 36n34
Moo, D.J., 67n73
Moule, C.F.D., 32n22
Morris, L.L., 65n65, 66n68, 67nn73–75
Moore, S.D., 14n62, 15n64, 16n3, 17n8, 18n11, 21n28, 24n40, 27n54, 119n227
Murray, G., 48n91

Nardoni, E., 40n53
Nineham, D.E., 71n13, 75n29, 78nn46 & 49, 82nn64 & 66, 83n72, 84n74, 85nn76 & 79, 86n82, 87n88, 90n98, 93nn113 114 & 116, 97n136, 98n139, 102nn150 151 & 154, 103n155, 106nn167–169, 109n186, 110n192, 111n197, 112nn199–201, 113n205, 114nn207 & 210, 116nn216 & 218, 117n220, 119nn227 & 230, 120n241, 121n244, 122n251, 123n254, 124n261, 125n264, 127n1

O'Connell, B., 98n140
Oepke, A., 152n3
Osburn, C.D., 71n8

Patte, D., 62n53
Perrin, N., 13, 13n57, 14n62, 137nn28 & 31, 141n48
Pesch, R., 4n19, 10n41, 58nn32 & 36–37
Petersen, N.R., 1n1, 14n62, 17, 17n9, 18n13, 20n20, 143n56

Porter, S.E., 11n48, 14n62
Prince, G., 16n3, 17n5

Radcliffe, T., 12, 12nn52 & 53, 13n54, 18n13, 141n48
Räisänen, H., 27n55
Reicke, B., 154n12
Resseguie, J.L., 17n5, 96n131
Rimmon-Kenan, S., 62n51, 65n62, 70n2, 75n31, 87n87
Rist, M., 65n65
Roberts, J.J.M., 72n14
Robertson, D., 14n60
Robinson, J.A.T., 80n57, 106nn167 & 168, 111n196, 151, 151n2, 152, 152n7, 153, 153n11, 154nn12 & 13
Robbins, V.K., 54nn15 & 16
Rowley, H.H., 67n74

Sandmel, S., 77n40
Savran, G.W., 63n57
Schneidau, H.N., 26n45
Schneider, C., 74n27
Schrenk, G., 76n38
Schweizer, E., 114n210
Scott, R.B.Y., 115n213
Silva, M., 62n56
Slawinski, J., 17n4
Smith, M., 12, 12n51, 18n13
Smith, S.H., 44n74, 45n79, 46n81, 47n88, 48nn90 & 91, 49n93
Stein, R.H., 61nn43–46 48 & 50, 64n60, 73n20, 83n69
Stock, A., 20n23, 114n210
Strathmann, H., 86n82
Suleiman, S.R., 16n3, 20n21
Suppe, F., 14n59
Swete, H.B., 110n190, 114n210

Tannehill, R.C., 19nn16 & 18, 28nn1 & 2, 29n4, 30n12, 31n16, 39nn44 & 48, 40n50, 45n80, 48n91, 52n7, 53n10, 54nn15 & 16, 55nn18–20, 61n49, 70nn4 & 5, 74n26, 98n138, 99n146, 103n158

Taylor, V., 4n17, 40n55, 42nn61 & 66, 53n11, 54nn12 & 14, 58n33, 64n58, 71n13, 75n30, 76n37, 78n46, 79nn47 & 49, 80n57, 82nn64 & 66, 83n72, 84n74, 85n76, 88n92, 89n96, 91n103, 93n114, 94n119, 98n141, 99nn142 & 144, 114nn208 & 210, 116n214, 117nn219 & 221, 118nn225 & 226, 119n228, 124n256, 135n22
Telford, W.R., 115n213
Tolbert, M.A., 114n210
Tompkins, J.P., 16n3
Torrance, J.B., 59n42, 64n59, 67n72
Trocmé, E., 127n1

Van Iersel, B.M.F., 12n53, 27n54, 29n9, 34n29, 114n210

Vielhauer, P., 13, 13n55, 137n31, 141n48
Vieth, D.M., 96n131
Von Rad, G., 72n14
Vorster, W.S., 17n10, 53n8, 131n9

Walhout, C., 66n71
Wenham, D., 1n2, 2nn8 & 10, 3n15, 4n19, 7n32, 11n44, 58nn32 & 36–37, 59n42, 122n251, 156n23
Wheelwright, P.E., 61n48
Williamson, L., 4n17, 114n210
Wimsatt, W.K., 17n17
Wittig, S., 20n21
Woodbridge, J.D., 15n65
Woodhouse, J.W., 105n163
Wright, A.G., 49n94
Wright, N.T., xiin2

Ancient Document Index

Old Testament

Genesis

8:22	115n213
14:10	97n135
19:17	97
41:19	99n144

Exodus

3:14	37n37, 79n47, 80n56
4	89n96
4:12	89n96
4:21	32n22
8:15,32	32n22
9:24	99n144
9:34	32n22
11:6	99n144
33:19,22	37n37
34:6	37n37

Numbers

22:35	89n96
27:17	36

Deuteronomy

13	105n162
13:7	112n200
17:14–20	80n58
29:17(16)	92n110
30:4	112n200

Judges

9:7–15	33n25

2 Samuel

4:12	102n151
7	72
13:20	93n111
16:1,2	115n213
17:13	73n23

1 Kings

8	72
11:5	92n110
11:7	92n110
19:2,10	41n57
22	111n196
22:17	97n135

ANCIENT DOCUMENT INDEX

2 Kings

2:9–10	43n69, 44n73
6:15–17	107n174
23:13, 24	92n110

2 Chronicles

15:6	82n65
15:8	92n110

Job

9:8–11	37n37
19:12	155

Psalms

2	155
2:7	29
22	43n68
22:1	141
31:5,21	155
32:4	115n213
48	72n15
48:12–14	72
74:17	115n213
110	74n27, 74n28, 141n49
110:1	48, 49, 137, 141, 157
110:2	74
118:25	80n56
119:46	85
125	72n15, 97n135

Proverbs

6:8	115n213
10:5	115n213
26:1	115n213
30:25	115n213

Isaiah

2:1–5	120n236
2:2–4	112n202
3:14	47n87
5:1–7	47n87
6	32, 33n23, 38n43, 111n196
6:9–10	33n23, 104
6:11–13	33n23
6:13	34n26
11:1–11	44n72
13	62n55
13:6–10	101n149
13:10	109n183
14:13	79n47
15:5	97n134
16:3	97n132
16:9	115n213
19:1	110n193
19:2	82n65
28:4	115n213
29:13–14	33n23
29:13,19,21	37
29:23–24	33n23
34:4	109n183
35:5–6	37n39
40:1–2	29n6
40:9	29n6
42:1–4	112n202
42:1	29
43:10–11	79n47
47:8,10	81n59
49:6	112n202
49:8,19	93n111
49:24–25	36
49:25	29n6
50:4–7	43n68
51:17–23	43
52:13—53:12	39n48
52:6–7	79n47
53	39, 130
53:7	140
53:12	43
54:1	93n111
55:2	36
55:8–13	32n21
55:10–12	36
55:10	32n21
56–66	112n202
56:7	46

ANCIENT DOCUMENT INDEX

61:4	93n111	30:7	101n149
63:14	29n8	31:29	109n183
66:3	92n110	32:34	92n110
		33:15–16	109n183
		40:10,12	115n213
		41[ET 34]:1	154n12

Jeremiah

1:9	89n96	48:32	115n213
1:18–19	155	49	82n65
1:18	80n58	49:8	97n134
2:8,26	80n58	52:7 A	154n12
3:15	81		
3:16,18	109n183		

Lamentations

4:1	92n110	1:4,13,16	93n111
4:6	97n132	3:11	93n111
4:9	80n58	3:1–8	155
4:19–31	82n65		
4:29	97n134		

Ezekiel

5:4–5	80n58		
5:21	38n43		
5:31	80n58	5:11	92n110
6	97	7:14–27	98n138
6:13	80n58	7:14	93n114, 97n134
6:22–30	82n65	7:16	97n134
7:29	40n51	7:20	92n110
7:30	92n110	9:3	75n29
8:8	80n58	10:18–19	75n29
8:13	115n213	11:1	75n29
8:20	115n213	11:18,21	92n110
10:21	80n58	11:23	75n29
13:13–14,18	80n58	17:22–24	33n25
13:27	92n110	20:7,8,30	92n110
14:9	80n58	32:7,8	109n183
14:14–15	80n58	34	80n58
14:18	80n58	34:5	36
15:4	80n58	34:11–16	36, 81
15:20	155	34:23–24	44n72
16:16	97n134, 97n135	36:4	93n111
16:18	92n110	37:23	92n110
17:19–27	80n58		
19:3–15	80n58		

Daniel

23:5–8	44n72		68, 145n63
23:5–6	80n58	1:1—2:4a	68
23:13 [LXX Aq],25–32	80n58	1:17	95n127
23:33–39	80n58	2:4b—7:28	68
26:7–9	80n58	2:21,23	95n127
27:14	80n58		
29:9,13	80n58		

ANCIENT DOCUMENT INDEX

Daniel (continued)

2:28,29	82n65
2:28	120n240
2:45	82n65, 120n240
4:10–12	33n25
4:20–27	33n25
7–12	107
7	4n20, 7, 39, 67n76, 68, 81n59, 83, 107, 108, 110, 111, 111n196, 113, 145, 157
7:1–14	107, 150, 156n18
7:8,11	79n47
7:12	41n58, 81n60
7:13–14	29n9, 40n55, 41n58, 108n182, 117, 144n61, 149n4, 152, 152n8, 155
7:13	7, 7n32, 74n27, 63, 106, 107–8, 107n172, 110, 137, 137n31, 141, 157n24
7:15–28	107, 156n18
7:15–27	149, 150
7:16	107n172
7:20	79n47
7:21–27	82n65
7:22	107n172, 111n196
7:25	79n47
7:26–27	108n182
7:26	81n60
7:27	41n58
8–12	68
8:10	79n47
8:13	153, 93n111
8:19	76n39
8:25	79n47
9:17,18	93n111
9:25	95n127
9:26,27	93n111
9:27	92, 92n109
10:14	120n240
11:20	120n240
11:31	92, 92n109, 93n113
11:36–45	105n162
11:36	79n47
11:44 Θ	82n65
12	40n55, 102
12:1–3	40n55
12:1	99, 100–102, 121n242
12:4	95
12:5–13	121n242
12:6–8	101
12:6	76n39
12:7	76n39, 102n152, 110n195, 118
12:8–9	111
12:8	76n39, 95
12:9	95
12:11	92, 92n109, 93n111, 93n113, 101
12:13	91n104, 95n127, 120n240

Hosea

6:2	144
9:10	92n110
10:8	97n136

Joel

2:2	101n149
2:10,31	109n183
3:15	109n183
3:9–16	82n65

Amos

2:16	135
3:15	115n213
5:19	97n134
8:1–3	115n213
9:12	80n58

Micah

1:2–7	101n149
4:1–5	120n236
4:5	80n58
5:4	80n58
7:1–7	46
7:1	115n213
7:2,3	90
7:6	90, 152n8
7:8,18	46n82

Nahum

3:6	92n110
3:18	97n135

Zephaniah

1:7,14	116n218

Haggai

2:15	73n23

Zechariah

	68
2:6	112n200
2:10	87n86
2:11	97n132
5:4	80n58
6–8	132n11
8:23	109n183
9:7	92n110
9:9	46n81
13:3	80n58
13:7	131, 135
14:2	82n65
14:4	74, 47n86, 74n28
14:5	97, 97n135
14:6	98n140
14:7	120n240
14:8	115n213
14:10	47n86, 74n28
14:16	87n86
14:23	75n29

Malachi

1:6,11,14	80n58
2:2	80n58
3:5	80n58
3:23	41n56

Apocrypha

Susanna

54	71n12

1 Maccabees

1:54–59	97n134
1:54	92n109
2:7	153
2:28	97n134, 97n136, 98n138
2:29–41	153
6:7	97n134
9:27	101n149

Pseudepigrapha

Assumption of Moses

8:1	101n149

Baruch

2:2	101n149

1 Enoch

61	112n199
68:1	34n29

Psalms of Solomon

17:23 [21 LXX]	44n72, 120n240

ANCIENT DOCUMENT INDEX

New Testament

Matthew

	44n72
8:27	71n12
10:5,6	152n8
10:16–23	152n8
10:17–21	152
10:17	152n8
10:18	86n82, 152n8
10:21–23	152n8
10:23	11, 153n10
10:34–36	152n8
13:11	34n28
13:13	32n22
14:25	124n257
16:28	153n10
22:6–7	153n10
23:35	153n10
23:38	73n22
24–25	152n6
24	7n32, 8
24:3	152, 152n6
24:14	86n82
24:15,20	153
24:22	102n151
24:25	106n166
24:26–28	153
24:27,29,30–31	152
24:30	117n223, 152
24:34	153n10
24:37—25:46	153
24:37,39	152
26:57–75,58	153
27:7	85n80
28:16–20	152
28:18–20	152, 152n8

Mark

1–13	127n1
1–12	Ch.3, xix, 23, 27, 28, 50, 127
1:1—8:26	28n2
1:1—3:35	29–32, 49
1:1–13	28n2
1:1	27, 29, 30n10, 45, 104, 142n53, 145n64
1:2–8	29, 41n57
1:2–3	30n10
1:2	112n198, 112n199
1:4	29n6, 31
1:5	97
1:7	29n6, 36, 36n32
1:8	29n6, 43, 97
1:9–11	29, 30n10, 39n48, 45
1:9	32n18
1:10	89
1:11	40, 121, 142n53
1:12–13	29, 31
1:12	89
1:13	112n199
1:14–45	28n2
1:14–15	29, 117, 117n221
1:14	32n21, 84n73, 133n13
1:15	29n9, 40, 85n78, 89, 144n61
1:16–39	76
1:16–20	30, 40n50, 44n74, 76, 89, 131n9, 145, 149
1:16	31n15, 75n32
1:17	70n3
1:19	75n32
1:21–45	30
1:21–34	31n15
1:21–29	81n60
1:21–28	85n75
1:22	31, 31n15
1:24	31, 31n15, 39n46
1:27	31n15, 35
1:29–39	75n32
1:32–34	31n15
1:33	31
1:34–44	31n15
1:34	31, 39n46
1:36	75n32
1:37	31
1:39	31, 85n75
1:44	86n82

ANCIENT DOCUMENT INDEX

1:45	31, 31n15	3:19	49, 51, 75n33, 84n73, 129, 133n13, 136
2–3	18n13		
2:1—3:6	28n2, 31n15		
2:1–12	31n15, 81n60	3:20–35	31
2:1	31n15	3:20–21	32, 32n18, 90n101
2:2	31, 31n15	3:20	31
2:3	54n17	3:22–30	32, 47, 81n60, 85n78, 97, 104
2:5	85n78		
2:6–9	31n15	3:22–26	96n131
2:6–7	31, 31n15	3:22–23	54n17
2:8–10	31n14	3:22	29n6
2:10	31n14, 31n15, 110n194	3:26	82
		3:27	35, 36n32, 39n46, 103n157
2:12	31n15		
2:13–27	81n62	3:28–29	137n32
2:13–17	81n60	3:28	118n224
2:13–14	30	3:29–30	89
2:13	31, 31n15	3:31–35	32, 32n18, 34, 34n26, 54n17, 90n101, 103
2:15–17	31		
2:15–16	54n17		
2:17	85	3:31	112n198
2:18–22	81n60	4	34n28
2:18–19	54n17	4:1–34	32, 38, 49
2:18	85	4:1	31n15
2:20	103n157, 133n13	4:3–9	32, 36
2:23–28	81n60	4:9	33n24
2:23–24	54n17, 85	4:10–12	33
2:28	39n46	4:10	75n30, 78n44
3:1–6	81n60, 85n75	4:11–12	33n24, 103, 139
3:1–2	54n17	4:11	33, 34, 34n29, 35, 35n30, 85n78, 89
3:4	91n105		
3:5	37	4:12	33n24, 37n38, 38n43, 79n52, 104
3:6	31, 36, 38, 39n49, 48, 48n90, 51, 133n13, 129, 136		
		4:13–20	33
		4:21–25	33
3:7–9	31	4:21–22	33n24
3:7	31n15	4:23	33n24, 38n43, 118n224
3:8	97		
3:11	39n46, 142n53	4:24–25	33n24
3:13–19	30, 75, 75n33	4:24	33n24, 79
3:14–19	36, 44n74, 90	4:25	47n86
3:14	70n3, 89, 112n198, 129n5	4:26–32	34
		4:26–29	33
3:16	75n32	4:26	34, 85n78
3:17,18	75	4:29	38n43, 84n73, 112n198
3:17	75n32		
		4:30–32	33, 87

ANCIENT DOCUMENT INDEX

Mark (continued)

Reference	Pages
4:30	34, 85n78
4:33-34	33
4:34	35, 96
4:35—8:26	35-38, 44, 49
4:35-41	35
4:35	31n15
4:38	71n9, 71n10
4:39	35
4:40	35
4:41	35, 39
5	45n77
5:1-20	39n46
5:2	36n32
5:3	36n32
5:4	36n32
5:5	36n32
5:7	142n53
5:10	112n198
5:19-20	36, 39n46
5:19	36n33
5:20	36n33, 37n39
5:21-43	36
5:23	91n105
5:25	36n34
5:28	91n105
5:34	85n78, 91n105
5:35	71n9, 71n10
5:36	85n78
5:37	75n32
5:42	36n34
6-8	18n13
6:1—8:26	28n2
6	38
6:1-6	36, 85n75, 90n101
6:2	89n94
6:7-13	36, 89, 90
6:7	112n198
6:11	86n82
6:12	70n3
6:14-56	81n60
6:14-29	36, 39n49, 41n57, 85, 133n13
6:14	85, 80n56, 85n80
6:17	112n198
6:22,25,26	85
6:27	85, 112n198
6:29	144
6:30	112n198
6:31-44	39n46
6:34	36
6:35-36	37n36
6:36-37	36
6:37,38-40,42-43	37n36
6:45-52	37, 39n46
6:48	37n37, 124n257
6:50	37n37, 80n56, 137n28
6:51-52	37
6:52	38
6:56	91n105
7	38
7:1-37	37
7:1-23	42, 97
7:1-22	81n60
7:2-5	85
7:5-6	54n17
7:6,8	37
7:13	37, 84n73
7:17	75n30, 78n44
7:18	37, 77
7:24-30	37
7:24	37n39
7:31-37	37
7:36	37n39
7:37	37n39, 39n46
8:1-21	81n60
8:1-10	37, 39n46
8:4	37n40
8:10	38
8:11-15	49n92
8:11-14	42, 77n42
8:11-13	38, 77, 139
8:12	118n224, 119
8:14-21	52n7, 77
8:15-18	79n52
8:15	38, 77, 79, 85, 91
8:16	38
8:17-21	77n43
8:21	38, 96
8:22-26	44n74
8:23-24	79n52
8:26	112n198

ANCIENT DOCUMENT INDEX

8:27—10:52	28n2, 39–45, 39n44, 44–45, 50	9:11–13	40n53, 134, 141, 142
8:27—9:29	39–41	9:11	40, 82n67
8:27–30	39, 39n45	9:12	41, 43n68, 110n194
8:27–28	39n47	9:13	41
8:27	39n49	9:14–29	41
8:29–30	104	9:17	71n9, 71n10
8:29	39n47, 45, 75n32	9:19	77, 104, 119
8:31—9:1	75n32, 89, 135, 149n3	9:22	41n59, 78n44
		9:23–24	85n78
8:31–34	131	9:26–27	41n59
8:31	39, 40n51, 41, 49, 51, 81n60, 82n67, 110n194, 129, 131n10, 132n11, 133, 136, 137, 141, 142, 142n54	9:26,27	41n59
		9:28	75n30
		9:30—10:31	42–43
		9:30	42n60
		9:31	42, 42n60, 51, 81n60, 84n73, 110n194, 129, 132n11, 133, 136, 137, 141, 142, 142n54
8:32	39, 40n51, 45, 75n32		
8:33	39, 56n23, 73, 82n63, 120, 138n34		
		9:33–37	42, 42n65
8:34—9:1	131n9	9:33–34	42n63
8:34–36	131n10	9:34,35–50	45n76
8:34	84, 138n34	9:35	42, 43
8:35	39, 39n49, 86n81, 89, 91n105	9:37	42, 80n56, 112n198
		9:38–41	42
8:38	39n49, 40, 40n51, 89, 110n194, 112n199, 119, 121	9:38	42n63, 71n9, 71n10, 75n32, 75n34, 80n56
		9:39	80n56
9:1	11, 40, 40n53, 85n78, 111n196, 118n224, 119, 119n227, 144n61, 153n10	9:41	80n56, 118n224
		9:42–50	42, 42n64, 135
		9:42,47	85n78
		10:1–12	97
9:2–13	40n53, 75n32	10:2–3	54n17
9:2–8	40, 45	10:5	42, 42n64
9:2	75n32	10:10	75n30, 78n44
9:5–7	75n34	10:13–16	42, 42n62, 44, 45n76
9:5	71n9, 75n32		
9:7	121, 142n53	10:13–14	54n17
9:9–13	160	10:14	85n78
9:9	40, 40n55, 110n194, 137, 137n28, 141, 142n54, 145	10:15	42, 85n78, 118n224
		10:16	42
		10:17–31	129n5
		10:17–27	43
9:10	40	10:17,20	71n9, 71n10

ANCIENT DOCUMENT INDEX

Mark (continued)

10:22	43n67
10:23	85n78
10:24–31	75n32
10:24,25	85n78
10:26	91n105
10:27	43, 135n19
10:28–31	131n10
10:28–30	43
10:28	75n32
10:29–30	149
10:29	86n81, 89, 118n224
10:30	99n147, 149
10:31	43, 44
10:32–52	43–44
10:32	45, 46n81
10:33–34	43, 81n60, 133, 136, 137, 142, 142n54
10:33	49, 51, 84n73, 87n86, 110n194, 129, 132n11, 141
10:34	138
10:35–45	75n32, 75n34
10:35–36	54n17
10:35	43, 71n9, 71n10, 75n32
10:36	44n73
10:37	43
10:38–40	135
10:38–39	29n8
10:38	43, 133
10:39	43
10:41	75n32
10:42–45	81n60
10:42	87n86
10:43–44	42n62
10:45	42n61, 43, 44, 110n194, 130, 133, 136, 139
10:46–52	44
10:47–48	44, 44n72
10:47	45n77
10:49	44n74
10:51	44n73, 71n9
10:52	44, 85n78, 91n105
10:53—15:47	20n23
11–16	12, 28n2
11–12	18n13, 28n2, 45–49, 45n80, 46n84, 50, 51, 52n3, 83, 97, 158, 159
11:1–11	52, 74n28
11:1–10	74n28
11:1	74, 112n198
11:3	112n198
11:9	80n56
11:10–11	48n89
11:10	46n81, 85n78
11:11	47n85, 69, 74n28
11:12–19	52, 74n28
11:12–14	74n28, 90, 114
11:13	23n35, 114
11:15–18	47n88, 74n28
11:17–18	81n60
11:17	46n84, 74n28, 86, 87n86
11:18	46n84
11:19	47n85, 69
11:20—13:37	52
11:20—12:44	47–49
11:20–26	47, 114
11:20–25	75n32, 115
11:21	71n9, 75n32
11:22	47n86, 85n78
11:23–24	85n78
11:23	74n28, 118n224
11:24	47n86, 98
11:25	47n86
11:27—12:37	104
11:27—12:12	90
11:27–33	47, 81n60, 104
11:27–28	54n17
11:27	48n89, 48n90, 49
11:31	85n78
12	47n85, 52n5, 71, 71n9
12:1–12	47, 47n88, 49, 74n28, 81n60, 133n13, 136, 137n30, 140, 141n46
12:1	48n89

190

12:2,3,4,5	112n198		147–50, 149n4,
12:6	121, 112n198,		158, 159, 160, 161
	142n53	13:1–4	5, 6, 56, 69–78,
12:12–13	48n90, 51		78n44, 92, 158
12:12	32n22, 48n89,	13:1–2	53–56, 58, 59,
	86n83, 129		64n58, 69–74, 75,
12:13–44	81n60		78, 80, 97, 120, 136
12:13–34	48, 129	13:1	47n85, 52, 53,
12:13–17	129n5		55, 59, 69, 71n9,
12:13–14	54n17		72n14, 72n18, 76,
12:13	112n198		78, 120n235
12:14	71n9, 71n10	13:2	xiin2, 59, 61n43,
12:17	86n83		64n58, 69, 72,
12:18–27	79n51		73n20, 74n25, 78,
12:18–19	54n17		80n53, 120n236,
12:19	71n9, 71n10		140n44, 156n22,
12:23–27	74n28		160
12:24	79, 85n78	13:3–37	130
12:25	112n199	13:3–4	55, 58, 59, 64n58,
12:27	79		74–78
12:28–34	51, 89n94, 129	13:3	53, 47n85, 74,
12:28–29	54n17		75n32, 124, 133
12:32	71n9, 71n10	13:4	52n3, 55, 58n35,
12:34	48, 48n91		58n36, 74, 74n25,
12:35–38	74		76, 76n39, 77n43,
12:35–37	48, 51, 74n28, 104,		78, 78n46, 92, 101,
	136, 137, 137n30,		105, 105n165,
	141		113n206, 116n215,
12:36	89n94, 137		120n235, 121, 122,
12:37	129		123, 139, 158
12:38–44	51, 129n5	13:5–37	25, 56–68, 135
12:38–40	49	13:5–31	5, 6, 10
12:38	77, 79	13:5–27	58, 118n226
12:39	85n75	13:5–23	3n13, 78–106,
12:40	74n28, 86n83, 104		110n191, 116n216,
12:41–44	49, 74		118n225, 159
12:43	118n224	13:5–22	4n16
13	*passim*, Ch.4, Ch.5,	13:5–13	5, 6, 52n3, 79–92,
	xix, 1, 2, 3, 4nn18		91–92, 102, 106,
	& 19, 10, 12, 13,		113, 117, 126, 148,
	15, 15n64, 18n13,		149, 149n4
	22, 23, 23n35, 25,	13:5–11	90
	26n47, 27, 28n1,	13:5–8	64n58
	32n19, 49, 50, 51,	13:5–6	29n6, 58, 58n33,
	61n45, 70n3, 108,		59, 79, 79n47, 81,
	127, 127n1, 131,		82, 84, 90, 92, 94,
	131n8, 132, 133,		103
	134, 134n16, 146,		

ANCIENT DOCUMENT INDEX

Mark (*continued*)

13:5	58n34, 59n39, 59n40, 64n58, 74n25, 80n53, 91, 106, 125	13:14–23	5, 6, 60, 64n58, 92–106, 109, 113, 126, 135, 148, 159
13:6	64n58, 79n51, 80, 81n59, 82, 104	13:14–20	9n40
		13:14–18	98
		13:14–16	61n43
13:7–20	58n33, 79	13:14	9n40, 26, 58, 58n34, 58n36, 59, 59n38, 74n25, 82n67, 92–97, 96n131, 97n136, 98, 103n157, 116, 141
13:7–8	59, 82, 109n186		
13:7	58n34, 58n36, 74n25, 80n53, 82n67, 82, 83, 83n68, 84, 87n88, 91, 91n103, 92, 134n16		
		13:15–18	97
		13:15–16	58n34, 98, 98n138
13:8	59, 61n43, 64n58, 83, 83n69, 85n78, 86	13:17	59, 98, 98n141
		13:18–19	102n153
		13:18	58n34, 98, 133
13:9–13	12n49	13:19–20	59, 98, 102n150, 109
13:9–11	84–89, 87n89, 90, 112, 152	13:19	59, 100–102
13:9–10	59, 89	13:20	59, 91n105, 102, 103, 112
13:9	58n34, 58n35, 59n39, 59n40, 64n58, 74n25, 80n53, 84, 86n82, 88, 91, 125, 136, 137n27	13:21–23	58, 58n33, 79, 104
		13:21–22	103, 139
		13:21	25, 59, 58n34, 64n58, 74n25, 85n78, 103n157
13:10	40n54, 64n58, 82n67, 86n84, 87n86, 89, 145	13:22–23	135n18
		13:22	59, 74n25, 103, 105, 112
13:11–13	59	13:23	58, 58n34, 58n35, 59n39, 59n40, 64n58, 74n25, 80n53, 106, 125
13:11	58n34, 58n35, 58n36, 59, 80n53, 84, 87, 88, 92		
13:12–13	59n41, 90–91, 90n97	13:24–27	*passim*, xi, xii, xix, xx, 2, 3, 4, 4n16, 5, 6, 7n32, 8, 10, 12, 13, 14, 15, 20n23, 60, 63, 64n58, 92, 106–113, 108, 109, 110n190, 110n191, 116n216, 124, 126, 144n61, 147, 159
13:12	58n35, 64n58, 84, 90		
13:13	61n43, 80n56, 90, 91n105, 102, 103, 134n16		
13:14–27	52n3		
13:14–26	149n4	13:24–25	59, 59n38, 61n43, 63, 109–110, 119n232, 141

13:24	2, 6, 12n49, 58, 62n55, 64n58, 110n190, 142
13:25	90n102
13:26	4n18, 11, 59, 59n38, 63, 74n25, 103n157, 106, 110–11, 110n194, 111n196, 113, 121, 133n14, 137, 137n31, 141
13:27	8, 59, 63, 103, 103n157, 111–13, 112n199, 113, 121, 145, 146, 149n4
13:28–37	58, 60, 64n58, 113–25
13:28–32	60, 114–16
13:28–31	3n13, 52n3, 121, 126
13:28–30	6, 6n26
13:28–29	58n34, 58n36, 114n207, 118
13:28	58n35, 117
13:29	58n35, 74n25, 114n207, 116–18, 116n216, 123n254, 125, 133n14, 144n61
13:30–32	114n207, 118–22, 118
13:30–31	118
13:30	xiin2, 2, 3n15, 4n16, 5, 11, 58, 58n35, 59, 61n43, 114n207, 119, 120n239, 121n246, 130
13:31	114n207, 120
13:32–37	3n13, 5, 6, 10, 159
13:32–33	6
13:32	2n6, 3, 6, 58n35, 59, 112n199, 120, 120n240, 120n240, 122n247, 125n263, 133, 133n14, 134, 137n30, 142, 142n53
13:33–37	52n3, 60, 114n207, 122–25, 124n258, 125, 133n14, 158
13:33	58n34, 58n35, 59, 59n39, 74n25, 80n53, 114n207, 122, 122n247, 123, 125n263
13:34	58n35, 74n25, 114n207, 122
13:35	58n34, 58n35, 59, 74n25, 80n53, 114n207, 122, 122n247, 123, 123n253, 125, 125n263, 128, 130, 132, 138, 142, 144, 144n62
13:36	124, 133, 133n14
13:37	26n28, 58, 58n35, 74n25, 114n207, 124–25
14–16	Ch.6, xix, 10, 11, 12n49, 23, 27, 47n88, 52n3, 135n21, 146, 147, 148
14–15	127n1, 140n42
14:1–40	132, 132n11
14:1–25	132
14:1–11	129
14:1–2	129, 133n13, 136
14:1	52, 129
14:3–6	129, 135n19
14:3	47n85
14:4–5	129n5
14:8	145
14:9	40n54, 118n224, 145
14:10–11	48n91, 129, 133n13
14:10	75n33, 84n73, 136
14:11	84n73, 129n5
14:12–25	130
14:12–16	130
14:12	130, 135n19
14:13	112n198
14:14	71n9, 130

ANCIENT DOCUMENT INDEX

Mark (continued)

14:16	130
14:17	130
14:18	84n73, 118n224
14:19	135n19
14:21	84n73, 110n194, 130, 141n46
14:23–25	135n19
14:23	85n78
14:24	130, 133
14:25	118n224, 130, 131n8, 142, 144n61
14:26–31	131–32, 134
14:26	130, 131n8
14:27–31	136
14:27	131, 134
14:28	131, 132n11, 135n19, 141, 145, 149
14:29	75n32, 131, 135n19, 138
14:30–31	131, 135
14:30	118n224, 131, 138
14:31	82n67, 131n10, 135n19
14:32–42	122n250, 133–34, 133n14
14:32–38	135
14:33	75n32, 133
14:34, 35	133
14:36	133, 137n30
14:37	75n32, 133
14:38	133
14:40	133, 135n19
14:41–42	133
14:41	84n73, 110n194, 128n3, 133, 134, 134n16, 136
14:42–43	136
14:42	84n73
14:43–52	134–36
14:43	75n33, 134
14:44	84n73, 134, 134n17
14:45	71n9, 134, 134n17
14:46	134
14:47	134, 135n19
14:48–49,50	134
14:53–72	136–39
14:53	136
14:54	75n32, 136, 143n58
14:55–59	136
14:55	85n75, 86n82, 136
14:56	86n82
14:58	73n22, 120n236, 136, 141, 142, 142n52, 156n22
14:59	86n82
14:60–61	136
14:61–62	13
14:61	136
14:62	7, 12, 74n27, 80n56, 110n194, 111n196, 141, 155, 157
14:63–65	137
14:63–64	137n27
14:63	86n82
14:66–72	138
14:66–67	75n32
14:67,68,69	138n34
14:70	75n32, 138n34
14:71	138n34
14:72	75n32, 138
15	144n61
15:1–39	139–43
15:1–5	139
15:1	84n73, 85n75, 139
15:2	85, 139
15:3–4	139
15:3	139n41
15:9–14	139
15:9	85, 139
15:10	84n73, 139, 139n41
15:11	139
15:12	85, 139
15:14	139
15:15	84n73
15:16–19	139
15:17	139
15:18	85, 139
15:19	139
15:20–39	142n50
15:21–32	139

15:21–24	140n45	9:51	155
15:23	142	10:9,11	155n15
15:25–32	140n45	13:27–31	155n17
15:25	140	18:8,16,17,24–27	155n15
15:26	85, 139	19:11–27	155n15
15:29–30	141, 142	19:11b	109n186
15:29	73n22	19:28–44	155n15
15:30–31	91n105	19:41–44	154
15:30	140n45	21:20–24	154
15:31–32	139, 139n41, 142	21:20, 21–24	155
15:32	85, 85n78, 140n45	21:28	155, 155n16
15:33–39	139, 140n45	21:31	116n218
15:33–38	140	21:32	119n227
15:33	12, 13, 140, 141, 142	22:37	134n16
15:34	140, 141	22:69	155
15:35–36	142	23:26–31	155
15:36	140n45, 142	23:35–39	155
15:38	136n24, 140, 141	23:42–43	155n15
15:39	20n22, 139, 140	23:46	155
15:40—16:8	143–46	23:48–49	155
15:40–41	20n23, 143, 144	24:21,45–49	155
15:42–47	20n23, 143–44	24:47	155n16
15:42	144	24:50	155
15:43	85n78, 143n59, 144		
15:44–45	143n59	## John	
15:46	143n59		119n230
15:47	144	2:13–22	140n44
16:1–8	20n23, 144–46	2:17–22	xiin2
16:1	144	2:18–22	156
16:2	144n62	2:19	73n22
16:7	75n32, 145, 145n64, 149	2:20–22	120n236
16:8	131n9, 143n56	11:23–24	40n55
		12:37–41	32n22
## Luke		14:3	156
		18:15–18,25–27	138n34
1:29	71n12	21:22–23	156, 156n20
2:25,38	155n16		
2:36	155n17	## Acts	
3:13–15	155n17		85n76
5:30–31	155n17	1:11	156
7:39	71n12	2	67n77
8:10	34n28	2:23	141n46
9:27	155n15	3:21	156
9:31	155, 155n16	4:2	156n18

ANCIENT DOCUMENT INDEX

Acts (continued)

4:23–30	155
7:56	155
12:4	124n257
14:22	156n18
16:31	156n18
17:31	156, 156n18
19:8	156n18
20:32	156n18
23:6	156n18
23:24	85n80
24:15,21,25	156n18
25:19	156n18
26:6–8,18,23	156n18
28:20	156n18
28:25–8	32n22
28:31	156n18

Romans

9:16–19	32n22
10:16–21	32n22
11:7–10	32n22
11:25–26	87n88

1 Corinthians

15:23–28	149n4

2 Corinthians

11:23–24	85n76
13:2	106n166

Galatians

5:21	106n166

1 Thessalonians

3:4	106n166

2 Thessalonians

2	109n186, 156
2:3	93n114

Hebrews

11:38	97n135

James

5:8,9	117n219

1 Peter

5:13	93n114

2 Peter

3:11	71n12

1 John

3:1	71n12

Revelation

	157
1:7,13	157n24
5:1–14	157n24
3:20	117n219
6:10	157
13:18	94n121
18:2	93n114
22:20	157

Dead Sea Scrolls

	101n149
1 QpHab 2:7, 7:2	119n227

Rabbinic Writings

Str.-B.	98n140, 123n254

Greco-Roman Writings

Josephus

AJ
2.184ff   93n114

BJ
4.155   93n114
1.12 (Proem 4)   101n149
5.442 (5.10.5)   101n149
6.429 (6.9.4)   101n149

Plato

Republic 6.492E   101n149

Potter's Oracle

                           98n140

Early Christian Writings

Eusebius

HE III 5.3   97n136

www.ingramcontent.com/pod-product-compliance
Lightning Source LLC
Chambersburg PA
CBHW070324230426
43663CB00011B/2213